An Introduction to the Theology of Karl Barth

An Introduction to the Theology of Karl Barth

by Geoffrey W. Bromiley

T. & T. CLARK LTD.
36 GEORGE STREET, EDINBURGH

Copyright © 1979 by Wm. B. Eerdmans Publishing Company

PRINTED IN THE UNITED STATES BY
WILLIAM B. EERDMANS
FOR
T. & T. CLARK LTD., EDINBURGH

0 567 29054 9
FIRST PRINTED 1979

F6277/6/2

For
Ruth and Timothy

Contents

Introduction   ix

The Doctrine of the Word of God

Chapter I   The Word of God and Dogmatics   3
Chapter II   The Revelation of God   13
     A. The Triune God   13
     B. The Incarnation   21
     C. The Outpouring of the Spirit   27
Chapter III   Holy Scripture *The word of God for the church*   34
Chapter IV   The Proclamation of the Church   45

The Doctrine of God

Chapter V   The Knowledge of God   57
Chapter VI   The Reality of God   69
Chapter VII   The Election of God   84
Chapter VIII   The Command of God   99

The Doctrine of Creation

Chapter IX   Creation   109
Chapter X   The Creature   122
Chapter XI   The Creator and His Creature   141
Chapter XII   The Ethics of Creation   156

The Doctrine of Reconciliation

Chapter XIII   The Problems of the Doctrine of Reconciliation   175
Chapter XIV   The Son of God   180
Chapter XV   The Son of Man   197
Chapter XVI   The God-Man   218
Appendix   Holy Baptism   239

Conclusion

245

Indexes

251

I. Scripture References   251
II. Proper Names   252

Introduction

AN introduction to Karl Barth's theology could take many different forms. One obvious possibility would be to focus on the background against which this theology arose and the historical forces which helped to produce it. Again, primary attention might be given to the relation between the theology and the theologian who engendered it. Or again, one might study the inner development within the theology itself. Among other options one might list a concentration on major concerns, an enquiry into the interaction with contemporary movements, or more specifically, an investigation of its influence on theological thinking.

These are valid approaches but the present introduction will not take any of them. Instead, it will attempt a simple presentation of what Barth is teaching and suggest some possible lines of evaluation. For this purpose, out of the great bulk of Barth's theological writings, only the twelve part-volumes of *Church Dogmatics* will be used. The aim is to give a direct summary of the material as Barth himself devised, organized, and presented it. Secondary sources will be ignored, not because they are valueless, but in order that nothing apart from the person of the introducer may stand between that which is introduced and those to whom the introduction is made.

Is this type of introduction necessary? One might argue that Barth already offers the best introduction to himself in his own volumes. Why not simply read these? The point is well taken, for first-hand evidence is always the best evidence. Nevertheless, the ordinary student of theology runs into an immediate obstacle here. The huge white volumes—the so-called white elephant—of the original *Dogmatics,* and the more modest but no less daunting black ones of the

English translation, demand far more time and effort than can usually be afforded when much else has to be read and done in learning theology. A few of the more interested and motivated might choose this better course. The many, however, will have little chance of gaining an adequate knowledge of Barth if they have to rely on their own firsthand reading.

All the same, might it not be better to use selected or sample readings for the purposes of introduction? Surely any student can read at least one volume of the *Dogmatics* and thereby acquire some understanding of Barth's essential message and method. Or perhaps even a series of representative extracts from the *Dogmatics* might open up the whole series in its systematic development. Barth's own *Dogmatics in Outline* could also serve as a supplementary guide in effecting the introduction.

These proposals have obvious merit. The present introduction is not designed to exclude or replace them. It is self-evident that there should be some accompanying engagement with the primary text in one form or another. Readers of this study would be well-advised to read through one or more of the part-volumes and to read extracts, as they are able, from the others. At the same time, merely to read a single part-volume, or to study individual passages in detachment from their context, hardly affords a proper grasp of Barth's theology, and unfortunately *Dogmatics in Outline* is a little too compressed to meet the need.

Why is it that the selective approach is not adequate? The reason lies in Barth's theological method. Barth does not simply deal with an individual doctrine in its proper sequence and then move on to the next. For him, God himself, not the doctrines, constitutes the theme of theology. Hence all the doctrines are closely interwoven. The individual teachings are constantly seen in new contexts and from different angles as the series continues. What does Barth teach about justification? It is not enough merely to read the appropriate section in IV,1. Barth has already said something very significant about the matter under the heading of the divine command in II,2 and he will have more to say in IV,2. What about the atonement? It, too, is a theme in II,2 before IV is ever reached, just as election belongs again to the context and content of reconciliation. What about incarnation? A first approach is made is I,2, but this can hardly be regarded as sufficient unless it is supplemented by the discussion in IV,1 and the detailed presentation in IV,2.

Sometimes, of course, the interweaving of themes does not bring out anything very new, except at the biblical and historical level. In other instances, however, what is said later may entail important modifications of earlier statements. Barth sharply rejects natural theology in I,1 and 2 and II,1, but sheds new light on this rejection by what he says about other truths in IV,3. The initial emphasis on the divine transcendence must be qualified or explained by the divine spatiality in II,1 and the humanity of God at a later stage. To read a given volume or a selection from different volumes in isolation from all the rest, is to run the risk of considerable misunderstanding, or at least misplacement of emphasis in relation to the theology as a whole. Ideally, no one should say anything about any of Barth's doctrines without first reading through the whole series at least once, and preferably more than once. This is not a rule that applies only to Barth; it is a principle of all good hermeneutics.

Conceding this, are there not enough secondary studies already available to fill the gap? At this point we run into a difficulty. Secondary studies abound. Some of them are valuable and certainly ought to be used, and almost all of them are stimulating and ought to be consulted if time permits. Nevertheless, they do not entirely meet the need of the average reader for several different reasons.

The first and obvious reason is that they do not provide the simple and straightforward introduction which is attempted in this volume. Instead they offer other (and useful) introductory material or, presupposing some knowledge of the text, they enter into learned discussions, criticisms, and developments which are of little profit to those without the initial information.

Nor is this the end of the story. Many of the studies which presuppose a knowledge of the text show no great evidence of a full acquaintance with it. A simple test will often make this clear. Is the writer trying to group Barth's theology under some master concept such as grace or covenant or history? Even a casual knowledge of the *Dogmatics* should quickly make plain that this is one of the things that Barth specifically wants to avoid, since God is the theme of theology and is not to be confused with anything else. It is for this material reason, and not just on methodological grounds, that Barth does not systematize. Nor does Barth do unconsciously what he does not intend to do. A broader reading of the *Dogmatics* clearly indicates that no single doctrine dominates the whole. Attention focuses on this or that theme from time to time, but the main spotlight remains constantly and consistently on God. Even Christ's centrality is meant to point to (and not away from) the centrality of the triune God. Hence secondary works which try to systematize the *Dogmatics* must obviously be treated with caution. Readers who have no comprehensive view, however, are in a poor position to discern or correct the distortions and false judgments which characterize so many of the secondary discussions.

The secondary works include some that even staggered Barth because of the magnitude and depth of their misapprehension and misrepresentation. In one of his prefaces, Barth complains of those who chew him up like cannibals. He can only conclude that if they will not read and try to understand what he is saying, there is no point in trying to talk to them. Unfortunately such studies, which vary in length and viewpoint, are common. The fact that they result in totally incompatible accounts of Barth, even sometimes in the same work, seems not to trouble the authors. Even students reading small parts of the *Dogmatics* for the first time, ask with wonder how obviously intelligent and well-trained scholars can commit such elementary blunders in the face of the clearest possible evidence. A failure to read and digest the *Dogmatics* has produced an enormous quantity of high-sounding and influential nonsense. This being the case, the need for a plain exposition needs no further justification.

It is, of course, a need for theological novices. Just as novices in biblical studies do best to begin with the Bible, or with a study of its contents, and not with the plethora of books that have been written *about* the Bible, so in Barthian studies the proper course is to begin with Barth's own writings, or with a study of their contents. Only in this way can a factual foundation be laid on which valid evaluation, development, and criticism may take place. A smattering of garbled, secondhand information about Barth and his teachings is worse than useless to the ordinary student. Perhaps it is better to have no knowledge than false knowledge, but better than both is a simple but real knowledge which, whether favorable or unfavorable, can be used in theological development and ministry. To provide some simple but real knowledge constitutes the compelling reason for this introduction.

If plain exposition is needed by the novice, one might plausibly argue that it is needed at a higher level as well. To a large extent, studies of Barth's *Church Dogmatics* still suffer from a series of false starts. Hence the addition of greater learning and acuity too easily results in compounding the confusion. Just as progress in the Christian life, according to Luther, consists in constantly going back to the beginning, so at this juncture the greatest progress in Barthian studies will probably come only with a modest beginning again at the beginning. Naturally the present introduction is not written for learned scholars. But if some of them have the humility to go back with it to the text of the *Dogmatics* on which it is based and to which it is meant to lead, then a new era could open up characterized by solid and profitable investigations and interactions grounded in real knowledge and understanding. It could very well bring about something of a dogmatic renaissance, not, of course, by the acceptance of all that

Barth says, but by the entry into authentic dialogue in which he is not misinterpreted but appreciated and appraised.

A final question is whether an introductory exposition such as this is really possible. After working through *Church Dogmatics* three or four times in the preparation of the English translation, after offering seminars and courses in the various volumes over a couple of decades, and after finally summarizing the whole material again directly from the text for the purpose of introductory presentation, the author is aware of the difficulties involved: the danger of misinterpretation; the risk of misplaced emphasis; the possibility of missing an important nuance or delimitation; the impossibility of compressing the richness of thought and subtlety of development into a series of bald and necessarily oversimplified statements. The small print sections, which form so vital and substantial a part of *Church Dogmatics,* have had to be largely ignored. Some of the sections or subsections, not without a certain arbitrariness, have had to be drastically cut down, although not completely eliminated.

Nevertheless, certain things may be said in reply. First, if the *Dogmatics* was a lifetime in the making, the introduction, although composed fairly quickly, rests on a lifelong encounter with Barth. It is more than a hasty and *ad hoc* selection of thoughts from various chapters. Even as the material was being prepared, the General Index to *Church Dogmatics* in English was also in preparation; thus, a new chance arose to examine the distribution of material over the whole series and to read the passages chosen as preachers' aids for the liturgical year. At the same time, another pack of more or less eager students was let loose on various Barthian scents in the *Dogmatics* and elsewhere, and this demanded new and fresh reflection.

Second, the necessities of hard and detailed study, along with a fundamental appreciation that falls short of naive and uncritical partisanship, provide some of the objectivity required in reliable exposition. What is thought to be dubious or speculative in Barth can be presented with no less directness than what is thought to be right and good. Even when there might be personal uncertainty as to the ramifications of what Barth is saying, the statements can, it is hoped, be factually conveyed with no attempt at gloss or commentary. An honest and not wholly incompetent study is not beyond the bounds of possibility.

Third, mistakes, defects, and omissions may easily be corrected or made good, since constant reference is made to the relevant passages in the text, and those who have the German can move fairly easily to it from the English translation. The work is not designed to replace *Church Dogmatics,* but is rather a preliminary presentation of what it is all about.

Fourth, the book is not meant, and, we hope, does not emerge, as either a commendation or a condemnation of Barth's theology. Certain lines of thought and questioning are occasionally suggested. These may stimulate readers to engage in interaction. The purpose of the book will best be served, however, by individual response, reflection, and more detailed investigation. *Church Dogmatics* contains such a varied wealth of exegetical and historical as well as dogmatic and ethical work that specific studies are needed, within a comprehensive understanding, for any authoritative assessment. Barth's theology is worth studying, knowing, and grasping, whether or not the verdict goes for or against it. This is the nature of the present introduction. It does not make any ultimate plea either one way or the other. It presumes that encounter with Barth is worthwhile in and for itself. Apart from a few remarks here and there, it allows the material the chance to make its own impact, first in this summary form and then, it is hoped, in Barth's own extended outworking.

Whether or not the introduction achieves its aims must be left for others to say. But the aims are "plain and unvarnished," as Luther said at Worms. If it does not make the present knowledge and understanding of Barth any better, it certainly cannot make it much worse.

The
Doctrine
of the
Word of God

CHAPTER I
The Word of God and Dogmatics

I N an important preface to the first volume of *Church Dogmatics,* Barth explains why he could not continue *Dogmatics* as originally planned, but had to make a fresh start. He had not changed what he wanted to say, but criticisms of his work had indicated that changes were necessary. Studying Anselm had also clarified his thinking and had shown him that he needed to express himself more correctly. Therefore, he had felt it to be both necessary and possible to attempt a fresh account of his essential theological concern and understanding.

First, of course, he defined his terms and explained his task. To do this he opened his new series of the relabeled *Church Dogmatics* with a relatively short introduction in which he discussed in two sections the task of dogmatics in general, and dogmatic prolegomena in particular. Both of the sections play a controlling role in the bulky volumes that follow, and should not be skipped by the reader.

1. The Task of Dogmatics (§1)

In subdividing the first section into three subsections, Barth deals first with the general relations between church, theology, and science. Theology consists of talk about God in the church. This may be either individual or corporate and it can have a very wide range. More narrowly, however, theology involves an element of self-scrutiny (3f.)* regarding the basis, goal, and content of this God-talk. It thus takes the three forms of biblical, practical, and dogmatic investigation (4f.). Whether or not this investigation may be described as scientific is not a matter of principle for Barth. Nor is it to be judged by whether or

*Note: Page references to *Church Dogmatics* I,1, are from the second edition translated by G. W. Bromiley and published by T. & T. Clark (1975).

not theology conforms to the criteria adopted by other sciences. What counts, as he sees it, is the relation between the investigation and its object (5–11). It is essential that the reader grasp this simple point.

Pursuing the thought of theology as enquiry in the second subsection, Barth advances the important presupposition that its content, which is the special concern of dogmatics, both may and must be known as divine truth (11f.). This truth has the distinctive character of being personal—truth in Jesus Christ—and for this reason it is known through the distinctive manner of obedience (14). At this juncture Barth adds that dogmatic theology will be the science of dogma, not dogmas, although he reserves the exploration of this distinction for a later point. His concern at the moment is that dogmatics should be seen as an investigation of the content of theology with the practical aim of considering how it is to be correctly stated and conveyed in each new age, language, culture, and society (16).

In his third subsection, Barth develops his thesis that theology, including dogmatics, can take place only in the church and only in obedience. This means that dogmatics has to be an act of faith. Outside faith, people may still talk about God but not in relation to the true object—divine truth (17). Faith ultimately depends on grace, but its human reference very pointedly raises the question of the personal faith of the theologian (18–21). This is a valid question, yet it is not the only one, for even the believing theologian can still engage in theology as though it were an abstract intellectual pursuit. In contrast, Barth contends that dogmatics itself must always be undertaken as an act of penitence, obedience, and prayer—all three of which are specific constituents of faith (21–23).

2. The Task of Dogmatic Prolegomena (§2)

Barth planned the first volume of Church Dogmatics as prolegomena. In the second section of the introduction he thus focused on the theme of the volume and considered the task of dogmatic prolegomena. Necessity and possibility engaged his attention in two subsections.

Regarding necessity, Barth begins with the simple statement that dogmatics does not in principle demand a prior discussion of methodology (25). Good dogmatics can be done, and has in fact been done, without it. Nor can it be argued with any cogency that the modern period has imposed a need for preliminary apologetics or polemics. Indeed, apologetics has suffered, and still suffers, from the disadvantage that it might become a diversion from the true dogmatic task and a substitute for dogmatics itself. Furthermore, although it aims at "relevance," it can easily miss this altogether by taking itself too seriously.

As Barth sees it, theology which does its own job will be the best apologetics. If prolegomena are needed, the necessity arises, not in relation to unbelief, but in relation to error in the church itself. Alongside truth in the church there is also heresy. Dogmatics, having a primary concern for the content of the church's confession and proclamation, must obviously learn how to distinguish between heresy and truth. In particular, Barth finds in the modern period two erroneous movements: Roman Catholicism on the one side, and Liberal Protestantism on the other. The presence of these movements constitutes the real necessity of dogmatic prolegomena (31–36).

When he discusses the possibility of dogmatic prolegomena, Barth immediately engages in debate with the two divergent movements. Liberal Protestantism tries to build up its prolegomena on general anthrolopology and history in order to present a purely human possibility (36–40). With far greater refinement, Roman Catholicism seeks a foundation in scripture, tradition, the church, and the faith of the church, but does so in such a way that in the end the possibility is still a human one, for while it finds a place for God's action, it merges it into man's (40f.). Barth locates the possibility of prolegomena in the speaking and hearing of Jesus Christ—the true being of the church (41f.). This points to the real question in prolegomena—the question of the dogmatic rule, criterion, or standard—which will be the theme of the first of Barth's long chapters on dogmatics. Following his reference to the speaking and hearing of Jesus Christ as the true possibility of prolegomena, Barth intimates that the true norm of dogmatics lies in the Word of God as holy scripture when this is seen "in the context of an embracing doctrine of the Word of God" (43f.).

The first chapter is entitled "The Word of God as the Criterion of Dogmatics." It contains five full sections which range from the material, form, and nature of the Word to its knowability and relation to faith and dogma. Each of these discussions has its own place in the comprehensive plan of Barth's prolegomena. Hence an attempt must be made to examine and understand each of them individually.

3. The Material of the Word (§3)

In the first section of the chapter, Barth finds the material of the Word in the church's proclamation. A first subsection here leads him back to the initial theme of theology as the church's talk about God. Talk about God, however, is the Word of God not in worship, education, social action, or even theology in the narrower sense, but in the commissioned proclamation of the church in its twofold form as preaching and sacrament (47–61). Here both Liberal Protestantism and Roman Catholicism fall into error. The former misunderstands preaching, rebels against it, and tries to replace it by action—this was already occurring in the fourth decade of the twentieth century. The latter overexalts the sacrament at the expense of the sermon, for which it usually finds a place, but only as apologetic instruction or moral exhortation. In his later years Barth was pleased to note a good deal of improvement in this regard. Barth himself does not wish in any way to minimize the sacrament; yet preaching, he thinks, has priority and the sacrament serves as a confirmatory act. Preaching can regain its proper place only if it is rightly understood as a repetition of the promise of God in which the Word of God and faith are in personal encounter (70).

The second subsection examines the relation between dogmatics and proclamation. While proclamation is God's Word, it is also man's, and highly responsible as such (72f.). The sharpest question that can be asked of it, and indeed of the church at large, is that of its truth (73f.). Dogmatic evaluation asks this question. Being human too, it lies under the question even as it asks it. Yet its main concern must be for the purity of proclamation. While theologians in the narrower sense have to bear this concern, no member of the church can evade it, or should try to do so (78f.). Nor can it relate to proclamation alone. Worship, hymns, social work, and many other forms of church activity are involved in proclamation. Hence they, too, must come under dogmatic scrutiny. In performing its task dogmatics has, of course, no right or commission to rule. It has no higher source of knowledge nor does it have any immanent end or law. In its concern for the truth of proclamation as man's word, it fulfils the role of servant and not of lord (85ff.).

4. The Form of the Word (§4)

The form of the Word, considered in the next section, is threefold. Barth devotes three subsections to these three forms and then a fourth to their unity. He bases his concept of the three forms—the preached, the written, and the revealed—on divisions already suggested and partly developed in reformation theology, for example in Bullinger's *Decades*. His originality here lies in the way in which he works out the concept and not in the concept itself.

Under the preached Word he considers the relation between the church's preaching and proclamation as God's Word. According to Barth, the decisive thing here is event. If proclamation and the church are to be true realities of revelation and not just human entities or enterprises, then the Word of God must happen (88f.). Barth suggests that this will entail four things. If proclamation is God's Word, then the Word will be its commission (89f.), the Word will be its theme (90f.), the Word will be its judgment (92), and finally the Word will be the event, so that as man's word is spoken, so, too, is God's (93–99).

The written Word next calls for discussion. Proclamation does not take place in a vacuum or begin again with every act. It rests on recollection of revelation that has already been enacted, not now in the church, but in a reality that is distinct from it—the biblical canon (99–101). Now scripture undoubtedly forms a part of proclamation. Nevertheless, in virtue of its apostolicity, it also plays a constitutive role in relation to it (102–104). Later proclamation cannot go its own way, but must follow the apostles and their writings. Tradition forms no substitute when taken in isolation, for if it breaks free from scripture it ceases to be in healthy dialogue and becomes unfruitful monologue (105f.). Nor can scripture be brought under a fixed exegetical yoke, for free scripture demands free exegesis (106). Scripture imposes itself on the church as canon. It does so, not statically or mechanically, but in virtue of its content and as an event (108). In this event we accept it in faith as God's Word (110).

In its third form the Word is the revealed Word. Scripture points to this—an important concept in Barth—and is indeed one with it as event (113–115). The differences as Barth perceives them are (1) that revelation is act and scripture record and (2) that revelation is directly God's Word while scripture is man's word (113). Revelation has ultimate priority even in the sense of engendering scripture (114). To express the relation Barth considers three senses in which the Word of God "holds" scripture. First, it holds it up on high, second, it holds it in place, and third it holds it in store (117f.). In the last analysis, revelation is Word in the absolute sense, namely, incarnation (119), whereas scripture and preaching attest and proclaim the Word (120).

A brief subsection on the unity of God's Word concludes this consideration of the threefold form. The Word does not have three separate forms in which we may have any one without the other two. Instead, the Word is the one Word threefold; thus, in analogy to the divine Trinity we always have proclamation and attestation with revelation, attestation and revelation with proclamation, and proclamation and revelation with attestation (121). This "perichoresis" should never be forgotten when the subject of scripture or proclamation is at issue in Barth, for misunderstanding inevitably follows if it is. Historically, Barth draws attention to the threefold form in Luther and the accompanying emphasis on unity in the Lutheran theologian Gerhard (121–124).

5. The Nature of the Word (§5)

In his study of the nature of the Word, Barth first explains why he has abandoned the order in the preceding *Christian Dogmatics*. Two commentators in particular, Gogarten and Siegfried, had disturbed him with their criticisms, which he discusses in detail (125–131). He rejects the criticisms because they are based on serious material misunderstandings, but he does concede that the misunderstandings could validly arise from the way in which he had expressed himself. For this reason he now introduces a new section on the nature of the Word. This, he believes, may be known indirectly from the three forms (132). He devotes the next three subsections to this question, first dealing with the Word as the speech of God, and then with God's speech as act and as mystery.

That the Word is God's speech is self-evident, for "God's Word means that God speaks" (132). As speech the Word has three important characteristics. First, although speech has a physical side, it is primarily intellectual or spiritual, communicating reason and person (133ff.). Second, speech is itself personal, so that the Word is not truth in the abstract but truth as the speaking person of God. Taking the form of words, it stands under personal control (136–139). Finally, speech has purpose and direction. The Word, then, does not float at random. It comes from outside, reaches us, and restores us. In virtue of the presence of the speaker it does all this definitively. A purpose is in view and this purpose is achieved (139ff.).

The purposiveness of the Word as God's speech leads naturally to the thought of God's speech as his act. The Word of God is not idle or empty talk. Here is a Word that makes history (143f.). It does so, not only once, but continuously by means of what Barth calls its "contingent contemporaneity" (145ff.). This means that its efficacy is not restricted to a single time. It makes time for itself in scripture, and for scripture in proclamation, so that it plays an active role in every time. In its contemporaneous operation the speech of God bears two additional characteristics. It is power to rule in the sense of accomplishing change, of bringing in a new man, and of effecting what it says whether in the narrower sphere of the church or the wider one of the world (145–156). It is also decision, for it has a free reality of its own, entails a choice of grace and judgment, and works on and in our own decision, which it does not, of course, eliminate, but establishes (160–162).

For all its powerful activity, however, the speech of God remains always the mystery of God. This means that we cannot prove or demonstrate it to be God's Word. The uniqueness or mystery may be seen, Barth thinks, in three areas. First, God's Word is his Word in secularity. Whether as Word revealed, written, or proclaimed, it bears the veil of humanity, so that what is discerned might simply seem to be man, human writing, and human address (165–174). Second, and consequently, Barth finds what he calls a "onesidedness" in God's speech. We do not perceive it as partly God's and partly man's, but as wholly God's or wholly man's; either unveiled in its veiling or veiled in its unveiling (176–181). If, however, it has for human sense only a human appearance, how can anyone pierce the veil? The third quality of the divine speech answers this question. This is its spirituality, not now in the sense of being a rational or personal Word, but in the sense of being spoken by the Holy Spirit in such a way that it is indeed heard as God's Word. In a fine phrase Barth argues that "the Lord of speech is also the Lord of our hearing"; this explains why the hearing of God's Word is always a hearing in faith (181–186). The mystery of God in the speech of God is the mystery of the Holy Spirit.

Three decisive elements in Barth's whole theology come to expression in this fourth subsection of §5. First, Barth sees no way in which ordinary modes of argument can demonstrate the Word to be God's. Second, and by way of explanation, God does not speak in immediacy but in human form which can conceal God even as it reveals him. Third, the Holy Spirit has a role of primary significance in the whole work of revelation, for the Holy Spirit alone gives eyes and ears of faith to see and hear what is actually there, though unperceived by the unaided senses of sinners. *The holy spirit reveiles to us the word of God.*

6. The Knowability of the Word (§6)

The emphasis on the mystery of God's speech raises the question of the next section, that of the knowability of the Word. The Holy Spirit forms the obvious answer to this question but Barth explores this answer more fully. Discussing the form of the question in a first subsection, he insists that the real question is not how we *can* know the Word. Through the Spirit's work certain people—believers—do in fact know the Word. Hence the true question is *how* they do so. If the question of the possibility arises, it does so only on the basis of the reality. Barth also makes here the significant point that in speaking of knowing God's Word we must not start off with a predefined sense of knowing. Knowing God's Word might have special characteristics as compared to knowing a star, a tree, even a human person, in accordance with the difference in the object of this knowledge (189f.).

In the second subsection, Barth relates the Word to man in general. The Word is, in fact, spoken to man. Man hears and receives the Word. But how? Does man have a unique capability to hear this Word? Barth rejects this answer (191–193), which he takes to be the basic mark of Cartesian theology (195). If man has any capability to be a hearer of the Word, this capability is given him by the Word itself (194ff.). From this fact alone derives the certainty that God's Word can be known, believed, and asserted (197f.).

Examining the relation in another way, Barth, in the next subsection, confronts the problematical area of experience. It was here that misunderstandings had arisen in his first draft. The notion that Barth is simply a theologian of experience (basically a follower of Schleiermacher!) in the new form of existentialist subjectivity still lingers in many theological circles. He thus deals with the matter very carefully and should be read and heard with equal care. He defines experience as a determination of human existence (198f.) and does not deny that it accompanies knowledge. Nevertheless, experience will have certain distinctive features when it stands in connection with the Word. First, this particular determination will not be a determination by the self, or by the self in cooperation with God, but by God alone (199f.). Second, no specific point in human life can be called the locus of this determination to the exclusion of other points; it is a total determination (202–204). Third, this determination may be generally characterized as acknowledgment, which for Barth covers the nine different but related aspects of cognition, personal knowledge, acceptance, encounter, obedience, decision, acquiescence, movement, and response (205–208). Fourth, acknowledgment has its basis in a being acknowledged (208). Fifth, it is not to be seen as the extraordinary possibility of certain people, as though it had human roots (210ff.). Sixth, it knows itself and its limits in the miracle—not the human faculty—of faith (223). Finally, it is given by the Word and can be affirmed only with affirmation of and in the Word (227f.). With this strict grounding of experience in God and the Word, to the exclusion of every possibility of autonomy, Barth has obviously tried to avoid the subjective and experientialist theology which he takes to be the very essence of Liberal Protestantism and a supreme manifestation of supposed human competence and self-sufficiency in the knowledge of the Word of God.

In contrast to autonomous experience stands the experience of faith. In a last subsection on the knowability of the Word, Barth examines the relation between the Word and faith. His opening thesis is that in faith we have valid experience of the Word (227f.). If experience in this context is acknowledgment, acknowledgment comes into effect when the Word is given as the object of faith's reference. Anselm and Luther offer helpful guidance here (230–236). In the last resort the knowability of the Word plainly comes from, and lives by, the Word itself. We have real experience of knowability in the form of acknowledgment as faith itself is given in conformity to God, through which God's Word can be spoken to man, heard by him, and dwell in him. Man exists by this object. Through it he is himself a subject (245); the man of faith; the man of experience. Yet this subject can never break loose and be an autonomous knower of the Word. For he is subject only as predicate of the original Subject, namely, God. This leads Barth to his ultimate and not unexpected conclusion. By way of the Word as object, which gives the faith by which experience comes— the divine determination of man in the form of acknowledgment— God creates "the possibility of knowledge of God's Word" (247). The knowledge is really ours and is thus experience. Nevertheless, it is not within our natural grasp, for we are sinners. Nor can it ever be an independent knowledge, self-grounded or self-controlled. A much more detailed reading and analysis of this crucial subsection is strongly recommended.

7. The Word and Dogma (§7)

Having given an extended account of the Word, Barth returns in the last section of chapter one to the initial question of the relation of the Word to dogma and dogmatics. He states the problem in the first subsection. Dogmatics has the function of testing proclamation by the criterion of the Word. But how does it do this (250)? Some dead ends are closed off first. It is not here a matter of congruity, philosophical adaptation, or relevance, as in Liberal Protestantism. To take this path is to be led into insoluble problems of knowledge, adequacy, relativity, and finally impossibility (251–254). It is to ignore the basic fact that God's Word confronts us as a concrete entity of its own which cannot be replaced by any other criterion and which does not have to answer to philosophy or ethics (255f.). Again, it cannot be a matter of letting the church play the role of surrogate, as in Roman Catholicism, which allows a place for the Bible but only under the judgment and control of the teaching office (257f.). To take this path is to change the Bible from a free and specific "other" into a domesticated instrument of the church (259f.). Scripture as a free factor represents God's Word to the church because it points to the truth of revelation by which may be achieved—not dogmas as supposed truths of revelation defined by the church, but dogma—the agreement of proclamation with the truth of revelation attested by holy scripture (265). Dogmas also have a place, but as a means, and not an end. They aim at dogma, which is personal, which goes out into the church as a command, and which is "the relation between the God who commands and the man who obeys this command" (274). In this light the dogmatic enterprise needs little elaboration. Dogmatics is the enquiry into the agreement of proclamation and revelation; it is the science of dogma.

What does it mean to call dogmatics a science? Tackling this issue in a second subsection, Barth first admits that dogmatics can take an irregular as well as a regular form. Regular dogmatics—that of the schools—does its work in the form of comprehensive and detailed investigation and instruction. It does not have to be done academically, for Calvin's *Institutes* qualifies as regular dogmatics; but mostly it will have a scholastic setting. Irregular dogmatics, in contrast, has no specific pedagogic purpose and does not aim at completeness. This by no means affects its value, for some of the greatest theology has been produced in occasional works by pastors and other non-academicians. Athanasius, Augustine, and Calvin also might be adduced in support (275ff.). Nor should one suppose that irregular dogmatics is any the less scientific than regular dogmatics. Only in the sense that it finally needs regular dogmatics might it be regarded as subordinate. Whether regular or irregular, dogmatics must answer three requirements properly to fulfil its function. First, it must stand in relation to proclamation (280). Second, it must engage, not merely in exposition, but in clarification and correction (281). Third, it must focus on agreement only with revelation (284). Barth concludes that only a scriptural theology can meet these demands and thus be true to itself (285f.)

In the last subsection, both of section 7 and of the entire chapter, Barth forges a link with the three chapters which follow and constitute the remainder of the first volume. Considering the route to be taken in dogmatic prolegomena, he argues that what is needed is a theology of the three forms of revelation (288–290). He now reverses the earlier order and proposes first to study revelation itself—the revealed Word. This will entail an analysis of the Holy Trinity, of Jesus Christ as the objective possibility of revelation, and of the Holy Spirit as its subjective possibility. In two further chapters dealing with the written and the preached Word, similar analyses will be offered, first of holy scripture, then of proclamation. To the formal treatment that has already been given, Barth will now add a much larger material exposition.

CHAPTER II
The Revelation
of God

A S explained at the end of the previous chapter, Barth divides his analysis of the revealed Word into three parts: Holy Trinity, Jesus Christ, and Holy Spirit. Since each of these is too bulky for a section, but all need to be kept together under the heading of divine revelation, he adopts an arrangement unique in the *Dogmatics* and interposes three subdivisions, each provided with its own sections and subsections. The first of these comprises the rest of Volume I,1, while the lengthy I,2 contains the second two. By dealing comprehensively with the Word of God in his prolegomena, Barth solves the problem of a starting point which has been much debated in theology. Instead of having to choose between an ontic beginning in God and a noetic beginning in scripture, he combines the two, since the Word of God in its threefold form calls for a discussion of both God and holy scripture as well as proclamation. God, of course, is finally both the ontic and noetic basis; thus, the theology of revelation must begin with the Word revealed.

A. THE TRIUNE GOD

1. God in his Revelation (§8)

Of the five sections devoted to the Trinity, the first (§8) deals with introductory matters under the general heading of "God in his Revelation." The placing of the doctrine in the prolegomena rather than in the body of the work constitutes the theme of the first subsection. Barth justifies his choice of location, which is certainly open to challenge, by showing how revelation leads us ineluctably to the Trinity. From scripture we learn that God is the self-revealing God. That *God through himself* reveals *himself* means that he is subject, act, and effect in a unity of revelation and revealing (296–299). Since God occurs at all three stages, as subject, act, and effect, we are led to the triune God as the controlling factor in revelation. A true doctrine of revelation cannot be attained in abstraction from the doctrine of the Trinity (300–303).

Barth delves more deeply into this relation in a second subsection on what he calls the root of the doctrine. In the Word, the Word is directly identical with God (304f.) as its own absolute ground (305f.). Hence when God reveals himself, he reveals himself as the Lord (306f.). Barth believes this to be the root of the doctrine. The trinitarian statement is not itself a direct statement of revelation. It "translates" the text of the witness to revelation and is indirectly identical with it (308f.). It has its basis in revelation, in the self-revealing God, according to holy scripture. For Barth this is not just a matter of hunting out direct trinitarian references in the Bible. There are some of these (313), but the basis lies primarily in the general presentation (314). This introduces us to God as the Lord in revelation three times, which Barth now defines as the self-unveiling, imparted to men, of the God who by nature cannot be unveiled. In the historical self-unveiling God is the Lord the second time, that is, in manifestation (315ff.). In being the one who by nature cannot be unveiled, God is Lord the first time, that is, in his inscrutability apart from his own free act (320–324). In his self-impartation to men, God is Lord the third time, that is, in his specific coming to us (324ff.). The third aspect leads Barth into a discussion of what is meant by the historicity of revelation. God's self-unveiling, he suggests, cannot be historically demonstrable in the way in which Jesus is historically demonstrable in his humanity. Certainly it takes place as a specific event at a specific time and place (326). It is thus history and not myth (327f.). Yet it is a particular event known by particular people in its own self-impartation in which its unveiling in veiling, or veiling in unveiling, is also known. Barth's concern here is not to deny or dissolve the historical facticity of the divine self-revelation but to preserve a proper place for the lordship of God in its self-impartation by denying that it comes within the category of events known through general historical demonstration.

Are we to attribute exclusiveness to the rootage of the trinitarian doctrine in the divine self-revelation? This is the issue in the third subsection on the so-called vestiges of the Trinity. Barth recognizes that many theologians have looked for, and supposedly found, reflections and even demonstrations of the Holy Trinity in many creaturely analogues (334), whether in the realm of nature (336), culture (336), history (336f.), religion (337), or human psychology (337f.). He concedes that these vestiges may not be dismissed out of hand and can indeed be helpful so long as they are seen in the light of revelation. On the other hand, he argues sternly that they cannot form the basis of dogmatics nor serve as another root of the doctrine (338–344). They give rise to the problem of the difference between interpretation and illustration. Both interpretation and illustration begin with a text or subject and then try to put the same thing in other ways for the purpose of better understanding. But whereas the former emphasizes the "same thing," the latter emphasizes the "other ways" and in so doing runs the risk of focusing attention on that which illustrates instead of that which it illustrates (344f.). For this reason Barth thinks it best not to use, even as illustrations, the vestiges of the Trinity that we might discover in creation, but to stick instead to the vestiges that God has specifically given us, namely, the Word as the one Word in threefold form as Word revealed, written, and proclaimed. As Barth states, we have here a plain and reliable vestige which does not set a second root alongside the first. From it one might be led to a second if more indirect vestige in theology, which is one discipline but takes the threefold form of exegetical, dogmatic, and practical theology (347).

2. The Triunity of God (§9)

Once these preliminary matters have been disposed of, Barth moves into the content of the doctrine with a section on God's triunity. He considers this first from the standpoint of unity in trinity. It must be established that in no way does the divine trinity conflict with the divine unity. Baptism into the triune name does not mean baptism into three names, for God is the one Lord in one—not triple—deity (349f.). What the trinity implies is that God is the one Lord in threefold repetition, with no addition, adulteration, or alteration. Each repetition is grounded in the one Godhead, and God is God only in this repetition (350). The unity must not be construed as a unity of species of which Father, Son, and Spirit are three examples, nor as a collective unity in which the persons are distinct personalitites, but as the unity in which we have the one divine I three times (351). Far from undermining or weakening the unity of God, the trinity, when properly understood, strengthens it. It points to that unity in trinity which is set before us in revelation, so that no choice has to be made between revelation and unity, as in the various monarchian heresies (352f.). In revelation, subject, predicate, and object are the same as revealer, revelation, and revealing. In his revelation, then, God discloses himself to be the God of unity in trinity in whom only the equality of Father, Son, and Spirit is compatible with true monotheism—not the monotheism of abstraction, but the monotheism of the true God in his self-revelation (353).

From this first subsection on unity in trinity it is a natural step to a second on trinity in unity which shows that the divine unity does not rule out the divine trinity. Many religions are explicitly or implicitly monotheistic, but at issue in the unity of the God of self-revelation is the unique revealed unity which must not be confused with the singularity or isolation of numerical unity (353f.). The unity of God includes a distinction and order in deity which is the distinction and order of the three divine persons (355). At this juncture Barth examines the concept of person in its historical trinitarian use and concludes that in addition to its generally admitted inadequacy, it has now become misleading due to the suggestion of personality and the consequent pressure toward tritheism (355–358). He proposes, then, to substitute the more colorless but also the more exact, if rather clumsy, expression "mode of being," which he explains and defends in a short historical note (359–360). The term raises its own problems. Where its orthodox credentials, both in the early church and in Protestant orthodoxy, are not known, and where the *Dogmatics* is read carelessly or superficially, or known only at second hand, the term is even cited in favor of the absurd idea that Barth advocates modalism. He himself, of course, excludes this with his definition that God is the one personal God in the three essentially and ineffaceably distinctive modes of Father, Son, and Holy Spirit. These "modes" are not parts or departments of deity, nor are they divine attributes, for the attributes of God are the attributes of each of the modes, and each of the modes is essentially God in unity and distinction. Where, then, does the distinction lie? In the divine self-revelation it is located in the relations of origin of the three modes in which we find begetting, being begotten, and proceeding, or in other words, fatherhood, sonship, and spirithood (361f.). Hence Father, Son, and Spirit are "three modes of being of the one God subsisting in their relationships one with another" (366). Naturally this type of statement does not explain everything, or even very much. The uniqueness of God means also the mystery of God. None of our terms and concepts can dispel this. They serve their turn if they finally help us to "know at least what we are saying when we say that what is at issue here is God's mystery" (368).

Unity in trinity and trinity in unity are brought together in the third subsection as triunity. Barth prefers this term to the more common trinity or other possibilities such as triplicity (369f.). Triunity as he understands it represents the movement of the two thoughts of unity and trinity (369f.). Each of the modes of being is known in its participation in the other two, that is, in their perichoresis or cicumincession. They are three in distinction but not in separation (370). This finds expression in the outer work by which we know the inner reality of God. The outer work of God is one; all outer acts may be described as acts of the whole trinity in which each of the persons is at work. This points to the inner unity in distinction (372f.). Nevertheless, individual acts are referred more specifically to one or the other persons by what theology has come to describe as appropriations, which are valid so long as they are biblical and not arbitrary or exclusive. This points to the distinction in unity. Both in his work and in himself, the one God is one in three and three in one in a movement of mutual interrelation. This is the divine triunity.

To round off the discussion Barth appends a fourth subsection on the meaning of the doctrine. The doctrine, or dogma, cannot claim to be a direct teaching of scripture. It is exegesis of the biblical text in a particular historical and social context. Questions inevitably arise, then, as to its authenticity and authority. Barth carefully considers the possibility of relativizing or even dismissing the doctrine (376–378). He concludes, however, that irrespective of the situation which produced it the doctrine answers a fundamental question that is posed by commitment to holy scripture. This is the question of the subject of revelation (379) whose self-disclosure embraces the three movements of self-veiling, self-unveiling, and self-imparting; of holiness, mercy, and love; of Good Friday, Easter, and Pentecost, so that he is named specifically the Father, the Son, and the Holy Spirit. In light of this subject, the doctrine of the trinity rules out the false answers of subordinationism on the one side, and modalism on the other. Subordinationism goes astray by subjecting God to creaturely ideas, thus making the three moments unequal (381). Modalism falls into the opposite error of relativizing God by making the moments alien to God (382). In contrast to both, the doctrine of the trinity shows how far the self-revealing God can be what his Word tells us he is, namely, our God, because in all his modes he is equal to himself, and his work for us has its basis and prototype in his own being as Father, Son, and Holy Spirit (383).

3. God the Father (§10)

The way is now cleared for a brief discussion of each of the three modes of being, and in §10 Barth begins with God the Father. In this and the next two sections he adopts the same schema, devoting a first subsection to God in his work and a second to God antecedently in himself. As God the Father this involves the presentation of God as Creator first and then as eternal Father. It should be understood, of course, that the material content of the doctrine of God the Creator forms the substance of a later volume III and is not at issue in this context.

Revelation, it has been argued, presents God to us as Lord. At its climax scripture points us to Jesus as Lord. But Jesus is primarily Lord in his execution, manifestation, and application of the lordship of the Father (384f.). In Jesus, of course, God as Father does not stand first for an affirmation of human existence, but for its radical questioning. As the Lord, the Father is the end of human existence known as death (387f.). Naturally this does not mean that God and death are identical. Yet neither are God and life. The point is rather that God is Lord of our existence (387f.). We exist as God wills and posits our existence. Our existence has an author who freely creates and sustains it. In this way God is Creator. As such, since our father is the natural human author of our existence, he may by analogy be called Father. Yet it is not from this analogy that we move to the concept of Creator, nor indeed by this analogy that he is known as Father. It is by revelation in Jesus Christ that God is known as Lord; Creator. And this Creator is Father as the Father of Jesus Christ (389).

God, then, is eternal Father. We may know God as our Father because he is first Father, not outwardly as Creator or as our Father, but inwardly as the Father of Jesus Christ (390–392). In this regard Barth makes the characteristic point that the term "father" finds its proper use, not in relation to our human father, nor even to God as our divine Father, but to God in himself as the eternal Father. God is Father in himself as the source or fount of deity. This does not imply the superiority or the superordination of God the Father in relation to God the Son and God the Holy Spirit (393f.). Since God in himself is Father irrespective of his being our Creator, it follows that an absolute equation of Father and Creator cannot be sustained. As God the Father is not the Creator of the Son or Spirit, so the Father is not alone the Creator, for creation as an outer work is also the work of the Son and the Holy Spirit (394f.). By appropriation, however, God the Father may be specifically seen as the Creator. Affinity supports this; it is fitting that the authorship of creaturely existence should be more associated with the mode of divine being by which God the Son is begotten and from which God the Holy Spirit proceeds (395–398).

4. God the Son (§11)

Turning in the next section to God the Son, Barth follows the same procedure. He has a first subsection on God the Reconciler and then moves on to a second one on the eternal Son. Here again he makes no attempt to develop the theme of reconciliation, which is reserved for Volume IV.

Beginning with Jesus Christ, as he did in §10, Barth points out first that in Christ God is manifested as Lord, not by adoption or personification, but by his reconciling self-revelation of God (399–408). Jesus enables sinners to hear God's Word by reconciling them to God (407–409). Compared with creation, reconciliation is a new work. It is not the work of man, nor of an impersonal revealer, but the work of God in his second mode of being, which in relation to God the Father is distinct in mode but one in being (410–413).

According to the confession of the church, God is this second mode of being as the Son, not just for us, but already in himself. Even Melanchthon, who would have us know Christ from his benefits, does not dispute this and it is the heart of the teaching of Luther and Calvin (414–420). In answer to the charge that only speculation can say this, Barth states that only speculation can *deny* it, for its rejection (1) makes God's being for us a necessary attribute, (2) does not derive from faith, and (3) can utilize only a human criterion (421).

What Barth has to say regarding the development of the eternal sonship is based phrase by phrase on the Nicene affirmations. Christ the "one Lord" is God (423). As the "only begotten," he is unique; the one God (424f.). "Before all time" points to much more than a being for us (424f.). "Very God of very God" suggests distinction within unity (425–427). "Light of light" supplies an illustration (429). "Begotten, not made" refutes creaturehood and yet establishes derivation from God the Father. "Of one and equal substance" refutes Arianism and subordination although it surpasses final comprehension in its uniqueness to deity (440). "By whom all things were made" stresses true deity in distinction and also the continuity of reconciliation with creation (443f.). In a fine and timely phrase, Barth describes Christ here as "the ground of our being beyond our being" (444).

5. God the Holy Spirit (§12)

A final section (§12) deals in similar fashion with the Holy Spirit, first as the Redeemer, and then as the eternal Spirit. Barth planned to fill out the content of redemption in his fifth and final volume. Health and time ran out before he could even begin this last part of his dogmatic enterprise.

As explained earlier, the Holy Spirit—the Redeemer—is he by whom we come to faith and in whom revelation is "being revealed." The Holy Spirit is God in life-giving presence (452f.). Although scripture can call him the Spirit of Christ, he is not Christ (452f.). In his redemptive work he serves as the threefold guarantee of (1) our participation, (2) our instruction, and (3) our witness (453f.). His special gift is the twofold one of sonship and freedom (456f.). In this he is distinctively the one God in his third mode of being (459ff.). From him faith arises with its eschatological reference (464). He himself, however is not our faith. No less than the Father and the Son, he is Lord.

The second subsection affirms of the Holy Spirit what has been affirmed of the Father and the Son. The Holy Spirit is not just the Holy Spirit in revelation to and in us. He is this because he is antecedently the Holy Spirit in himself (467), distasteful though this may sound to an autonomous faith (468). The Holy Spirit is the eternal Lord, distinct from the Father and the Son and yet related to them as their common factor or fellowship. He is God as the act of love (469).

To complete what he wants to say about the eternal Spirit, Barth follows further statements of the Nicene confession. As the "giver of life," the Spirit is the subject of creation from which redemption is distinct, yet with which it is also connected (471–473). "Proceeding" signifies, not creation, but emanation from the other mode or modes of being, and hence distinction (in unity) from them. The precise meaning of the term, and its difference from begotten, necessarily remains a mystery for us as it was for Augustine (474–477). "And from the Son" *(filioque)* may rightly be included, Barth thinks, since it has an economic basis in the twofold sending of the Spirit, it recognizes the communion of the Father and the Son, it relates the Holy Spirit to revelation and reconciliation as well as creation, and it sees in the Holy Spirit the love of the Son as well as the Father (480ff.). In reply to the argument that logically there should then be a procession of the Son from the Spirit, particularly in view of the fact that the Son was conceived by the Holy Spirit at the incarnation, Barth has a double answer. Regarding the incarnation, he contends that the reference here is not to the origin of the Son but to the assuming of humanity into his mode of being, and that in any case the Spirit is not to be viewed as replacing the earthly father. Regarding the logic of a double procession of the Son, he does not think that perichoresis demands this. Expounding the "worshipping and glorifying" of the Spirit together with the Father and the Son, Barth points out that the Latin is *simul,* not *cum,* so that "together with" or even "like" expresses the meaning better than a plain "with" or "alongside" (487). Three matters are emphasized in this final clause: first, the deity of the Spirit;

second, the personhood of the Spirit; and third, the identity in the Spirit of gift and Giver.

Barth, it will be seen, stays very close to the orthodox formularies in his trinitarian teaching. His only substantial polemic is against the idea of natural or human vestiges when this carries with it the suggestion of another root. His reservation concerning the term "person" aims to defend rather than subvert the orthodox position. Here and there he attempts new forms of expression, but in his main position he accepts and develops the creedal affirmations.

Methodologically, Barth sees that he has to begin with the economic Trinity. The very knowledge of God as the triune God comes from revelation—not just from the statements of revelation, but from its very structure. Similarly, what we know of the persons, or modes of being, may be read off from the divine activity in revelation, both in the general sense that this activity takes the form of creation, reconciliation, and redemption, and also in the more detailed sense that the incarnation points to the Father-Son relation and the outpouring of the Spirit carries a hint of the twofold procession. At the final extreme individual biblical statements give direct evidence of the Trinity, although they obviously do not develop the doctrine of the divine triunity.

From the economic Trinity Barth moves on at each point to the essential Trinity: God is what he reveals himself to be. Revelation in its three moments leads us to Father, Son, and Holy Spirit. Creation pushes us toward God the Father, reconciliation toward God the Son, and redemption toward God the Holy Spirit. The outer activities do not simply point us to a single God playing three different roles in his dealings with the world. God does not just become Father to be our Father, or Son to be the incarnate Son, or Spirit to be the Spirit poured out on the church. He is Father, Son, and Spirit in his dealings with us because he is already Father, Son, and Spirit eternally and antecedently in himself. In his inner being he is authentically Father, Son, and Spirit. Because he is so, he reveals himself and acts as Father, Son, and Spirit in his outward dealings with us. Noetically the economic Trinity forms the starting point, but the eternal Trinity has ontic priority.

B. THE INCARNATION

1. God's Freedom for Man (§13)

Continuing in Volume I,2 his presentation of the revealed Word, or

God's revelation, Barth considers next the role of Jesus Christ from the general standpoint of the objective possibility of revelation. He divides his treatment into three sections: God's freedom for man, the time of revelation, and the mystery of revelation.

Typically the section on God's freedom for man (§13) opens with a subsection, not on the objective possibility of revelation, but on its objective reality (I,2,3). This, says Barth, is the order prescribed for us by holy scripture, which is witness, not opinion (6ff.). Revelation is a reality in its fulfilment in the incarnation of the Son. Everything hinges, then, on the simple twofold fact that the Word became a man, Jesus (13ff.), and that the man Jesus is the Word (19ff.). New Testament quotations are adduced in support of this, particularly from John and 1 John in relation to the first aspect, and from the Synoptists in relation to the second (22f.). The two aspects must not be regarded as antitheses that have to be brought into a synthesis, but as "two testimonies to one reality" summed up in the name of Jesus (23f.).

A second subsection then follows on the objective possibility of revelation. How *can* God reveal himself? The incarnation, which is the reality of revelation, obviously constitutes the answer. Hence a proper reply to the question of possibility will simply exegete the reality (24ff.). The reality has five implications that display the possibility. It shows us (1) that God can indeed cross the boundary to meet us because in the freedom of his gracious condescension he wills to do so, and in fact does (31–33). It shows us (2) that God has the freedom to do this by becoming man in the person of the Son or Word. It is not, of course, the deity of God that is made flesh. It is not the Father as the Who of revelation, nor the Spirit as the How, but the Son as the What. Nevertheless, in the incarnation the Son is not without the Father and the Spirit. It is God in his mode of being as the Son who is thus free for us (33–35). Whether he could have revealed himself in other ways is impossible to determine or even discuss (35). The reality, according to the biblical witness, tells us that he could and did do it this way. Again, the reality shows us (3) that the Son became man; a perceptible being whom we may know by analogy with other such beings, although the possibility of revelation does not rest on the basis of a known analogy of being between God and man (35–37). It also shows us (4) that the Son remains God in his incarnation as man, so that he is veiled even in his unveiling (37–39). It shows us finally (5) that he becomes what we are—flesh. He is not sinful himself, yet he stands with us under the judgment of God (39–41), veiled in the divine unveiling (41f.). In conclusion Barth comments on the divine necessity whereby revelation, to be revelation, had to be incarnation. This does not mean, of course, any restraining of the divine freedom.

It certainly does not point to any inherent capacity of humanity for revelation. It rests on the basic fact that God wills to reveal himself in such a manner. On this the necessity (and therewith the possibility) of incarnation rests (43f.).

2. The Time of Revelation (§14)

Incarnation or revelation means God's coming to us in time, and the time of revelation is the difficult theme which Barth goes on to tackle in §14. He opens the first subsection by comparing and contrasting God's time and ours. As an event the incarnation has a proper time. This is distinguished as the time of God for us, which Barth characterizes as our only true time (45). There are, he suggests, three times: created time; fallen time, which is our present time; and revelation time, real time constituted by God's coming to us and to our time (47ff.). This new time has two features: It is that of the Lord of time, and it is fulfilled time. In it we too can have a present, a past, and a future as contemporaries of Jesus (55). The change brought about by revelation may be seen in the relation between revelation and history, since revelation is not a predicate of history, as other events are, but history a predicate of revelation (56ff.). This sheds a new light on the problem of revelation and history, which is usually approached with the false notion that we can start with the general phenomenon of time or history, that revelation is something problematic, and that it can be viewed as an absolutizing of a specific bit of history (56–58). Revelation as fulfilled time means three things: (1) that time is mastered (59f.); (2) that all other time is shown to resist God's time (61f.); and (3) that new time breaks into the old (63f.). This new time—the time of God—is, Barth believes, real time. It takes our time from us, although, since this is as yet only intimated and not completed, our time remains until the redemption (66–70).

The new time has what Barth calls a pre-time and a post-time. In the second subsection he discusses the first of these—pre-time—as the time of expectation. Pre-time has the form of a specific history, that of the Old Testament, which revelation shows to be the time of the manifestation of Jesus as the expected One (72ff.). Centered on Jesus Christ, the Old Testament constitutes a unity, as the New Testament indicates, and as theologians have consistently recognized from Irenaeus and Augustine to Luther and Calvin (74–78). Three points must be grasped here. First, the Old Testament, like the New, bears witness to revelation, as may be seen from Israel's being a congregation and particularly from the covenant on which it rests and moves historically toward its expected fulfilment in Jesus Christ (81–84). Secondly, the Old Testament is witness to revelation as God's veiling in unveiling. Because of man's sin, the God of Israel allows catastrophe in nations and even Israel so that the expected Christ, who was to die under Pontius Pilate that we might be reconciled to God, is typified in the suffering servant (84–89). Finally the Old Testament bears witness to revelation in the form of God's presence as the coming God, as seen in the people (96), the land (96), the temple (96f.), the divine lordship (97), the divine judgment (97f.), and the monarchy (98). All of these have their reality as God's, yet still await their fulfilment in the time of Jesus Christ. In this light, the Old Testament is shown to be the pre-time, the time of the expectation of revelation (99–101).

The third and last subsection deals with the post-time of revelation, which Barth, adopting once again a category familiar from the reformation, describes as the New Testament time of recollection. Here witness is again borne to Jesus Christ, but now as the recollected Christ (101ff.). Again there are three points for consideration. First, the New Testament directs us to revelation in the incarnation, in the particular name of Jesus as the name, not of a symbol or cipher, but of a particular man in a particular place and time (103–106). Second, the New Testament directs us to the revelation of the hidden God. The story of this particular man is the story of righteous suffering in which the one man Jesus died for all those under divine judgment, bearing away their sin (106–113). Third, the New Testament is witness to the revelation in which God is present to man (in the incarnation) as still the coming God (in the *parousia*), for to the recollection of the past event of Christ's birth and death is added the recollection of the Easter event, of God's pure presence, of eternal time which implies expectation of this time at the consummation of revelation (113–121).

3. The Mystery of Revelation (§15)

From examining the time of revelation Barth turns to a study of its mystery. He here engages in a preliminary christological discussion (his full christology will be presented in Volume IV) in which he deals successively with (1) the problem of christology, (2) very God and very man, and (3) the miracle of Christmas.

The first subsection on the problem of christology opens with the observation that since revelation means incarnation, dogmatics has to be fundamentally christological, not just generally but also expressly and specifically (122ff.). The content of christology is God's becoming man in Christ (123). This can be stated and understood only in New Testament terms—the event of very God and very man described in the conception by the Holy Spirit and the virgin birth (125). In this respect Barth defends the early christological statement of the creeds against the charges of intellectualism and metaphysical abstraction which have been brought against it in the modern period from Herder to Harnack (125–131). True christology has to stay with its object. In so doing it faces the problem of a limit or frontier, as Grünewald so finely depicts it in his famous altarpiece at Isenheim (125). This problem is the problem of the mystery of revelation. Modern christology goes astray because it drops the problem. Early christology, for all its detailed faults, confronts the problem (132).

The second subsection on very God and very man consists of a tripartite exegesis of John 1:14: "The word was made flesh." Discussing "the Word" first, Barth notes that the Word is very God. Analyzing the statement, he then makes four points. First, the Word is the subject of what happens (134). Second, the Word as subject acts in divine freedom (135). Third, the Word does not cease to be free and sovereign in becoming flesh (136), so that the Liberal cult of the historical Jesus and the Roman Catholic cult of the heart of Jesus are both theologically in error (136–138). Fourth, the fact that the Word is subject justifies the use of *theotokos* (God-bearer or mother of God) in relation to Mary (138–141), although the extravagant development of mariology in abstraction from christology is to be deplored and resisted (141–146).

"Flesh" is the second term to call for comment. Again Barth has four points. First, flesh means true humanity (147–149). Second, it denotes participation in our human nature or essence in which the Word, without ceasing to be such, is now what he was not before, namely, man (149–151). Third, it means sharing, not neutral flesh, but flesh that in the form of human nature is marked by Adam's fall and subject to God's wrath and judgment; thus, while the man Jesus is himself sinless, he accepts the situation of, and is reckoned as, a sinner (151f.; cf. the important historical discussion 152–155). Fourth, flesh denotes likeness to us but not identity, since Jesus is flesh in a different way, that is, sinlessly and obediently and savingly as the Word who in a reversal of Adam's fall, "willed to be and was ... the divine bearer of the sin which man as a sinner must bear" (156).

"Was made" or "became," the verb between Word and flesh, points to the central mystery. Here Barth insists first that "became" does not imply any surrender of being as the Word (159). For this reason he approves of the common equivalent "assumed," which offers protection against any idea that the Word ceased to be wholly and equally himself. God as God may also be man, but he cannot cease to be God (160f.). As man he is not, of course, a third thing. The unity of God and man in Jesus is thus presupposed in the "becoming"

(162). This finds expression in the doctrine of enhypostasis, which holds that the man Jesus has no separate mode of being as man but that his mode of being is always that of the Word (163–165). A further point is that the verb "became" indicates a complete event (165). Since the event is completed, the Word must not be sought elsewhere than concretely in the man Jesus (166). Since it is an event, however, it is dynamic and not static, an act in which God may always be seen as Lord; thus, while the Word is made flesh, he is not confined to flesh (168–169). The so-called Calvinistic extra, which derives from the fathers and is found even in Luther, expresses this truth with its perception that the Word is outside (extra) the flesh as well as in it (168–170), though this runs the obvious risk of leaving us with a twofold Word and a dissolution of the unity (170). Historically, Lutherans have stressed the completed nature of the event, Calvinists its dynamic aspect. Barth suggests that both emphases are needed so long as they are kept in tension (171).

In the last subsection Barth looks at the mystery of revelation in the form of the Christmas miracle. The texts in Matthew and Luke provide the biblical basis and starting point. Barth concedes that in view of textual problems the evidence has a certain thinness (174–176). All the same, one cannot dismiss the dogma of the miraculous conception and virgin birth on exegetical grounds (176). As a sign, the miracle of Christmas denotes the mystery of revelation, the fact that God himself does this real act of incarnation which means the coming of revelation and the effecting of reconciliation (177). Like the empty tomb at the end of the earthly life of Jesus, the virgin birth at the beginning is distinguishable but not separable from that which it denotes (178f.). The virgin birth cannot properly be understood in the context of natural theology (180f.), and it is not to be rejected (cf. Brunner) as a poor attempt at explaining the incarnation biologically (183f.). If the dogma cannot be proved, it demands acceptance because it answers to the biblical attestation and is analogously related to the mystery.

After these preliminary remarks Barth devotes a special passage to the "born of the virgin Mary." The virgin birth, he thinks, signifies five things. First, that Jesus was born as no one else was (185). Second, however, that he was born as real man (186). Third, it implies a judgment and limitation of human nature, or, more strictly, of sinful human nature (187). Fourth, and more positively, it marks a new beginning of human life (189). Fifth, it shows that this new beginning is not due to human will and achievement but to the free grace and act of God (190ff.). The exclusion of the male, discussed in an interesting excursus, gives this truth historical form, although it must not be taken to imply the merit of virginity or the exclusion of the female from God's saving work, or indeed from the need for it (192–196).

In conclusion, Barth has a similar passage on the "conceived by the Holy Spirit" (196ff.). This denotes first that the incarnation is God's work, for the Holy Spirit is God (196f.). Conception by the Spirit does not mean, of course, that the Spirit is the husband of Mary or the father of Jesus, but that he is the transcendent cause, or, better, God's creative command (200). The conception, then, is spiritual. It takes place in grace and faith and hearing (Augustine), for, as John of Damascus noted, it is by believing that Mary takes the eternal Word into herself (201). At the conception God assumes the creature and imparts his own existence to it (201). A final point to be noted is that the mystery does not rest on the miracle but the miracle on the mystery, to which the miracle bears testimony. Apt quotations from Turrettini, Quenstedt, and Peter Lombard are adduced in support of this final consideration.

C. THE OUTPOURING OF THE SPIRIT

1. Man's Freedom for God (§16)

To conclude his long chapter on the revelation of God, or the revealed Word, Barth has a third part on the outpouring of the Holy Spirit. In formal parallelism to the second part he includes first a section on the freedom of man for God, or the subjective possibility of revelation. He then introduces a discussion of the relation between revelation and religion. To round off the part, and the whole chapter, he has a first look at the ethical question in a section on the life of the children of God.

Like the parallel section on God's freedom for man, the section on man's freedom for God (§16) consists of two subsections on the reality and possibility of revelation from the subjective angle, so that the Holy Spirit, not the Word, is now the reality and possibility. The reality, of course, is dealt with first and Barth locates this in the outpouring of the Spirit (204f.). Scripture tells us not only about Jesus Christ but also about the recipients of his word and work (206ff.). These recipients—specific people at a specific time and place—constitute a specific community, the church (209ff.). The church derives, of course, from Jesus Christ himself, and this has four implications for Barth. First, it means derivation from the incarnate Word (214f.). Second, it means the law and limit of an existence for Christ's sake (216f.). Third, it means a common life in dependence on the incarnate Word

(217f.). Fourth, it means not only divinity, eternity, and invisibility, but also humanity, temporality, and visibility as a historical reality (219ff.). Yet this is not the whole story, for when we turn from the originating Word to human receiving and believing, we find that even this subjective side has an objective side, for here revelation means God's giving by the Holy Spirit as well as man's receiving in the Holy Spirit (222ff.). What Barth says here is of crucial importance. Opponents frequently accuse him of an ultimate subjectivity in which the Holy Spirit is equated with human reception and his objectivity as the self-revealing God is obscured. To support his contention that reception, too, has genuine objectivity as the gift of the revealing Spirit, Barth argues that even in its subjective reality revelation bears definite signs of its objective reality in the events, relations, and orders of the world of nature and history in which it is an objective reality. These signs, which include circumcision, prophecy, the sacraments, and the church (225–227), serve as instruments whereby the Word seeks to be apprehended by men and thus to do the work of grace on them and in them (228). Barth has an excursus on the sacraments which merits careful attention (228–232). Yet in its subjective reality revelation also consists of recipients or believers who see themselves in the light of the objective reality. How this comes about we cannot finally say. It rests on the mystery of God's grace and freedom (233–235). What we can say is that the existence of these people in whom objective revelation is also subjective revelation involves the ministry of the Holy Spirit as impartation; as Christ's ongoing work in adoption, calling, union, and faith (240–242). The distinction but inseparability of objective and subjective revelation must never be forgotten (238f.).

Turning to the subjective possibility of revelation in the second subsection, Barth begins by saying categorically that in and of himself man has no freedom for God. This does not negate the possibility, however, for God in his freedom can reach man in three successive ways by the Holy Spirit (242ff.). He can reach him (1) by bringing the Word to his hearing (246ff.; the close relation between Christ and the Spirit must be underlined here, as it obviously is not in so many pietistic hymns of the modern period, 250–257). He can reach him (2) by making man a humble, penitent, and believing hearer through the Word and Spirit. The biblical and reformation teaching that this is God's work warrants some attention (260–265). He can reach him (3) by causing the Word to become his master by the Holy Spirit (265), a master from whom he cannot withdraw (270f.); to whose supreme authority he is subject (271f.); whose command he must obey (272ff.); who frees him from all other masters (274–276); who fashions and directs him (276ff.); and whose concern is his only concern, requiring, not anxiety and activity, but simple faith and obedience (278ff.).

2. Revelation and Religion (§17)

From an early period in his work as a minister and theologian, Barth frequently dealt with the question of the relation of revelation and religion. Religion clearly belongs to the subjective side of revelation. In dealing with the outpouring of the Spirit he discusses this question in §17. He gives the section the striking title "The Revelation of God as the Abolition of Religion." It should be noted, however, that the word abolition is used here for the German *Aufhebung*, which in good Hegelian fashion can mean elevating as well as abolishing. Barth undoubtedly has this double meaning in mind.

The first subsection states the problem of religion. Revelation as God's act meets man as an event that has at least the aspect or character of the human phenomenon of religion. At this level we clearly have to think of religions in the plural, for there are other religions that display the same or similar human features (280–282). The question, then, is whether or not to regard revelation as one among the many world religions—a particular specimen of the general category which is finally to be understood and expounded in the light of this category. Aquinas, Calvin, and the older orthodox refrained from taking such a course, but some of the later orthodox, such as van Til and Buddaeus, opened the door to a general discussion of religion, and modern Liberal Protestants have pushed the door wide open (284–291). According to Barth, a serious theology that remains true to its object—the revelation of God in Jesus Christ—can and must refuse to go through this open door. Religion has to be considered (293), but it cannot be coordinated with revelation (294). If revelation on its subjective side becomes religion as event, God himself is always the subject of the event. The question, then, is not that of relating revelation to a known factor of religion, but of finding out what religion is from the standpoint of the disclosed factor of revelation and faith.

A second subsection states the negative side: religion is unbelief. The church, not the best human religion, constitutes the locus of true religion (298f.). The church tolerates religion because it sees that God has graciously reconciled sinful man along with his religion (299). Religion needs this toleration, for in itself, as a concern of ungodly man, it is shown, not by human judgment but by revelation itself, to be essentially unbelief (299–301). Two elements in revelation make this clear. First, revelation opposes man's arbitrary idea of God, which religion opposes to revelation (301–304). The biblical testimony against idolatry in the Old Testament and in Romans and Acts expresses this contradiction of religion by revelation (303–307). Second, revelation as God's act of reconciliation opposes man's self-righteousness of works, which religion opposes to God's revealed work (307–310). The Old Testament, properly understood, gives evidence of this contradicting of religious self-righteousness no less than the New. This exposure of religion by revelation must be distinguished, of course, from human criticism of it. Human criticism points to a twofold weakening of religion. First, it does not meet an authentic need and hence is ultimately unnecessary (315). Second, it is a culturally variable expression of variable man (316). Under the pressure of this twofold criticism, however, religion can seek refuge from externality on a road that has two forks (318). The first and conservative fork is mysticism, which does not negate religion but attempts to bring out the inner meaning of the external (318ff.). The second and radical but also naiver fork is atheism, which comes out openly with a negation, and lives only by this negation, but finally results in a new religion (320–323). Both mysticism and atheism bring religion into crisis, but neither of them can undermine its power, which is man's power to devise and be his own god. Only revelation can bring religion into true crisis, for revelation alone, coming from outside, sets it under the judgment of idolatry and self-righteousness, thus leaving no refuge to which to flee. Neither mysticism nor atheism can genuinely disturb or abrogate religion. Revelation does this even as in its coming to man it takes the form of religion.

There can be true religion as well as false. Religion is elevated as well as abolished. This is the positive theme of the final subsection on true religion. If revelation denies that any religion is true, it also means true religion (325f.) In what sense? Not as the Christian religion, for in and of itself this comes under the judgment of revelation too (326ff.; cf. Exodus 32 and the examples of the earlier Peter, Ananias and Sapphira, and Simon Magus). Religion has to be "justified" to be true religion. This involves faith—not the faith that lives by Christian self-consciousness, but the faith that accepts Christianity's weakness and therein displays its true power (331–333). Problems arise when Christianity tries to prove itself to be the true religion, as in the early apologists, the later concept of Christendom, and modern defences of Christian superiority (333–337). Grace contradicts such contradiction of grace (337ff.). Yet not by the fact that Christianity is a religion of grace, for the example of Yodo-Shin in Japan shows the difference between a religion of grace as a human possibility and grace in itself (340–344). That there is true religion is an act of God's grace in Jesus Christ and an event in the outpouring of the Holy Spirit

(344). Christianity is true religion because it rests on the act whereby, through Christ's name, people believe in his name (346). According to Barth we have here an act that has four specific aspects. It is an act of creation (346–348), election (348–352), justification (352–357), and sanctification (357–361). Only in virtue of this fourfold divine act, and not of any inherent religious qualities of its own, is Christianity authentically described as true religion.

3. The Life of the Children of God (§18)

As Part B of the chapter on revelation closed with a section on the person of Jesus, Barth closes Part C with a section on the recipient of revelation. He thus has a final discussion (§18) of the life of the children of God which also serves as an introduction to the ethical chapters in the succeeding volumes.

The first subsection raises the general question of man as a doer of the Word. Revelation aims at a recipient. Hence man becomes a theme of dogmatics, although not independently of revelation (362–364). Man is a being that constantly achieves his existence in free acts of self-determination, but in this self-determination he is an object of the divine predetermination in the grace of revelation (362–365). This predetermination is for doing, but for doing on the basis of being, in what Barth, borrowing a phrase from Harnack, calls the life of the children of God (367–369). As children of God, believers, in a divinely given freedom, are claimed by God for being and doing: for being as the inward aspect, the seeking and loving of God (369f.); for doing as the outward and social aspect, the attesting and praising of God (370f.). From this twofold characterization derive the titles of the second and third subsections, the first on the love of God and the second on the praise of God.

Barth defines love as the beginning, essence, and totality of the Christian life (371). We love, however, only as we are first loved. If love can be called a creaturely reality, it is not so as an extension or transformation of natural human capacity but as a new creation of God through faith, which works by love, in the miracle of the Holy Spirit (372–375). Even our knowledge of Christian love rests on God's love for us (375f.), for love is no master concept embracing God's love and ours and knowable apart from either. God is love, and so knowledge of love derives from his unique love (376f.). The love of God means first his intrinsic love as the Holy Trinity wherein he loves without and before loving us and without having to love us (377). Then it is his electing love expressed and summed up in the name of Jesus, in whom he takes upon himself "the sin and guilt and death of man" (378). Our love for God answers to this love of God for us. Barth describes it in a brief exposition of Christ's first and great commandment found in Mark 12:29–31.

First, the command is given a specific target in the preamble; it is addressed to God's people (381f.). Second, and again in the preamble, it requires love for him who alone is Lord, so that no act of repayment is required but only the love that corresponds to the uniqueness with which God is Lord (382–384). Third, the "shalt" contains a future yet this does not weaken the imperative nor does a contradiction arise between love and demand, for real obedience is possible only in love, and real love is obedience (384–386). Fourth, the command shows that love must always be for another, so that there can be no such thing as self-love, as Augustine and later Kierkegaard believed, but not Luther and Calvin (386–389). Fifth, love consists in joyful seeking and finding in which there is no self-righteousness but a constant looking to the divine forgiveness and trusting in the grace of God (389–394). Sixth, loving with all one's heart, soul, mind, and strength means total and voluntary obedience (394–397), once-for-all commitment (397–400), and exclusive orientation to God in gratitude for his revealing and reconciling work (400–401). In conclusion Barth points out that love of God, while not a self-justifying work, is nevertheless a work which produces works in witness to God's work (401). In view of this, one wonders why the odd idea persists in some circles that Barth has no concept of Christian works.

One wonders even more so when reading the last subsection on the praise of God—the doing side—in which Barth expounds the second and similar commandment on love of neighbor. Here he comments first on the relation between the commands. The second command, Barth thinks, should not be seen as a second absolute (402), nor as identical with the first (402–406), nor, conversely, as relative and derived (406–409). Instead, three features demand emphasis. First, the second command, relating to our earthly walk as members of Christ, must be genuinely distinguished from the first. Second, we have in both "the one claim of the one God on the whole man" (409f.). Third, since the first command relates to the coming world and the second to the passing world, the two are not in equilibrium but constitute, in order not quality, a first and then a second which is comprised in the first, which exists for the sake of it, but which is also like it—absolute and imposing full responsiblity (410–411).

Again drawing his points from the text, Barth believes that here (1) the "thou shalt" points to a concrete task of witness in the relation of God's children to the present world (411–414). He then engages in a long discussion (2) of the term "neighbor," whom he describes christologically as our benefactor, a hidden representative of Christ (416ff.), and then as our fellow in need or suffering, representing Christ in his affliction (427ff.). (3) What, then, does love mean in this context? It means readiness to live in coexistence with our neighbors as those who both show us our need and also show us Jesus Christ as the One who is for us, so that we are both discomforted and yet also served (430–434). Love in this sense takes three forms: talking about Jesus Christ (441–444); giving help as a sign of God's promised help (444–447); and backing up the word and act by an appropriate attitude and disposition (447–450). Finally (4) Barth tackles the concluding clause "as thyself." He argues again that this does not legitimate self-love. Instead, it limits it (450ff.). Self-love exists as a reality. This reality, however, reminds us that in ourselves we are loveless sinners. Thus we can obey the command only on God's responsibility and not our own. If obedience is to be rendered, then, two things, Barth believes, are indispensable: the courage of humility (453) and the assurance of prayer (453f.). To fully appreciate this subsection, and particularly Barth's remarkable discussion of the neighbor, readers will undoubtedly have to study and ponder the details for themselves. The final sentence, perhaps, will give some indication of the attractively devotional note which typifies much of Barth's discussion:

> Praying can consist only in receiving what God has already prepared for us, before and apart from our stretching out our hands for it. It is in this praise of God that the children of God live, who love God because He first loved them (454).

CHAPTER III
Holy Scripture

1. The Word of God for the Church (§19)

HAVING finished his long chapter on the revealed Word, Barth now has a briefer one (just short of three hundred pages!) on the written Word. This chapter, by the way, should not be wrenched from its context for independent study and appraisal, as is sometimes done by those who do not seem to have as much interest in the Word of revelation or proclamation as in that of scripture. For Barth it forms an integral part of the discussion of the one Word in its threefold form. Similarly the first section on the Word of God for the church, which deals with scripture as God's Word, should not be detached from the succeeding sections on authority and freedom in the church, for in these Barth deals with matters of high importance in the doctrine, and perhaps even more so in the practical function, of holy scripture. The mistake of isolation can lead only to an incomplete and misleading understanding and evaluation.

Barth entitles the first section on scripture "The Word of God for the Church," which immediately relates scripture to its specific role in the preaching, doctrine, and life of the community. He divides the section into two subsections: a shorter one on scripture as witness to revelation, and then a longer one on scripture as the Word of God. The first of these obviously forms a transition from the previous chapter on the revealed Word and should be read in sequence with it. Incidentally, the title does not imply that scripture is one among many witnesses to revelation, as the English rendering might suggest. It simply describes the (unique) relation of scripture to revelation. The German has no article.

34

Barth opens the subsection with a preamble on the crucial importance of scripture, as well as of the scripture principle of the reformation (459f.), in relation to revelation and all that it embraces and entails (457–463). He then discusses the term "witness," which he sees as taken from scripture itself. On the one hand, it implies a limitation: scripture cannot be equated directly with revelation itself but bears witness to it (463). On the other hand, it has a positive side, for even in its differentiation scripture is in unity with revelation as this comes to us through the written words of its immediate recipients, the apostles and prophets (463). In virtue of its human form, scripture obviously must be studied historically (464). For Barth, however, truly historical study means hearing what scripture says about itself (466ff.). He refers approvingly to Calvin in this connection (467f.). Reading the Bible historically and reading it biblically are one and the same thing. Scripture, however, understands itself to be God's Word. Hence good hermeneutics cannot assume the comical position of pretending that neutral impartiality underlies sound exegesis but must accept the fact, whether one likes it or not, that materially the human word of scripture seeks to be heard as the Word of God (468ff.). Reading scripture as merely the human words of the human authors in their human situations is not truly historical and is, in fact, poor hermeneutics in which we do all the talking instead of genuinely listening (469f.). Biblical hermeneutics as truly listening to what the Bible says forms, in Barth's view, a model of all good hermeneutics. There is, of course, a distinction between what others say and what God's revelation can be in holy scripture. Thus biblical hermeneutics must be on guard against "the totalitarian claim of a general hermeneutics." It must dare to be a special hermeneutics "for the sake of a better general hermeneutics" (472).

In the second subsection Barth raises the crucial question of how the human witness of the Bible can be heard as more than human witness; how the word of man can itself speak as the Word of God. He does not give here an immediate material answer, postponing this for the next two sections. But under the heading of scripture as God's Word, he attempts some more precise definitions which he hopes will clarify the question (473).

First, Barth points out that when we speak of scripture we refer, with the church, to canonical scripture (473ff.). Scripture is to be accepted as canonical when revelation bears witness to it (a reversal of roles—revelation, too, can be witness to scripture), and when the church confirms this testimony (474f.). Many theologians, including the Roman Catholic Bartmann, can be adduced in support of this conclusion. The canon is closed relative to the witness of revelation.

Relative to the church's confirmation, since the church's hearing may be faulty, the canon has been, and still is, a debatable question (476–478). Nevertheless, it is not for individuals arbitrarily to change the canon by inclusion or exclusion. The voice of the whole church, in time as well as space, must always be respected even if views may differ concerning the utterances of this voice and their consonance with the canon to which revelation testifies (478–481).

Second, we refer in the canon to the scriptures of the Old and New Testaments, the witness of expectation and recollection, which Barth declares to be in irreversible distinction and yet also in indissoluble unity (481–483). The unity, of course, is that of revelation itself, or of witness to it, not of a system of imposed or extracted doctrines which much of the older orthodoxy espoused and which, when it crumbled, left the field open for what Barth describes as "the Philistines of the eighteenth century" (483–485).

Third, we follow what scripture says about itself. We find this implicitly in the unique and contingent revelation to which it bears witness, or, more simply, in the true humanity of Christ as the object of this witness (485f.). To this implicit material testimony corresponds an explicit formal witness: that of humanity represented by specific men who had the unique and contingent function of being the first witnesses to the unique and contingent revelation (486). First of all, these men are apostles (487f.), although not to the exclusion of the Old Testament writers or prophets (488–490). Their witness has a passive form—they witnessed what took place—and it also has an active form—they bore witness to it (490). Barth stresses the point that they are the authors of scripture only as they discharge their office of witness, not as the thinkers or religious geniuses or moral heroes that they might also have been.

Fourth, we accept a unity of scriptural form and revelational content, so that we are, as Barth strongly states, "tied to these texts." Luther is quoted here (492). In this connection Barth warns against trying to find facts above or behind the texts, such as a history of Israel or a life of Jesus, for which the texts may be merely regarded as more or less trustworthy original sources (492f.). From a purely literary or historical point of view this might be helpful. Theologically, it misses the point. Certainly one can and should make use of the findings of biblical scholarship. One must not use them, however, to mediate a supposed truth behind the texts. The historical truth to be mediated is "the true meaning and content of the biblical texts as such." For this reason Christianity is a living religion only when "it is not ashamed to be actually and seriously a book-religion" (494f.).

Fifth, we ascribe to scripture a unique position, not in virtue of its superlative intrinsic qualities, but in virtue of its unique function: it is both divine and human in analogy to the incarnation (496). Barth realizes, of course, that one cannot speak of a unity of person between God and the biblical writers. Nevertheless, there is a likeness to the incarnation. Scripture is neither divine only, nor human only, nor a mixture of the two. In its own way it is very God and very man. It is witness to revelation which is itself revelation; it is also a human historical document. Barth can thus speak of "an indirect identity of human existence with God himself . . . by the decision and act of God" (500).

Sixth, we believe that scripture "has priority over all other writings" and as the "original and legitimate witness is itself the Word of God" (502). It is this, not statically, nor as a compendium of human knowledge (508), but dynamically in the act of the Holy Spirit. Barth offers here an exposition of 2 Timothy 3:16 and 2 Peter 1:10–21 in support of his dynamic understanding (503–506). Scripture has been God's Word, it will be so again, and it is so, not as a lasting state, but at the living point between the "has been" and the "will be." He does not think that this being of scripture as God's Word endows it with inerrancy, although he issues a warning against the idea that we have any superior platform from which to judge it to be in error (510–512). To get at the meaning of scripture we have to study it in its human historical context. Nevertheless, it is by the miracle of God that the human words with their given contextual meaning are to us also the Word of the God of scripture (513).

In this connection Barth introduces a biblical and historical excursus. He first seeks additional support for his view in 2 Corinthians 3:14–18 and 1 Corinthians 2:6–16 (514–516). He then surveys the teaching of the early church, in which he finds a focus on inspiration, an interest in grammatical inspiration, and a docetic tendency (516–519). The reformation rightly accepts verbal inspiration but lays new emphasis on Christ as the content of scripture and on the work of the Holy Spirit not only in its composition, but also in its right hearing and reading (520–522). In Protestant orthodoxy the pressures of Socinianism and Roman Catholicism produce, he thinks, a desire for security which finds expression in a tight identification of man's word and God's. Consequently, this brings about the disastrous Liberal reaction of a purely human treatment of scripture and the virtual denial that it is specifically the Word of God (522–526).

Barth sums up his own understanding of scripture as God's Word in eight propositions. First, the Word of God means the control of God (527). Second, it means the work or act of God (527f.). Third, it means the miracle of God (528). Fourth, it means also a human form (528–

530). Fifth, the presence of God's Word is not an intrinsic attribute (530). Sixth, the Word, or God, decides when scripture is the Word (530–532). Seventh, the Word is through the text: God "says what the text says" and "the work of God is done through this text" (532f.). Eighth, inspiration cannot be reduced to, or made dependent on, our own belief in it, for God's Word is recognized as such simply "by the fact that it *is* the Word of God." To Strauss, and to many others who have followed him, this circular reasoning is "the Achilles' heel of the Protestant system." In contrast, Barth believes that at this apparently weakest point "Protestant doctrine has all its indestructible strength" (534–537). Why? Because it dares to let God's Word be truly God's. God can and will speak his own Word through scripture and therefore it is no illusion to begin with the fact that he does.

2. Authority in the Church (§20)

Having cleared the ground in this way, Barth develops the substance of the doctrine of scripture, and of the scripture principle, in a second section dealing with the issue of authority in the church (§20). In two subsections he approaches the matter from two angles, that of the authority *of* the Word, and that of authority *under* the Word. [If the witness of scripture is that of the Holy Spirit, so that hearing scripture is hearing Jesus Christ, then scripture has objectively an overruling authority in the church by which the church's own authority is limited but by which alone it is authentically established.]What is this authority?

First, Barth does not think that it consists merely of the historical precedence enjoyed by scripture or its authors. Certainly the apostles are historically closer to Christ and on that ground (as even Schleiermacher could admit) their writings carry special weight. In itself, however, this confers on them only a higher degree of indirect, relative, and formal authority—not the direct, absolute, and material authority that they enjoy as God's Word (540f.).

[Ultimately, of course, it is revelation itself that has direct, absolute, and material authority. This means that the apostles can have such authority only by reason of a unique relationship with Christ as the revealed Word.]They have this relationship by their unique calling and commissioning as his witnesses, so that as the church hears them, it hears God's Word (542–544). This is the scripture principle which Barth discusses historically in a long and important excursus (544–572). The fathers, he thinks, held the principle, although not unequivocally (548–551). The reformation confessions stated it clearly and forcefully (546f.). The Tridentines did not reject it but weakened it by exalting tradition, not as another form of the same apostolic witness, but as a second source of revelation (547f.), and also by trying to bring scripture itself under the final hermeneutical authority of the church (551f.). Some of the older orthodox, particularly Grotius and Calixtus, made unfortunate if well-intentioned concessions to the Roman Catholic position along the lines of a supposed early catholic consensus (554ff.). A few Roman Catholics, like Simon, pressed home the resultant advantage by drawing attention to the textual and even the historical fragility of scripture (559). Finally Sailer, Drey, Möhler, and Scheeben developed a theology of the church as the living interpreter of scripture and voice of the Holy Spirit. This theology came to a head in the Vatican Council of 1870 and its hotly contested but finally accepted decree of papal infallibility. Papal infallibility undermines the scripture principle, not so much by setting alongside it a second source, but by bringing scripture definitively under the exegetical rulings of the teaching office (560–572). Fortunately, since Barth wrote, scripture has been able to display the freedom of which he speaks in the next section and has broken loose from this yoke by the astonishing development of biblical studies in the Roman Catholic world.

In contrast to the Roman Catholic understanding, the scripture principle, proclaiming the living presence of the Word in and with holy scripture, resists the autonomous authority of the church while giving this authority an authentic ground as the authority of obedience (573f.). Scripture continuously confronts the church as an ongoing entity of its own, embodying the unique witness to revelation through which God speaks his own Word to the church (580f.). The reality of the prophets and apostles "has the form of book and letter" in which they themselves continue to live without being absorbed or subsumed by the church. Authority in the church consists in this book and letter, not as such, but as the book and letter through which their voice is heard, and through their voice "the voice of Him who called them to speak" (581f.). In this function scripture maintains its own integrity and autonomy irrespective even of all exposition (583). The true vitality of the church depends, Barth thinks, on its being by the Word of God, which means by holy scripture (584). The ongoing presence of scripture gives it constant assurance of God's own gracious presence in a concrete authority different from and far above its own (584f.).

The higher authority of scripture necessarily limits the lesser authority of the church. Yet it also establishes it, just as the first commandment establishes even while it limits the fifth. Hence a second subsection is needed to deal with what Barth describes as authority under the Word.

In a general sense, Barth has in mind what he was speaking of at the end of the first subsection, namely, the authentic obedient authority of the church which recognizes the absolute authority of the Word (586ff.). This authority is set up by common hearing and receiving of the Word (588). In practice, then, it takes the form of the basic confession of the church within which each individual Christian makes his or her individual confession (589ff.). Debate in the church, Barth believes, should always be with a view to authoritative common confession (592) and the call for decision issued in relation to specific historical forms of authority (593ff.).

Barth goes on to discuss three of these historical forms: the canon, the fathers, and the confessions. Regarding the canon, he does not add a great deal to his discussion in the previous section, but examines it from a different angle. The church proposes the canon for the Christian. Clearly the authority of the church is subsidiary here to scripture itself. Hence one might always challenge the common decision, particularly if appeal can be made to the self-testimony of scripture on which the church's canon finally reposes. Nevertheless, the church has authority here in relation to the individual. Any challenging of the church's common decision can be done only as a serious and responsible enterprise and not as a matter of mere whim, caprice, or arrogance. Even if secondary, the authority of the church may not be lightly disregarded. The church's proposal holds until agreement, or at least a measure of agreement, leads to a new decision (601f.). Barth does not take the view, however, that the same principle applies (at least to the same extent) in relation to agreed texts or agreed translations of scripture, although here, too, there must be regard to what others have done or are doing in the church at large (602f.).

Next, Barth defines the fathers, among whom he reckons the leading reformers, as teachers in the church who across the years have been accorded special authority because their word has been commonly received with "attention and gratitude" (603ff.). After some interesting historical discussion (603–606, 607–609, 610–612), he advances four criteria by which to recognize authentic fathers. First and fundamentally they must be correct expositors of holy scripture (613). Second, although with no restriction of time or place, they must stand the test of the evangelical confessions (614). Third, they must be responsible to the church in their work and witness (615). Fourth, they must speak a word that calls for decision (616ff.). Those who might have a claim to be regarded as fathers should be brought under rigorous scrutiny according to these criteria, for many teachers have made significant contributions to the church without enjoying the authority of true fathers. Even when the test is successfully met, it should always be understood that the authority of fathers of the church is an indirect, relative, and formal authority which stands always under the direct, absolute, and material authority of the Word.

Finally, Barth considers the subsidiary authority of creeds and confessions. As one who had a hand in framing a significant confession, the *Barmen Declaration* of 1934, Barth had much interest in this topic. What constitutes an authoritative statement of this type? He singles out, and discusses at considerable length, five necessary characteristics. First, the authoritative creed or confession must be a common statement expounding holy scripture (620–622). Second, it must confess an insight that has been given to the church (622–624). Third, this given insight must owe its material content to holy scripture as illuminated by the Holy Spirit (624f.). Fourth, the confession must express this insight in definite limits, that is, limits of time, place, and debate which impart to it not only a positive aspect but also a decidedly negative and polemical side as well (625–637). Finally, the authentic confession must be a public statement which derives from the church and which is ultimately ratified by it in spite of every possible counterpressure (633–657).

In conclusion Barth repeats the point that all these authorities, in distinction from holy scripture, are indirect, relative, and formal. They cannot be regarded as infallible and therefore they are always in principle reformable (657–659). The difference between Roman Catholic and Evangelical teaching on this issue comes up for treatment in a brief excursus which includes apt citations from Luther, Calvin, Hollaz, and representative reformation confessions (657f.). Nevertheless, Barth sees fit to issue a warning against hasty and frivolous changes. An inner necessity must exist if, for instance, a confession is to be altered or replaced. Holy scripture, and indeed all past and present voices, must be heard publicly in the church before a new statement is ventured (659). Liberal Protestantism, for all its noisy revolutionary utterances, has never reached the point of seriously proposing a new canon, new fathers, or new dogma. This may be due in part to a rejection in principle of all such authorities. In Barth's view, however, it rests on the wise if not wholly conscious realization that the movement has in fact no real authority for its radical ideas about canon, fathers, and dogma (660).

3. Freedom in the Church (§21)

From authority in the church Barth moves on in the third section (§21) of the chapter to the complementary theme of freedom in the church. Here again he has two subsections: the freedom *of* the Word, and freedom *under* the Word. The written Word in its relation to the church is still, of course, the subject of discussion.

Freedom is linked to authority because the authority of the Word calls for free obedience (661f.). In this respect Barth makes the perspicacious observation that authoritarian churches need to learn true authority while churches which emphasize freedom need to learn true freedom (663ff.). True freedom, like true authority, is first and supremely that of the Word in which the authentic freedom of the church is grounded. The Word itself is the free Word for free men (669ff.). What this freedom means for the Word is that it is a truly living, acting, and speaking subject which only as such can be heard and received by and in the church (672).

Analyzing this freedom of the Word, Barth finds it first in the unique and divinely given theme which constitutes it a subject, namely, the revelation to which it bears direct witness (673f.). He then discovers it in the power of the Word in relation and opposition to all other powers, a power (1) to maintain itself (680f.), (2) to assimilate alien elements (682f.), and (3) to change its own form and effect in the world (683f.). As Barth states, holy scripture "has more power than all the rest of the world together" (678). He finally sees the freedom of the Word in its operation in the sphere of the church, which, he maintains, it chooses, defines, claims, and conquers (686f.). This activity comes to expression in its founding (687f.), its preserving (688f.), and its ruling of the church (692–695). In order that the church may respect this freedom of the Word, and maintain a fundamental openness to the leading of scripture, two things are demanded: constant exegesis and constant prayer (694f.).

Freedom under the Word results from the Word's own freedom, which constitutes its basis and limit. Barth defines this freedom as freedom to accept the Word as well as the responsibility to hear and understand it (695ff.). Giving itself to us in human form, the Word comes as a claim, command, and law which frees us to hear and apply it. In this way the divine determination makes possible our own self-determination, both corporately as the church and individually as its members (699ff.).

Barth works out five implications of freedom in this sense. First, it means the common participation of believers in hearing and receiving the Word as those who are given an active and responsible part in "the great event by which holy scripture lives and rules in the church and in the world" (710–715). This participation of ours consists predominantly of the interpretation of scripture. This leads to the second implication, namely, that in this task true freedom means the subordination of all human concepts, ideas, and convictions to the biblical witness to revelation (715–722). In discussing this point Barth issues the sober reminder that even in what may seem to be "its most debatable and least assimilable parts" the message of scripture is always "truer and more important than the best and most necessary things that we ourselves have said or can say" (719).

As interpretation, freedom has three phases which constitute the three remaining implications. Exposition comes first as the investigation and exegesis of scripture (722–727). Then comes meditation or reflection, in which we put the teaching of scripture into our own words and concepts, although with constant awareness of what we are doing, having no independent interest in the words and concepts as such, nor preference for them, and keeping them continually under the control of the text itself (727–736). Barth's more positive assessment of philosophy in this context as well as its specific limitation should be noted (735). Finally, interpretation means application or appropriation (736ff.). In authentic freedom this cannot be assimilation or adaptation of the Word to ourselves, to our own concerns, to modern man, to the new generation, or to the burning issues of the day (738f.). It involves instead a transposition away from self to the Word, to the questions and concerns of the Word, and supremely to its object—Jesus Christ. Faith is the prerequisite in this transposition, for faith sees in scripture the focal point of our attention. By faith we ourselves think what scripture is saying to us and thus attain to what Barth calls "contemporaneous homogeneity" with the witness of revelation. For Barth, then, obedient faith—note the familiar juxtapositon—constitutes the exercise of the freedom that is granted to us in and under the Word.

The demands of introductory exposition rule out any extended evaluation of Barth's doctrine of scripture; nevertheless, a few comments are in order. It must be remembered that in the context of the revealed Word, and by the ministry of the Holy Spirit, scripture is for Barth genuinely and objectively God's Word, although he resists any static conception of it which might abstract the written text either from God or from his Word in its threefold totality. This means that he tends to ascribe more validity to the present inspiring of scripture by the Spirit in its reading and hearing, although he finds a satisfactory objectivity both in the person of the Holy Spirit and also in the authors as the unique witnesses to Christ who are given a place in the event of revelation itself. In no sense does he think of a constitution of scripture as God's Word by subjective experience of it. He has little time for inerrancy, which he seems to regard as both irrelevant and even misleading. On the other hand, while thinking that the possibility of error must be accepted, he can see no absolute position from which to establish actual errors and he sets no store by the emphasizing of alleged mistakes or difficulties. Indeed, he does not follow here his own rule and deduce the possibility of error from its reality!

To some this might all seem to be unsatisfactory and even ambivalent, but in what he has to say about the authority and freedom of scripture as God's Word, Barth leaves little room for complaint. He wisely recognizes a qualitative, not just a quantitative, distinction between this authority and freedom and all other authorities and freedoms in the church. He no less wisely perceives that as divine authority and freedom, the authority and freedom of the written Word do not have to conflict with these others. The important point is that things be set in proper order, the supremacy of God's Word being acknowledged and the subordination of the church accepted. When this is done, the apparent bondage becomes genuine freedom, while self-grounded authority is exposed as empty pretension and tyranny, and autonomous freedom is exposed as real enslavement. Both in teaching and life the church and individual Christians attain to their own freedom and authority only as they subject every thought and act to the obedience of scripture and engage in the objective scriptural exegesis in which holy scripture can speak God's Word.

An odd thing happens here, for as Barth develops authority and freedom in this way the two finally amount to very much the same thing. In its authority the Word is free—in its freedom it exercises authority. So, too, the church achieves its freedom when it is subject to the authority of the Word, and in this freedom of obedience it can speak and act with genuine authority. Today, as always, the church and the Christian are hard pressed by the questions of authority and freedom in both thought and life. Under current pressures the two tend to fall apart, and with authoritarianism on the one side and self-will on the other, there is in the last resort neither freedom nor authority. Forgotten in this dilemma and conflict are the authority and freedom of the Word under which the church's freedom and authority can be reconciled. Perhaps the best aspect of Barth's total doctrine of holy scripture as the written Word is that it drives us back beyond the interminable squabbles about inspiration and inerrancy to this concrete issue of the authority and freedom of the Word. When this is recognized, the authority and freedom of the church can be restored, and the confusion of much of its teaching and practice can be healed.

CHAPTER IV

The Proclamation of the Church

1. The Mission of the Church (§22)

IN his material presentation of the threefold Word, Barth dealt first with the revealed Word in chapter two and then with the written Word in chapter three. To finish his doctrine of the Word of God he needed a parallel discussion of the preached or proclaimed Word and he supplied this in chapter four under the general heading of "The Proclamation of the Church." He divided this chapter into three sections: the mission of the church; dogmatics as a function of the hearing church; and dogmatics as a function of the teaching church.

In this chapter Barth seems to have had in mind a question which had occupied him as a preacher and had helped to push him into serious theological reflection. This was the question of the possibility of the word of man also being the Word of God. He thus opened his first section (§22) on "The Mission of the Church" with a subsection on "The Word of God and the Word of Man in Preaching." Preaching or, more generally, proclamation, is no less God's Word than the revealed or the written Word. It is so in a different form yet no less integrally (743f.). God proclaims himself in the proclamation of the church, as Luther and Calvin both declare (746f.). Now obviously we cannot measure or test this pragmatically (748). Nevertheless, we believe and accept it as God's grace in Jesus Christ (748f.). The human impossibility of speaking of God in such a way that others hear of him (750) cannot alter the fact that "God in the freedom of his grace makes good what we do badly," so that the true impossibility is known only from the reality (750f.). This reality has to be described as the miracle of God himself in both speaker and hearer (751f.). Hence the confidence of preachers must be tempered by a sense of their need for forgiveness as they reflect how little their own words correspond to what is required (752f.). Dependence on prayer in both speaking and hearing necessarily calls for emphasis (755). At the same time, Barth issues a warning. Prayer does not eliminate the summons to serious and honest work undertaken, not in self-confidence, but in the confidence in God which will tolerate neither indolence nor indifference (755ff.).

What is entailed in this serious and honest work forms the subject of the next subsection. Here Barth comes to his special concern in the chapter, namely, the role of dogmatics in this whole matter. Under the heading of "Pure Doctrine as the Problem of Dogmatics," he examines the human requirements of our human speaking if it is to be the Word of God. First, our human speaking about God must receive a specific goal and rule, and then it must examine its correctness. Next, it must be set under a definite responsibility toward God. Always it must seek to be the true and pure doctrine or teaching which the Augsburg Confession describes as an essential mark of the church (758–762). Right teaching, Barth suggests, must always have right hearing in view as well. This is why he prefers the term "pure," for it suggests transparency as well as truth and correctness (764). Whether or not doctrine achieves this depends finally on God's own speaking in and with our speaking (765), yet trust in God's gracious action demands our human activity along the lines suggested. In Barth's view, the essential task of dogmatics is to ensure that as far as humanly possible, our speaking and teaching is pure. The problem of preaching is the problem of dogmatics; the problem of dogmatics is the problem of preaching.

But why dogmatics? Why not theology as a whole in the threefold task of interpretation of which he spoke in the preceding section? Barth recognizes that preaching depends on exposition (biblical theology) and application (practical theology) as well as reflection (dogmatic theology). If he assigns a central role to the last of these, it is because it actually does come in the middle, supervising the transition from exposition to application that has to be made in preaching and teaching (766f.). Pure doctrine, he points out, is dynamic, not static. It is achieved by the gift of the Holy Spirit in the fulfilment of the task of dogmatics (768). Dogmatics as the seeking of pure doctrine is thus preparatory to proclamation as the word of man in which the Word of God speaks and is heard (770). Dogmatics may, of course, be preaching, just as preaching may be dogmatics, but the two are separable inasmuch as dogmatics forms the essential base for the front-line job of preaching (769f.).

Standing in the middle between exposition and application, dogmatics has to maintain relations on both sides. Not being directly confronted by either scripture or congregation, it can easily wander off into abstraction or fall victim to the invading forces of philosophy (773f.). On the other hand, it must resist the tendency to abandon its own proper task. This consists of first hearing the word of proclamation (775f.), then praying (776), then asking basic and rigorous questions about what is being said on crucial issues (777ff.). Barth insists that these questions must not be asked in judgment or correction but in a process of weighing and testing (779f.). The questions, which good dogmatics will always address to itself first, finally boil down to two: the question of the dogmatic norm, which is the objective possibility of proclamation; and the question of the use of that norm—of dogmatic thinking or method—which is the subjective possibility.

Before taking up these questions of norm and method in the next two sections, Barth interposes a third and very short subsection on the relation between dogmatics and ethics. He opposes any independent ethics based on general anthropology. His main reason for this is that anthropology will tend to absorb dogmatics and ultimately swallow up biblical and practical theology as well—an insight that is no less true today than at the time of writing (782f.). To back up his objection, Barth offers a historical survey which ranges from Basil of Caesarea, by way of Aquinas, Luther, and Calvin, then Melanchthon and Calixtus, to Schleiermacher, Nitzsch, Wendt, and Kähler (781–786). A further important point for Barth is that separation of dogmatics and ethics is harmful to both, for dogmatics becomes intellectualistic without ethics, while ethics adopts the wrong approach to conduct without dogmatics (787f.). Historical examples are again adduced in explanation (788–790). Of course, ethics necessarily arises in dogmatics, for the Word of God comes to man as doer, not just thinker or hearer (792f.). Thus the question of right doing is posed for dogmatics as well as that of right thinking or hearing (793f.). Technically ethics can be treated separately, but not materially. Barth proposes to deal with the two in integral relation, thus bringing method into conformity with matter (795f.).

2. Dogmatics as a Function of the Hearing Church (§23)

In the next main section (§23) Barth begins his final and most detailed exposition of the work of dogmatics and its relation to the preached Word. If he tends to be repetitive here, there is some excuse. As noted already, the problem of preaching God's Word led him to dogmatics in the first place and his exposition of the task obviously serves the purpose of self-clarification. It also brings to light for all of us the essential if often concealed and neglected participation of dogmatics in the church's ministry and mission of evangelism, pastoral care, and practical activity.

From the general standpoint of the section, Barth has a first subsection on the formal task of dogmatics. Dogmatics starts with preaching and its ambiguity in relation to scripture (798f.). Dogmatics constantly reminds us that God speaks in man's word. It aims at better speaking about God and to this end issues a call to unity and order (800–802). To achieve this, the teaching church must be a hearing church, and if dogmatics is to serve it as such, it, too, must be a hearing dogmatics (805–807). The service of dogmatics consists negatively in a summoning of the church away from self-will in the form of heresy (807f.) or of pre-heretical deviation (808f.). It consists positively in a constant calling back to hearing (810). Strictly, dogmatics itself does not define or proscribe heresies and their proponents; this is a job for the whole church. Instead, dogmatics warns against emerging heresies, draws attention to their possible consequences, and shows what is the right decision in relation to them (811f.). It does this on the basis of a fresh hearing of Jesus Christ in holy scripture (810).

The second subsection follows up this final point with a renewed discussion of the dogmatic norm. Dogmatics teaches by listening. Its job is that of a sign or witness in the church (812ff.). In this capacity it functions as a gateway which is also a barrier (815). Since it sets up as a norm the revelation attested in scripture, it is itself theonomous and not autonomous, but with heteronomy as a counterpart and basis, that is, as the recognition of another law to which it, too, is subject (815f.).

Concretely, three things are demanded of an obedient and exemplary dogmatics. First it must be biblical, which in turn implies three things: (a) it must adopt the attitude and orientation of the biblical witnesses; (b) it must hear their witness; (c) it must not merely exegete this witness but take up questions and concerns that cannot be answered directly from biblical texts and contexts, and yet answer them in a way that conforms to the witness of scripture (816–822).

The second demand is that dogmatics be confessional. This means a determination in part by the fathers, councils, and creeds. To this extent one might call a true dogmatics ecumenical (822–824). It also means a determination in part by prior conflicts and controversies. For Barth this means that dogmatics will be Evangelical, not Roman Catholic, Eastern Orthodox, or Neo-Protestant (826). It will, of course, remain dogmatics in the broader sense and not become narrowly specialized in the form of symbolics (827f.). It will also embrace all the Evangelical churches, for example, the Reformed, Lutheran, and Anglican, although for Barth personally dogmatics has to mean Reformed dogmatics (829–831). The same applies to the different Evangelical schools within the churches (833ff.). A final point is that, while incontestably and unashamedly confessional, and rightly so, dogmatics cannot be merely a confessional reiteration of dogmas laid down by, for example, the reformers or the reformation confessions (837ff.).

This leads on to the third and final requirement that dogmatics be modern, or, better, that it be churchly in the sense of listening to the church of today and its situation (839ff.). Dogmatics can never with a good conscience pretend to be timeless (841). It can never think and speak aesthetically (841f.). It must not ignore the present and seek refuge in a romantic or romanticized past (842f.). At the opposite extreme, of course, it is not allowed to become secular and merely to serve the spirits of every passing present (843). Praying in and with the church, dogmatics will not listen to the voices of today but will seek "the voice of God for today." In solidarity with the church, churchly or church dogmatics tests the spirits of the age. In so doing, it does not become their witness. It gives the witness which these spirits need to hear and which only the church and a churchly or church dogmatics can give (843).

3. Dogmatics as a Function of the Teaching Church (§24)

In the last section (§24) Barth looks at the other side of the coin, dogmatics as a function of the teaching church. This time the first subsection deals with the material task of dogmatics. The church must teach as well as hear. Dogmatics, then, summons it to a better presentation of its theme (844). Authentic hearing imposes a demand for service, that is, for teaching (845). But why is this so? Might it not seem that the church can hear without teaching? The answer is this: God wills to speak, and he wills to speak his own Word in the church's word. He has given the church a promise to this effect in Jesus Christ who is the theme as well as the norm of proclamation. The dynamics of doing the Word—of teaching it—is the dynamics of its theme (848). The presence of Jesus Christ means that the church has no option but to preach, and a primary task of dogmatics is to remind it that the Word of God goes out as a living message in the active teaching and preaching of the church. The divine theme or object is thus the subjective possibility of pure doctrine as a human activity. If dogmatics calls the church to the Word as a norm to be heard, it also calls it to the Word as a content to be taught (850). It does not do this only from outside. While dogmatics is not itself preaching, it has a part to play in teaching, namely, that of unfolding and presenting the content of the Word in the power and freedom of the Word. In doing this it also encourages and empowers the whole church in the feeble but divinely constrained and encompassed discharge of its teaching and preaching mission (851–853).

The last subsection, which concludes the section, the chapter, and indeed the whole volume (I,1 and I,2) of prolegomena, serves as a link to the volumes that follow. In it Barth considers what he calls "The Dogmatic Method" and he is thus led to an exposition of the method which he proposes to adopt. He begins with some general reflections. Dogmatics, like preaching, is an instrument. Its way or method is determined by the Word (856). It will consist of an exposition of God's Word and work. It is thus theonomous, taking its law from God. True theonomy, however, means a legitimate autonomy, a human freedom, although naturally a freedom that is rooted in obedience to the object (860f.). By reason of this freedom, method is "arbitrary." At the same time a considered decision has to be made if dogmatics is to be what it is required to be, namely, biblical, confessional, and churchly (862).

What about system? Barth has two counterbalancing thoughts here. System is to be avoided in the sense of focusing on a specific article or articles (862), with a clear-cut distinction between the basic and the non-basic. It militates against the freedom of obedience, not allowing the Word itself to be truly basic and central (863). Nevertheless, this does not rule out a systematic or architectonic handling either of the whole or of specific doctrines. If it did, Barth would come under his own criticisms, for *Church Dogmatics* and its individual volumes give ample evidence of careful planning and balanced structuring. Barth's point is that since the Word constitutes the norm and core, the dogmatician can find no outside platform from which to survey the field. Instead, he is under the direction of the Word and in authentic freedom of obedience he will work out his dogmatics in the form of *loci* or tenets which do not proceed from a higher unity or express a transcendent synthesis, but simply arise out of the Word itself (867–870).

In this connection Barth asks himself whether reconciliation does not seem to form a central doctrine to which all the others should be related. He acknowledges that it stands at the heart of dogmatics but not in such a way as to subsume either creation preceding it, redemption following it, or God himself as the God of creation, reconciliation, and redemption (870ff.). (Those who criticize Barth on the ground that he has no real doctrine of creation should note that, if this be true, it is not at least by intention.) We are led, then, to four basic *loci* or tenets: God, creation, reconciliation, and redemption. These four might seem to derive from the doctrine of the divine unity and trinity, but Barth does not accept this in the sense of deliberate systematization. The four *loci* and the doctrine of the divine unity and trinity all derive, as they should, from the same source—the Word and work of God in his self-revelation—so that any structural parallelism is not imposed *by* us on the matter but imposed *on* us by the matter. In other words, it is not by conscious systematization, but under the pressure of the actuality of the Word that we are led to the Trinity and then to the four *loci* as the authentic themes of dogmatics (878f.).

Is there any essential reason to deal with the four themes in the order already suggested; namely, God first, and then successively God the Creator, Reconciler, and Redeemer? Barth thinks not. Barth stays with the order because it represents the most unpretentious and yet also the most meaningful choice (879f.).

Preparing to embark on the dogmatics proper, Barth concludes his prolegomena with a brief account of what he aims to do under each of the four heads (881–883). In giving this account he stresses the central position of Jesus Christ as the Word by whom errors may be detected and avoided. Even here, however, he steers clear of his supposed mistake of christomonism—an abstract isolation of the second person of the Trinity. For, he says, we shall avoid errors in the autonomy of our human words and thoughts only as God speaks his own words and thoughts in the autonomy of the Holy Spirit. In all its work, dogmatics can speak legitimately only as it speaks of the God who is the revelation of the Father in Jesus Christ by the Holy Spirit (883f.).

Barth raises many interesting and important issues in this whole chapter. The most immediately pertinent, perhaps, is that of the function of dogmatics. Brought up in theological circles that had little use for dogmatics, Barth makes a significant contribution to its rehabilitation earlier in Volume One with his discussion of the nature of dogmatic science. Now at the close of the volume where he develops points already made earlier, he issues a strong plea for the practicality of dogmatics in relation to the church's ministry and mission.

The plea is no less timely today than when it was first issued. For many people dogmatics is outdated; for many it is esoteric; for many more it is useless; and for many it is all three. Among those who still have a concern for it, its main purpose seems to be to answer their intellectual questions and to provide material for apologetics or polemics. What purpose it can serve in the real life and work of the church at large is not perceived. Teaching dogmatics may be ranked at the top of the ecclesiastical ladder by some but then more as an escape from the hurly-burly of true mission than as engagement in it, and only with a very secular and not at all a biblical sense of values.

Barth, however, sees things very differently. The dogmatician serves no doubt at the base, but he performs there a task that is essential to activity at the front. This is the task of shaping the word and work of the church in such a way that even in new forms of thought and speech, and even in new situations which have no direct precedent in scripture, right things are said and done. It fulfils this task by keeping both itself and the church at large subject to the right norm and in a relation of scientific objectivity to the authentic content.

Dogmatics has this function for Barth because of two convictions he holds most strongly. First, our own preaching and teaching can be God's Word only as they are tested by the norm and brought into conformity with the object, namely, the revealed Word as this is authoritatively attested by the written Word. The ministry of the Word, then, cannot escape the theological question, or it can do so only to its detriment. Second, every practical issue, as World War I so vividly brought home to Barth, is basically a theological issue. In face of wrong developments, and indeed of practical problems in general, the most practical course is to explore first the theological basis of action. For the church to rush into action without considering what it is doing theologically is the height of folly. Dogmatics has the task of aiding the church at large both to know and to do the gospel in its ministry of both word and act.

The servant role of dogmatics calls for notice here. Far from assuming a role of mastery, dogmatics gives itself to the service of the whole church in order that the church may truly be the church in the service of the world. The true dogmatician claims and accepts no eminence. He does not even see himself as a being apart, for in some measure dogmatics is the responsibility of every Christian. Barth could never abide ordinary church members excusing themselves from the theological task as supposed "laymen." Nor does the dogmatician see his work as an end in itself. At the same time, he will not be content to be pushed into a quiet backwater. With the church and on the church's behalf he has the job of meeting the needs of the church's mission. He does it, not as the superior critic and adviser on the outside, but as the involved and responsible participant on the inside without whose counsel and example the ministry of the church would be less faithfully discharged.

Whether or not dogmatics in particular has this function rather than theology in general may well be disputed. Barth has something in his favor when he argues that dogmatics stands at the middle point between biblical and practical theology. Nevertheless, as he sees only too clearly, dogmatics cannot be done without biblical and practical theology and the ancillary but indispensable discipline of historical theology. Perhaps what Barth says about dogmatics and its function actually applies to theology in its totality. Perhaps biblical and historical theologians might be profitably recalled from more esoteric intellectualized pursuits to their proper work in the service of the Word of God and the church. Perhaps practical theologians should be shown again the practicality of theology so that they do not slip into a supposed theology that is dominated by practice. Theology as a whole and not just dogmatics in particular has been regarded for too long and in too many circles as a luxury which can be allowed only to the few, and to many of the few only for limited periods of time. It will surely be for the better health of the church and the integrity of its ministry if the servant function of theology can again be grasped, if theologians can give themselves to its fulfilment, and if the church as a whole can learn to welcome and utilize the service that they render.

The
Doctrine
of God

CHAPTER V

The Knowledge of God

1. The Fulfilment of the Knowledge of God (§25)

HAVING dealt with the Word of God first, Barth immediately confronts the question of the knowledge of God. This follows very naturally, of course, from his presentation of the revelation of God in the first volume. He divides the subject into three sections: the fulfilment of the knowledge of God; the knowability of God; and the limits of the knowledge of God. The first of these (§25) is made up of two subsections with the somewhat enigmatic titles of "Man before God" and "God before Man."

In the light of the self-revelation of God, on which dogmatics rests, Barth believes one must obviously begin with the reality of the knowledge of God and not with its mere possibility. God is known in the church through his Word (II,1, 3ff.). If dogmatic investigation is to follow the actual situation, then it, too, must put the reality before the possibility. The knowledge of God that is bound to the Word of God stands secure against every threat of impossibility and therefore against every actual or possible attack upon it (6ff.). This security, grounded as it is in simple fact, is of great importance to Barth. As he sees it, the basic error in defensive apologetics is to let go of this security—to set aside the reality for strategic reasons, and to begin by trying to demonstrate the abstract possibility (6ff.).

In the knowledge of God, God himself is the object. This means that man is made the subject of this knowledge; he is set before God. A distinction of known and knower is thereby established which safeguards the authentic objectivity of the knowledge. The knowledge has to conform to the object. Nevertheless, God as object demands a special form of knowledge, namely, the knowledge of faith, faith being the relation of the knower to the God who gives himself to be known (10f.). If, then, a difference arises between the knowledge of God and the knowledge of other things or persons, it arises out of the prior difference between God as object and all other possible objects (14f.). Here is an absolute difference—the difference of Creator and creature—in contrast to all the relative differences between creaturely objects that naturally involve differences, but only relative differences, in the knowledge of these objects.

God as object is primarily objective to himself in his triune being as Father, Son, and Holy Spirit. Of this primary objectivity we cannot speak and need not try to do so. Secondarily, God makes himself objective to us (16). As distinct from his immediate objectivity to himself, this secondary objectivity is mediate in accordance with the epistemological equipment of sensory creatures. God chooses creaturely objects to represent him, as may be seen both in the Old Testament (18ff.) and also in the New (25ff.). His own presence in the incarnation, life, words, and works of the incarnate Son—the man Jesus—forms the climax of the creaturely representation whereby God is objective to us. This links up with the whole understanding of revelation as both unveiling and veiling, as will be seen later. It might be added that in the light of this emphasis on God's objectivity, it is hard to understand the persistent idea that Barth's teaching on the knowledge of God falls into the category of pure subjectivity. Is it that people misread him because of prior misconceptions? Or is it simply that some people do not read him?

Even the very real subjective aspect is not to be thought of as self-generated. By reason of their fallen and sinful nature human beings are not in themselves subjects of the knowledge of God even though God presents himself to them as object. God constitutes them subjects of this knowledge by grace (25ff.). This is why the knowledge of God is the knowledge of faith, faith having in this context the sense of obedience to God himself in his Word. The obedience of faith in the knowledge of God means that those who know God are bound to the Word of God, without which there is neither object nor subject.

This leads to the reverse side which is handled in the second subsection under the heading of "God before Man." While God posits himself as the object of knowledge before whom we stand, he always remains the subject too. In this sense the subjectivity of the knowledge should certainly be given prominence, that is, with a reference to God as subject. As subject, God confronts us, shows himself to us, and opens our eyes to see him so that we may truly know him as God (31f.).

As this active subject confronting us, God in the reality of his being stands before us, Barth thinks, in two specific ways, each of which has a twofold aspect. First, he is the God whom we must fear above all things because we may love him above all things (32ff.). We may love him above all things because he is worthy of love, he offers himself to be known, and he gives us the possibility of knowing him (33). We must fear him above all things because this God whom we may love is in himself to be feared, wills to be feared, and opens our eyes to his fearfulness. Fear of God means recognition that we can expect only the end of our existence at his hand. It is set in relief by the love of God in which we may see that the freedom to love comes by unmerited grace, without which we would be doomed to destruction (34f.). When this is understood, it is again understood that "knowledge of God is in obedience to God"—the obedience of faith evoked and determined by its object (36f.).

Second, the God who is subject as well as object of knowledge of himself is the God who remains a mystery to us because he has made himself so clear to us. We must acknowledge this fact as we are bound to God's Word (38f.). We have the knowledge of God from God. Acknowledgment of it is faith and this knowledge is the knowledge of faith (40). Nevertheless, the limitation remains that we know God in his mystery. The knowledge and the clarity are his, not ours. Bound to God's Word, we have to admit that our knowledge of God is only the knowledge of faith (40f.). We know him in the mystery of his making himself known, in the mystery in which he exists for us. This does not contradict the clarity, for we know him with clarity and certainty in this very mystery. If we did not know him in this mystery, we should not know him clearly. Indeed, we should not know him at all (41f.).

The point behind this is, of course, that God is known through God and through God alone. This thesis does not rest on an epistemological assumption about the knower. It rests on the object of knowledge, on the God self-revealed in his Word (44). In his Word God tells us about himself as the one true Lord (45). He demonstrates himself in his lordship, in his eternal being as the triune God (47). Standing before us as the triune God, he stands as the one who stands before himself (49). His secondary objectivity is rooted in his primary objectivity. We may truly know God because he gives himself to be known by us as he knows himself. To us is given a share in the truth of this self-knowledge (51).

The importance of the incarnation comes out here. God does not give only a part of himself to be known. He gives *himself* to be known. Yet in his secondary objectivity he does this in the mediate form which entails veiling as well as unveiling (52ff.). Revelation means sacrament—the objectivity of God in the form of creaturely objectivity adapted to our creaturely knowledge. Hence a limitation is involved, but of what kind?

Barth offers a threefold answer. First, God in choosing something creaturely to speak for him renounces the visible distinction between himself and the creature, and so, even when it comes to the incarnation, unbelief may see only the medium and not God himself who institutes and uses it (53ff.). Second, while God reveals himself as the eternal, original, and incomprehensible I that he is to himself, he also reveals himself as a Thou or He—one Thou or He among many others—so that he may be hidden and unknown as the I he truly is (57–61; cf. the exposition of Exodus 3:6ff.). Third, while it is the eternal God who makes himself known to us, in so doing he lowers himself into time in order that he may be known in the temporal way appropriate to our cognition, and so we know him in succession and not eternally. Thus we may know God truly, for he has time for us. We do not just know him partially but participate in his own self-knowledge. Yet we do so under the limitation of the sacramental reality at the heart of time (61f.).

It might be noted in passing that the principle that God is known through God underlies Barth's whole conception of dogmatics as a science. No scientist can escape subjective pressures but the validity of his work rests on his being taught by the object of his study. In the human sciences the object may also be a subject in the interplay of known and knower. It is crucial for Barth that theology should not consist in the spinning out of our own conceptions or the exposition of our own experiences but that, with all due allowance for the distinction of its object, it should engage in a true "divinity," that is, in a scientific presentation of God. It can do this, however, only if there is real knowledge of God. There can be real knowledge of God only as God is objective to us, and God is object to us only as he, as subject, makes himself object and makes us subjects in relation to himself. The supremacy of God both as object and subject guarantees the real fulfilment of the knowledge of God. True knowledge of God does not spring from the knower. Whether relative to objectivity, or, finally, to subjectivity, God is known through God.

2. The Knowability of God (§26)

From the reality of the knowledge of God Barth moves on in §26 to the knowability of God. Obviously, the question here is not whether there *can* be knowledge of God. In face of the real knowledge of God enjoyed in the church, discussion of that question would be a waste of time for both writer and reader, although it might seem to make sense to the unbeliever or the secular philosopher. Existent knowledge, however, does not rule out epistemological enquiry, for the pertinent question remains: how can God be known or how far can God be known? To Barth this seems to be a meaningful subject of dogmatic investigation.

The starting point of an answer naturally lies in God himself. For this reason the first subsection bears the title "The Readiness of God." Primarily, properly, and decisively, God may be known because he is ready to be known. This readiness is the ground and source of his knowability.

In the first instance God is ready to be known eternally in himself (cf. his primary objectivity). This is why a readiness of man does not similarly constitute a presupposition of divine knowability. Apart from man—from knowability to him—God is knowable to himself. We know little about this, but at least we know it, for God has disclosed it to us in his self-revelation as the triune God (67).

The knowability of God to himself means that God is ready to be known with an eternal readiness that is grounded in his very nature, being, and activity as God. His readiness to be known by us does not arise with the existence of the creature. In no sense, then, is it contingent, or dependent on a corresponding human readiness. It forms the unshakable foundation of knowability which gives the knowledge of God its unique and enduring strength (67f.).

Analyzing this readiness, Barth characterizes it first as the readiness of truth (68), and second as the readiness of grace (69f.). Truth means openness and grace means openness to us. In all this we have to do with the truth of God and the grace whereby this truth of God comes to us as revealed truth, or truth for us. Here again the rooting of the knowability of God in God himself, or in the truth and grace that came by Jesus Christ, takes on decisive importance, for without it the authenticity of the knowability always stands in question.

Barth finds a special reason for this. Man in his resistance to God, to the readiness of God, to this readiness as truth and grace, sees the alternative possibility of pursuing an inauthentic knowability in the self-originated movement of thought which has no true object but simply takes the form of an absolutizing of his own being and nature (71f.). The eighteenth-century reaction against revelation offers an example of this "encroachment on God," as Barth calls it.

Both positively and negatively this discussion has great importance for Barth. Positively, the readiness of God in his encroachment on us justifies the grounding of the knowability of God in God's self-knowability. Against the charge that to speak of this is to speak speculatively and barrenly, Barth argues that revelation both enables and indeed constrains us to do so without illegitimate encroachment on the divine mystery. Negatively, rejection of this basis, and the resultant attempt to ground the knowability of God in a religious *a priori* in man, represents the true encroachment on God which stands at the very heart of natural theology.

Bound by the Word of God, we neither can nor should begin at this point with concepts and analogies of our own, as natural theology does. We have no analogies by which to know the nature and being of God as Lord, Creator, Reconciler, and Redeemer (75–79). Roman Catholic theology, in Barth's view, makes its fundamental mistake when it supposes that we have. In so doing it encroaches on God instead of accepting his own encroachment on us (79–84). It dabbles in natural theology instead of sticking to the simple theology which thankfully receives the knowledge of God, and therefore his knowability, from God himself.

In this connection Barth poses an astonished question. Since natural theology is so patently impossible, to what does it owe its enduring attractiveness and vitality? He suggests four answers. He presents three of these in some detail, while merely indicating the fourth and reserving discussion of it for the second subsection.

First, natural theology seems to owe its force to its alleged factual possibility and practicability and its consequent self-demonstration (85ff.). This might be convincing but it runs up against the rock of holy scripture and therefore crumbles. Scripture shows this alleged reality to be a sham. This deprives the self-demonstration of its apparent cogency.

Second, natural theology derives its vitality from its supposed pedagogic, pastoral, and apologetic usefulness as at least a prelude to the full knowledge of God. Barth concedes that some of the issues raised in this connection have their own weight and seriousness. Yet he finds it difficult to understand how, by adopting for tactical reasons the premise of unbelief, faith can lead the unbeliever to the premise of faith, or even give the unbeliever the assurance of a candid or authentic discussion. No indispensability can be claimed for natural theology on this ground of usefulness. On the contrary, its usefulness is by no means clear and its dispensability is apparent (88ff.).

Third, and with a greater show of truth, natural theology persists because it can appeal to scripture for support (97ff.). In his consideration of this explanation Barth offers a running commentary on the so-called nature psalms (cf. particularly 111, 113–116) and he also examines the relevant passages in Romans 1 and Acts 17 (118–123). He allows that the Bible has what he calls a second line or strand that sees man and creation as a witness to the gospel (99). He denies, however, that this line constitutes a parallel to the main line or that it leads us to the knowledge of God independently of the main line, for we have also to take into account the passages which deny any knowledge of God to the natural man (103–105, 109f.). This second strand cannot serve, then, as evidence for even a preliminary knowability of God that is not given with, and bound to, the knowability that he bestows in his readiness to be known, and in his making himself known in his gracious revelation in Jesus Christ.

Fourth, the persistence of natural theology may perhaps find a very different explanation. As noted, this explanation belongs to a different context, that of the readiness of man for God. Discussion of it must be postponed, then, until the new theme has been developed. All that Barth does here is simply to note again the real historical power of natural theology notwithstanding its self-evident impossibility. He then moves on to the second subsection on human readiness in which the fourth point will be presented.

He begins the subsection with the positive thesis that man's readiness for God is given with God's readiness for man, on which it depends (127). Since God's readiness is that of grace, it follows that man's is a readiness for grace (128f.). At this point, however, one must guard against a simplistic understanding of this openness to grace. The process suggests itself: need of grace, knowledge of the need, knowledge of the grace that meets the need, and readiness to receive the grace (129f.). In a sense all of this is correct, yet in itself, as a purely human reading of the situation, it might signify an ultimate closedness to grace, a mere covering up of the real need, which is simply that man in himself is neither ready for grace nor open to receive it (130ff.).

This sheds light on what Barth regards as the real problem of natural theology. It occupies a central position because it envisages a second knowability of God that has its origin in man and not in God (135f.). Even in the church, even in the context and the doctrine of grace, man will always jump at this possibility, even to the point of bringing grace itself into the context of his own possibility (136). Natural theology in this sense may begin by introducing the second possibility but it quickly assumes a monopoly, for here, it seems, one has the real possibility which excludes or absorbs all others. It may pretend at first to be no more than a preamble but it will end up domesticating revelation (139).

If, however, the readiness of man must not be understood in a way that opens the door to natural theology, does this mean that there is no readiness at all? Of course there is (139ff.). But how are we to understand it? Barth characteristically gives a christological and not just an anthropological answer. Not man, not even Christian man, but Christ alone, as true man, "is the knowability of God on our side, as He is also the knowability of God on God's side" (150).

How can we say this? We can say it because Jesus Christ is the Lord, the eternal Son, God himself, who is always open to God and to whom God is always knowable. We can say it because this God is God who is man, bearer of our flesh. Bearing our flesh, he bears us and our enmity against God. He reveals its depth but bears it away by bearing the righteous wrath of God (151f.). We can say it because he is risen in self-revelation as the new man who is ready for God and by participation in whom we also may be ready (153f.).

How does this participation take place? Correctly we say "by faith." But like the correct reference to grace, the correct reference to faith can be rendered invalid and ineffective by being made into a reference to a human possibility. First, then, we must refer to Christ and his representing of us as the object of faith. Our participation consists objectively in our being effectively represented by him (156). Subjectively it consists in the ministry of the Holy Spirit which gives the church and the individual Christian the life in Christ that is the life of faith (157f.). Thus our being inside with God consists of three things: (1) We are inside because Christ is for us; (2) we are inside in the Holy Spirit; (3) we are inside in faith (160).

Here, Barth thinks, is man's authentic readiness for God. This positive understanding offers the best protection against natural theology. It discloses the true nature of the inauthentic readiness which natural theology proposes (163f.). It shows that its vitality is simply that of man himself in his powerful but illusory autonomy (165f.). It does not fall into the trap of playing at natural theology by replying to endless detailed arguments (166f.). Starting out, not from independent man, but from the man for whom Christ died and rose again, it rules out natural theology in advance, conceding that this is a natural and necessary enterprise when God is sought outside his revelation in Christ (168f.), but denying that it has any legitimate function or ongoing place in the church (170f.). Barth closes the subsection with a historical illustration taken from his own experience in National Socialist Germany. Quoting the *Barmen Declaration,* he contrasts this with the position of the so-called "German Christians," that is, those who wished to come to terms with Hitlerite ideology. It is a serious mistake, he suggests, to treat the German Christian movement as a highly exceptional one. It is instead only the final development and culmination of natural theology, to which the clear and trenchant statements of Barmen must always be opposed (172–178).

3. The Limits of the Knowledge of God (§27)

Having considered the knowledge and knowability of God, Barth has a final section on the limits of this knowledge. Here again he divides his material into two subsections, a first on the hiddenness of God, a second on the veracity or authenticity of our knowledge of God. He sees the former as the backward limit, the *terminus a quo,* and the latter as the forward limit, the *terminus ad quem.*

First, then, we learn from God that his hiddenness is the *terminus a quo* of our knowledge of him (179ff.). The certainty of the knowledge of God rests on God's being not only the object but also the primary subject (181). (It might be noted that Barth's concern for subjectivity is predominantly a concern for the subjectivity of God!) We come in only as secondary subjects, so that, while we exercise our cognitive functions in knowing God, we do not owe the knowledge to our cognitive capabilities (182), for God is known only by God (183). Any attempt to understand God using our own views and concepts is an attempt undertaken with insufficient means. For this reason, true knowledge of God necessarily implies a knowledge of the hiddenness of God, not as a natural insight, but as a recognition of faith.

God's hiddenness means his incomprehensibility. God is incomprehensible even to the point that we do not comprehend how we come to know him (184). The divine incomprehensibility can easily be misunderstood philosophically. It has, however, a biblical derivation and when understood biblically it is of central importance (184–186). What we comprehend, Barth suggests, we resemble, control, and possess. Originally and properly we are one with it. God is outside our comprehension in this sense (187–189). We do not resemble, control, or possess him and we are not one with him. If we do nevertheless comprehend him, it is only because by revelation he lets us do so, or causes us to do so. The beginning lies with him, not with us (190ff.). For this reason one can say that negatively God's hiddenness is his judgment on us.

Yet God's hiddenness is not only judgment. It is also, and primarily, grace. Knowing God's hiddenness, we know God (192). We comprehend the incomprehensible. Even though our views and concepts are imperfect and inadequate, this does not reduce us to silence (192f.). We do not have terms of our own, whether naive, theological, or even biblical (194ff.), but God in his self-revelation gives us terms. As Father, Son, and Spirit, he alone can properly speak of himself and he has in fact spoken (198). He has made himself apprehensible in the revelation of Jesus Christ (199).

This being so, the hiddenness of God does not rule out our thinking and speaking about God. A naturally perceived limitation might seem to do this. But this limit, being itself revealed in revelation, authorizes and indeed commands us to think and speak about God. Even though the approximate nature of our knowing is recognized, we are not to treat this knowing sceptically. On the contrary, we can be obediently confident of its truth, for the God who alone may judge it has made it real by his grace (202f.). Theology can indeed be human vanity, but when it humbly acknowledges its grounding in revelation, and finds in the exposition of revelation its exclusive task, then it can seek a closer and closer approximation of our views and concepts to their object and therefore a greater and greater fulness and clarity in the witness to the reality of God. In his revealed hiddenness God is incomprehensible. Nevertheless, this forms no reason for silence. For God permits us to conceive and praise the inconceivable and ineffable God in faith and obedience (203f.).

What about the forward limit, the *terminus ad quem,* the goal and end of the knowledge of God? The second subsection on the veracity of man's knowledge of God deals with this question. Moving from the knowledge of God, we follow a circular course toward this knowledge (204), this time not in the form of hiddenness, but in the form of the authenticity of our knowledge as true knowledge of a true object.

Now obviously, true knowledge rests on God's revelation whereby he becomes object for us through the witness of creaturely reality (207). On this basis, by God's gracious act, our knowledge of God may be true knowledge in the twofold sense that we truly know *God* and that we know him *truly,* although always incompletely (208).

Barth develops his thesis step by step. First, the truth of revelation consists in its being God's truth (209). Second, as God's revelation it is correct and trustworthy (210f.). Third, it verifies itself by verily claiming our thinking and speaking (211). Fourth, it makes good the impotence of our own views and concepts, so that while we cannot shirk the task of finding views and concepts, we give God the credit for their truth. In this regard Barth argues firmly that we do not achieve authentic words and concepts merely by repetition of those we already have (215).

In what way does our knowledge share in authenticity as its goal? To answer this question Barth recalls that revelation, the source and basis of knowledge, means unveiling in veiling and veiling in unveiling (215f.). Veiling is the beginning, but by it unveiling is the goal. Participation in this goal may thus be described first as an act of thanksgiving, that is, an evoked response and acknowledgment under the order of revelation and with an accompanying joy (216–219). It may then be described as an act of wondering awe, the sense of an overcome incongruence, inadequacy, and distance, in which we let the overcoming grace be truly grace and accept the permission to use the means that we are given (220–223).

What does this permission mean? How can we use the terms and concepts at our disposal, as indeed we do? Obviously they do not have parity of meaning when applied to God on the one side and the creature on the other. Yet obviously they do not suffer from total disparity (224f.). We have to speak, then, of analogy, which implies both similarity and dissimilarity (225ff.). But how does the analogy arise (227)? Not from us, nor from within the creaturely objects, but from God himself, both because he is properly what the creature is only improperly and also because he says primarily, truly, and infallibly what we say only fallibly in secondary and derivative truth (228ff.). Father, son, arm, mouth, and ear are offered as examples (230f.). God dynamically restores to their proper use the words of analogy that we employ by referring them to himself (231), by presenting himself as their true object (231f.). Hence a partial correspondence of our words and God's being may be achieved. This is not, of course, an intrinsic analogy of being; it is the analogy of grace (231ff.).

But what is the meaning of "partial" in this connection? It cannot denote a quantitative similarity and dissimilarity, for God is one and cannot be dissolved into quantities (236f.). Instead, it denotes the dialectic of veiling and unveiling to which the dissimilarity and similarity correspond (236). The "partial," then, may be properly interpreted as a reminder of the limitation of our knowledge but also of the promise that it has when undertaken in obedience (236). Barth finds it rewarding at this point to enter into a comparison and contrast with Quenstedt as a representative of the older orthodoxy (237–243).

If the veracity of the knowledge of God rests on the revelation of God, in which we participate in thanksgiving and awe by means of a similarity between our speaking and its object, we are clearly moving in a circle. How do we know that this is not a vicious circle but a circle of truth (244ff.)? Obviously, Barth thinks, the question can be answered only as one that is put by faith under the assault of temptations. Yet the answer does not come from us—not even from our faith. It comes comfortingly from outside us (246–249), from that to which we look in faith (246–250). Specifically, the answer lies in Jesus Christ as the divine reality that encompasses the circle of truth in which we move (250f.). Jesus Christ experienced the assault of temptation for us in his crucifixion and he received comfort for us in his resurrection. With him, therefore, we may go through the tempting assault of questioning and receive the comfort of reassurance. Faith accepts this rule. Accepting both temptation and comfort in Jesus Christ, it knows not only the question and the answer regarding our knowledge and its limitation, but also its authenticity.

The referring of faith to Jesus Christ in his representative work preserves the final answer from what seems to be the dangerous threat of subjectivity. In this entire chapter Barth plainly shows how far he has clarified his thinking since the early days of an apparent orientation to experience. The knowledge of God starts with the divine object set before us in creaturely signs of God's own choosing. Man as a knower of God is not man in his autonomy but man in Jesus Christ. Readiness for knowledge has its source in God's own readiness as subject. Nor is this balanced by an independent human readiness, as natural theology supposes, but by the readiness of Jesus, and of others in him. Again, the knowledge of God implies first a knowledge of his hiddenness which pinpoints the inadequacy of our words and concepts. If we may still think and speak of God, we may do so not because we have words—even analogous words—but only because God chooses words and makes them analogous by restoring them to their proper use. Finally, assurance of the authenticity of our knowledge cannot be located in human experience, even the experience of faith. Faith undoubtedly plays a central role, yet only as a tempted and comforted faith which has its ground in the temptation and comfort of Christ for us. At every point the spotlight focuses on Jesus Christ both as the God who is before man and ready for him, and also as the man who is before God and ready for him. In Jesus Christ, both known and knower, God truly makes himself known and is known, utilizing for this purpose the world of perceptible creaturely objects and comprehensible creaturely words. It is on this basis and in this way, not with a human subjective reference, but with a divine reference, both objective and subjective, that God is known, knowable, and known to be known.

CHAPTER VI
The Reality of God

1. *The Being of God as the One who Loves in Freedom (§28)*

FROM the knowledge of God it is a natural step to the reality of God. Barth considers this in four carefully constructed sections. He first examines God's being as the One who loves in freedom. He then has a brief discussion of the perfections of God (§29). Last he has two series: the first on the perfections of the divine loving (§30), and the second on those of the divine freedom (§31).

Since God is known by us in his revelation, Barth concludes that one cannot speak of his being in abstraction from his act (257ff.). Hence the first subsection of §28 deals with God's being in his act. God is God. He is not being in the abstract nor indeed God in the abstract. He is God in his act or, concretely, in Jesus Christ. Hence his being is known in his act (260ff.).

From his act, God's being may first be defined as life. God is the living God. His word is the word of the living God, his work is the work of the living God, worship of him is worship of the living God, and knowledge of him is knowledge of the living God. To be more precise, God is act, event, and life not only in a general sense, but in a unique and distinctive sense (264). In this context unique has the force of spiritual, not in distinction from natural, but with the connotation of personal (265f.).

This means that God is neither a personified nor impersonal being. Nor is he personal as creaturely beings are. God is authentic I, self-sufficient to himself. His being, which knows, wills, and decides in and of itself, is thus an unmoved or self-moved being to the exclusion of all forms of deism or mystical pantheism (268f.), and in opposition to the humanism which thinks it can talk about God by speaking loudly about man (269f.). Even in calling God personal, we do not personalize God. God is real person. He exists in his act. He is his own decision. He lives from and by himself. On the validity of this depends every further statement about God, and every possibility of avoiding confusion between God and us. God is who he is in his act, and in his act he is who he is. Grasped by this act of his, our thoughts about him cannot become thoughts about ourselves (272).

In a second subsection Barth makes the important additional point that in his act God is revealed in his love. He seeks and creates fellowship with us (273). He does this in an overflowing of the inner love in which he wills and fulfils fellowship in himself. In himself, before us and apart from us, he is love—not in an abstract sense, but according to the expression of his love in his loving of us in Jesus Christ (275).

Barth offers four elucidations of this active divine loving. First, God in his love does not seek and create fellowship with us for its own sake. He does not just give us something. Giving, he gives himself, and in himself gives everything (276–278).

Second, in his love God does not seek and create fellowship with us for any worthiness in us or with any thought of reciprocity. He seeks and creates fellowship where none exists and where no possibility of it exists apart from his love (278–279).

Third, God in his love has love as the source and end. In his loving he wills his own glory and our salvation. Nevertheless, he does not love us for the sake of these. Instead, he wills these because he loves us (279–280).

Fourth, God in his love is under no necessity apart from love. He does not need us to be able to love, for in himself he is eternally love. Our being loved by him is our being taken up into the eternal fellowship of his love (280). The necessity of God's love lies in God himself, not in the created object of it (281f.).

"God is" implies "God loves." Barth finds here the real meaning of speaking of God as person. It is from God, of course, that one learns what true person is, namely, the true I willing, knowing, and acting in love (284ff.). In this regard Barth offers a long and important excursus on modern criticisms and defences of the personality of God in such theologians as Hegel, Strauss, Biedermann, Lüdemann, Siebeck, Lotze, Ritschl, and Feuerbach (287–296). He reaches two conclusions. First, the term has no intrinsic importance. What counts is that God is he who loves. Only in this context can and should one say that God has or is personality (297). Second, the term "personality" does not properly apply to the three "persons" as though Father, Son, and

Holy Spirit were three personalities (cf. his earlier discussion of this point in I,1). The one triune God, who is self-revealed in Jesus Christ as the living and loving God, is the personal God (296f.).

A third and last subsection considers the self-revealed God from the angle that he is Lord as well as love in his act. God is who he is— not only loving but also free and sovereign.

This freedom may be seen in the uniqueness of God's act and God's love as God's alone (297). The life and love of God are not abstractly divine. They are the life and love of God. For Barth this means that they are the life and love of the God who is sovereign subject, who freely lives and loves in this distinctive way, who manifests the lordship or freedom of his being in his unique life and love (298–302). Negatively, this freedom is freedom from compulsion, the divine transcendence (301f.). Positively, it is freedom unconditioned by this very freedom, as though God were not free for immanence as well as transcendence (303f.). God's freedom embraces his freedom to reveal himself in the sphere of the created reality distinct from himself, as well as his freedom in and for revelation as this may be learned from revelation itself (304f.).

God's freedom, then, is true freedom to be, not just in the sense of freedom from outward necessity, but even in the sense of freedom from having to be in order to be (305f.). Here Barth discusses the idea of the aseity of God—the concept of God as his own cause, and particularly the idea of the necessary being of God. He suggests that the idea of God's necessary being has to be carefully understood if the genuine truth behind it is to be properly grasped and expressed (306f.).

If God is free in himself, this entails his absoluteness in the sense of his transcendent independence of created reality and the total dependence of created reality on him. It entails, too, his absoluteness in the sense of his immanence in relation to created reality and the existence of created reality in virtue of it (308f.). Properly grounded in God's being in freedom, the absoluteness of God may be asserted in both senses without the risk of self-deification which arises if transcendence and immanence are no more than human concepts to which God is conformed.

The freedom of God has two implications, the one noetic and the other ontic. Noetically, it implies that God cannot be classified with what he is not. This takes place in the analogy of being when being is treated as a superior concept embracing both God and creature. It occurs, too, in Kant's intolerable doctrine whereby God's freedom and immortality are lumped together in subordination to reason (310f.). Ontically, it implies the decisive distinction of God from what he is not—on this the noetic distinction finally depends. All forms of pantheism are hereby excluded (311f.).

God has the freedom to be what he is not. He has the freedom to do this without being in any way bound by it. He also has the freedom to do it in different ways. His freedom means also freedom from inflexibility (313f.). God's presence is his personal presence taking different forms according to his own freedom of will, intention, and decision (314). Yet his rich multiplicity is not speculatively open (316). It centers on the fulfilment of union between God and man in Jesus Christ. In this all other possibilities have their meaning, norm, and law (317). A freedom of divine immanence detached from Jesus Christ exists only in the false constructions of idolatry or heresy (319f.). Without Jesus Christ there is no fulness of the divine presence. God's freedom consists in Jesus Christ and in him he has exercised it.

2. The Divine Perfections (§29)

Barth now has a short section on the divine perfections. This forms a link to the more detailed grouping of the individual perfections as those of the divine loving and freedom. Departing for the second time from his usual practice, he does not divide his material into subsections but handles it all in a single discussion.

The opening thesis is that as the one who loves in freedom God is perfect. His perfection may be known, however, in the abundance of his perfections (322). God is one, yet also many. He is not all things, of course, for he is not creature, sin, or death. He is the many, and the many are his perfections (323). As previous theologians emphasized (cf. Anselm), he does not merely have his perfections; he is his perfections (323). In being his perfections he is the Lord of glory (324).

Two opposite dangers must be avoided here. First, we are not to think that there is a God behind his perfections who differs essentially from what he is economically in his perfections (324). Second, and conversely, we are not to see God only in his perfections and not also in himself, as though we had to do only with a world of forces and not with the person of the living Lord of glory (325f.). From holy scripture we learn to see both the Lord as the Lord of glory and also glory as the glory of the Lord.

Can we validly speak of perfections in the plural? The objection can be made that God is simple, and hence his so-called perfections are merely subjective descriptions, as later nominalism supposed (327ff.). Or, it might be argued, the perfections express our view of God according to his accommodations to us. John of Damascus, Aquinas, and Calvin took this line and many Evangelical and Roman Catholic theologians have followed them (327–330). In reply Barth offers some explanatory observations.

He points out first that the plural perfections are those of the one divine being, not of another divine nature related to God (330ff.). He then maintains that the many and varied perfections are those of God's simple being; multiplicity and simplicity do not stand in antithesis here, for God includes them both in himself. He insists finally that the multiple perfections all have their root in God's being—not in his sharing in the characteristics or qualities of other beings (333f.). As the being of all being and the nature of all nature, God is in himself rich and multiple, individual and diverse (333f.).

How, then, do the perfections exist? How do we know them as such? What is their derivation and distribution? At this point Barth analyzes the erroneous groupings of the perfections in psychological, religio-genetic, and historico-intuitive categories (335–340). He then presents the orthodox distinctions between positive and negative, absolute and relative, communicable and non-communicable perfections. He also considers such modern variations as the distinction between absolute and personal perfections, or formal and material, or ontological and actual, or perfections of holiness and of love (341). He adapts this line of treatment to his own concept of the being of God as the one who loves in freedom. As he sees it, God reveals himself in a unity and distinction of his perfections corresponding to the unity and distinction of love and freedom in his own being (341ff.).

He concludes the section with three observations. First, he points out that the distinction between God's freedom and his love is not to be equated with the distinction between his transcendence and his self-giving. It does not rest on a distinction between God in himself and God for us. Such a distinction can have heuristic significance, but not essential significance (344f.). Second, while conceding that one might take the two paths of negation and eminence in the knowing of the divine perfections, Barth denies that these ways can be specifically related to freedom and love (346–348). Finally, he argues that the proper noetic order is from God for us to God in himself, since his being in freedom is self-revealed along with his being in love.

In his view, then, it best accords with the subject matter to begin with the perfections of love and then to proceed to the perfections of freedom. Nevertheless, this should not be done without a constant counterbalancing (as in Anselm's *Proslogion*) to show that, as the God who loves, God is free, and that as the God who is free, God loves.

The main problem in §28 and §29 is whether Barth actually succeeds in justifying the preeminence that he gives to love and freedom. Can one say, as Barth would say, that when describing God as love and righteousness, or as freedom and power, righteousness can be brought under love and power under freedom? Can any grouping of perfections, whether in two or more series, be finally upheld when it is seriously and properly maintained that God is and does not merely have his perfections, that he is not just this or that perfection but each and every perfection? Even if an appeal be made to the distinction between God for us and God in himself as a basis for distinguishing the perfections, this hardly seems to lead necessarily and specifically to love and freedom, for in the knowledge of God, does not revelation teach us that God is free for us and also that he loves in himself? Indeed, does it not tell us that God is righteous, wise, and powerful for us and also righteous, wise, and powerful in himself?

In fairness to Barth it should be recognized that this is a problem for all theologians and not just for Barth. It seems that the perfections do fall very naturally into two groups and various attempts have been made to categorize these groups. A merit of Barth is that he does at least try to relate them, not just to human concepts, but to God in his self-revelation. If an arbitrary element creeps in when he singles out love and freedom as master-concepts, perhaps the arbitrariness is simply that of method. Certainly the method selected yields by no means unimpressive results. More important from Barth's standpoint, it stands in some correspondence with its theme, for God is self-revealed as essentially and economically the God of love and the God of freedom. Hence it can hardly be wrong, even if it is not overwhelmingly necessary, to see the other perfections from the standpoint, first of the love of God that is also free, then of the freedom of God that is also loving.

3. The Perfections of the Divine Loving (§30)

In his third section (§30) Barth first examines the perfections of the divine loving. He takes three pairs of perfections, that of grace counterbalanced by holiness, that of mercy counterbalanced by righteousness, and that of patience counterbalanced by wisdom. He devotes a separate subsection to each of the pairs and within each subsection has a separate discussion of each perfection.

Beginning with grace and holiness, Barth states his principle that love precedes but also includes freedom. Hence love as grace, mercy, and patience embraces freedom as holiness, righteousness, and wisdom (351ff.). He then moves on to grace, which he views from three angles. He first defines it as love seeking unmerited fellowship (353f.). He then expands this: Grace is a gift in which the Giver turns in loving condescension to the unworthy, that is, to sinners (354f.). This identification of gift and Giver leads him to the final point that God is eternally grace in himself. If grace in the form that it takes in God's own being is hidden from us and incomprehensible to us, grace in any form is known only by grace and in faith (358f.).

The grace of God is the grace of the Lord. This means that God's loving is holy loving. The divine freedom constitutes the factor common to both grace and holiness (360). In his grace God affirms his victorious will; he does not surrender to the creature. The revelation of his love is the revelation of his opposition to man's opposition to him (361ff.). Judgment and grace unite in holiness. God is holy (a) because his grace judges and (b) because his judgment is gracious (363). In a concluding excursus Barth reveals the relation of this to Christ. Christ is the holy one of God as God is the holy one of Israel (363–367). In all this God loves. His love, however, is holy love, for God himself, and in himself, is holy.

Turning next to mercy and righteousness, Barth observes that grace implies mercy, for in it God meets a need (369). Through sin man has brought himself into a miserable plight and God has compassion on him in this plight (370). Hating sin, he loves and pities the sinner. We do not know this by logical inference. We know it from the reality of mercy as this is demonstrated in the name of Jesus Christ, in whom God has mercy on us (373f.).

As God has mercy in love, he also has mercy in freedom and its power. He does not have to have mercy because he is free, but he does so effectively because he is powerful. Freely and powerfully he bears and bears away our sin and guilt (374f.). This leads us to God's righteousness. Righteousness must be seen as a determination of the love of God. There is thus no disunity in God, as though his righteousness were not merciful and his mercy were not righteous (376ff.). In Barth's view, a failure to bring out God's unity here marks many orthodox theologians, Quenstedt and Polanus being cited as examples (377–380). In contrast Luther, and Anselm before him, teach us that "there is no righteousness in God which is not also merciful and no mercy which is not also righteous" (380). As both the Old Testament and the New declare, God is Judge and his revelation is law. Yet this finds its strongest affirmation in his mercy (381f.). The righteousness of God is Jesus Christ (384). Faith in him means decision for God's righteousness and not our own, so that faith is at one and the same time both "the source of all comfort and the epitome of God's most zealous demand" (385). The needy seek God's righteousness; for them it is mercy (387ff.). Yet it is justice, too, in its just judgment on sin (390ff.). The reason why it can be sought and found as mercy without in any way losing its character as justice or judgment is that in Jesus

Christ love and grace and mercy meet us "as the divine act of wrath, judgment, and punishment" (394).

Anticipating the doctrine of reconciliation, Barth develops this briefly under four heads. First, the bearing of our sin by the Son of God manifests to the full the wrathful righteousness of God (398f.). Second, the taking of our place by the Son of God means that God's righteous justice can take its course without our destruction (399f.). Third, the vicarious action of the Son of God implies the satisfaction and indeed the fulfilment of the righteousness and faithfulness of God (400ff.). Fourth, the death of the Son of God for us results in our reconciliation to the righteous God and therefore in the securing of our righteousness before him. No other could effect this act of righteous mercy and merciful righteousness, but "God's own Son could do it" and he did (403–406).

In his third subsection on the perfections of the divine loving Barth pairs the perfections of patience and wisdom. As God's gracious and merciful love comes to expression in Jesus Christ, it shows itself to be patient (407f.). God's patience means that he grants us time and space. He does not impatiently consume us but accompanies us (410ff.). Suffering for us in the Son, he accepts, transforms, and renews our reality instead of bringing it to a sudden end (411). The Old Testament stories of Cain, Noah, and Jonah are adduced in illustration (412–414). Problems arise: Will people really repent? Does patience sometimes have an end and judgment fall? The answer lies in the way in which God is patient. He upholds all things by his Word, which is Jesus Christ (416). In Jesus Christ God does not just wait in his patience. He acts to bring about our awaited penitence and obedience (418f.). If his patience includes temporal judgments, as is clear from scripture, in the shadow of Christ's death these do not have to be eternal judgments; indeed, they are tokens of life (419ff.).

Like his grace and mercy, the patience of God is that of his freedom as well as his love. This comes out in the counterbalancing perfection of the divine wisdom. As we have seen, God exercises his patience by the Word. The Word declares the logic, meaning, intention, and purpose of God in and behind his concession of time and space (424). It thus confronts us with his wisdom. His wisdom does not act capriciously, tyrannically, irrationally, or paradoxically (425). If there is mystery to his action, it is that of his own reason, meaning, and purpose in which he himself is wisdom. (Critics who accuse Barth of irrationalism should read and ponder this crucial passage, for in it he clearly portrays the rationality of God which should be reflected in the rationality of theology.) Wisdom is the truth and clarity of God's self-justification and the criterion of everything that is clear and true

(426). It signifies God's self-consistency, gives meaning to his patience, and is thus the meaning of the world (427). This is not an immanent meaning, but rather an acquired meaning (427ff.). God is no slave of his patience. He is self-moved to it by his wisdom, by the "holy and gracious, righteous and merciful meaning" which is "the wisdom of his being and his works" and the true "philosophy of the created universe and . . . human life" (432). Scripture teaches the identity of the wisdom of God and Jesus Christ (Colossians 2:3; 1 Corinthians 1:30) and Barth closes the subsection with a more detailed study of wisdom, first in Solomon and then in Jesus Christ, according to the united testimony of the Old and New Testaments (432–439).

4. The Perfections of the Divine Freedom (§31)

The second series, that of the perfections of the divine freedom, occupies Barth in the final section (§31). Here again he has three pairs in three subsections: unity and omnipresence, constancy and omnipotence, and eternity and glory. He begins by pointing out that as God's love includes his freedom, so his freedom includes his love. Hence freedom as unity, constancy, and eternity carries with it omnipresence, omnipotence, and glory, although it is not so obvious, perhaps, why the latter set particularly should be seen as perfections of God's loving. Barth candidly admits that his selection is not sacrosanct. Scripture lies behind the perfections chosen, but others, he says, may do things differently so long as the result is biblically and materially satisfying (441f.). For the perfections of love in this grouping he offers no specific explanation but simply comments that God's love is divine as the love of his freedom and that in these perfections we are glancing back from God's freedom to his divinity (441).

Regarding unity, Barth in the first subsection points out that God is one in the sense of uniqueness and simplicity (442). Uniqueness does not mean that he alone exists but that he alone is God in his life of love and freedom. None can be compared to him and none can compete with him. No other is to be worshipped and glorified alongside or in place of him (442ff.). Simplicity means that in all he is and does he is wholly and undividedly himself (445). In relation to the world he cannot be identified with it nor can emanations of the divine be isolated in it (446). Recognition of the simplicity of God is, he thinks, recognition of the trinitarian and christological unity. Philosophical concepts can help to explain it but they cannot form a foundation for it. The simplicity at issue is that of the divine triunity, of the consubstantiality of the Father and the Son, and of the hypostatic union in Jesus Christ. Only thus is it God's simplicity (446f.).

Barth is led, then, to oppose an understanding of divine unity in terms of a general concept that might apply to other things as well. God is not relatively unique as is the individual specimen in a genus. He is absolutely and uniquely unique. Similarly, he is not relatively simple but absolutely and uniquely so (447). He is truly individual and not just an absolutized or divinized unity—as in the abstract monotheism of Islam. Nor is God mere simplicity, as in equally abstract philosophical conceptions (448–450). Knowledge of God's unity comes from meeting with the one God who shows himself to be the God of electing love. At this point Barth includes an examination of Old and New Testament sayings on the unity of God (451–457). In scripture God's simplicity is his own. It is God in the actuality, power, and facticity of his presence and dealings according to the testimony, not of logical or mathematical reflection, but of what the apostles and prophets say about God himself (457–461).

Being unique and simple, God is omnipresent. Omnipresence, Barth suggests, is a determination of his freedom. He is everywhere present as Lord in a unity of proximity and distance which is first that of himself—near and distant in the one being (461f.)—then that of his relation to the creature (462f.). This unity of proximity and distance reminds us that God is love, for omnipresence implies love both in God himself and outward to what is other than himself (462f.). For this reason Barth resists the common equation of God's omnipresence either with his eternity or, more generally, with what is called his infinity (464–468). Omnipresence means that God has his own place in which he is present to himself and his creation (468f.). In his own way God is spatial; being present everywhere does not mean being present nowhere (469ff.). He is present everywhere as fully God whose space is himself and who creates space (470). At the same time he can also be present in specific ways, that is, in differentiations of his presence (472ff.). Thus he is distinctively present in and to himself (474ff.). Outwardly he is then present (1) in creation (476f.), (2) in his revealing and reconciling work (477ff.), and (3) at the core of this work in Jesus Christ, in whom he is present to himself (483f.). Barth concludes the subsection with a discussion of the threefold outward presence (484ff.) and a conciliatory appraisal of the ubiquitarian debate between the Lutherans and the Reformed in the context of the eucharistic presence (487–490).

The constancy and omnipotence of God occupy Barth in the second subsection. God's constancy means that he remains who he is. Since he is the living God, it does not entail immutability in the abstract sense of immobility (491–493). The immutable as such cannot be equated with God. Nevertheless, God is immutable; he is immutably the living God in his freedom and love (494). He is what he is in being and actuality (494). Barth believes that passages like Exodus 3:4 and Psalm 18:25ff. support this understanding of immutability (495ff.). If God is said to repent in the Old Testament, he is still immutable; that is, he is the one God in his freedom, and indeed in his love, for primarily and properly he repents of his threatened judgments (497f.). Again, when he becomes the Creator, God does not change, for he does so not under constraint, but in his unchanging love and freedom (499f.). Two errors must be avoided here: first, the monistic one of regarding the world as an integral part of God's essence, and second, the dualistic one of abstractly opposing the world's mutability to God's immutability, as though the world did not live by the constancy of God (500ff.). If creation does not change God, his constancy does not prevent him from having a real history with it in revelation and reconciliation. The creature's resistance to God, and his own resistance to this resistance, bring no conflict or change in God (502f.). But they do not leave him untouched, for in his constancy he is active, not passive, even to the point of the new creation in Jesus Christ (505ff.). This action may be seen in salvation history, which for all its particular characteristics displays the same constancy. This history finds its meaning and secret in Jesus Christ as the history in which one and the same God, active in his love and freedom, becomes a creature— one with other creatures—yet without ceasing in any way to be God (514ff.). He does this in a free decision that we must also recognize to be an unalterable decree, although not the abstract and inscrutable decree of the older Reformed teaching (cf. Wollebius, 518–522).

Constancy means omnipotence (522). In his constancy God can do all that he wills to do, and not do what he does not will to do, in a power defined by himself (522ff.). Since God's omnipotence is his own, it must be distinguished from neutral power (524) or purely physical power (526). It is moral power, exerted in God's acts and not in a general omnicausality (cf. Quenstedt, Schleiermacher, Lipsius, Seeberg, 526ff.). Its criterion does not lie outside God (cf. Augustine, Aquinas, Heidanus, Mastricht, 528ff.), but in God himself. Thus "God cannot do a thing because it is impossible; it is impossible because He cannot do it" (535). "The limit of the possible is not self-contradiction . . . but contradiction of God" (536).

God's power is power over everything, the power of all powers, in and over all powers, whether created or permitted. Here Barth accepts the distinction of Aquinas between absolute and exercised power. He rejects, however, the interpretation of this as a distinction between extraordinary and ordinary power (539ff.), for this has unfortunate implications, as in supernaturalism (540) or nominalism (541). The real point of the original distinction is that God's omnipotence cannot be absorbed in omnicausality. The error in the second distinction is that of not seeing God's omnipotence in its actual operation (542).

A final point regarding omnipotence is that as God's power it is personal power, the power of the knowledge and will of God in which God is God (543). As the power of knowing and willing it takes the two interrelated forms of omniscience and omnivolence. In relation to the former Barth has a penetrating discussion of the traditional distinctions of the divine knowing (567f.) and of the implied problem of divine foreknowledge and human freedom, with particular reference to the issues raised in Molinism (569–573), Reformed and Lutheran theology in the seventeenth century (576f.), and modern Roman Catholic teaching (577–586). In relation to the latter he offers a briefer but not unimportant excursus on the traditional distinctions of the divine willing, that is, the distinctions between God's necessary and free will, his hidden and revealed will, his absolute, antecedent, and efficient will, and his conditioned, consequent, and permissive will. All these Barth finds to be helpful, but not so the distinction between God's efficacious and his non-efficacious will (591ff.). These historical analyses should be read carefully and in detail by those who wish to delve more deeply into these matters, or into Barth's thinking about them.

In conclusion—and this is the needed link—Barth points out that omnipotence, being God's, is the omnipotence of love. Hence it does not endanger or destroy the freedom of the creature; it is omnipotent in it (598f.). The knowing and willing God is the loving God and *vice versa* (599). How do we know this? We know it by divine revelation as scripture bears witness to it and as it climaxes in the personal omnipotent Logos—the crucified and risen Jesus (599ff.)—by knowing whom we know, not a nameless knowing and willing, but the omnipotent knowing and willing of God (605ff.). Omnipotence can be understood properly only when it is understood christologically as the omnipotence of the one God who is free in his love and loves us in his freedom.

The third and last subsection deals with the final pair of perfections, the eternity and glory of God. Barth first defines eternity as a perfection of God's freedom. It means duration in which beginning, succession, and end are one and not three, as they are in time (608). It thus means simultaneity. God has and is this simultaneous duration and he is free in it (609). If time, which he created, might be called the principle of his free activity outwards, eternity is the principle of his free activity inwards (610). Eternity is no mere opposite of time. It does not negate it; it includes it (612). One must not describe it as nontemporality but as God's duration which includes his origin, movement, and goal in ordered simultaneity (614f.). As the eternity of incarnation it could and did become time. God became temporal, "permitting created time to become and to be the form of His eternity" (616). In so doing God mastered time (617).

The temporality of God's eternity takes the threefold form of pretemporality, supratemporality, and posttemporality. The eternal God manifests himself as the who who precedes time, accompanies it, and is there after it (619; for the bearing of this on providence see Vol. III,3). He creates, preserves, and rules time as the one who was, is, and is to come (620). In the pretemporality of his eternity he was before us as the beginning of all beginnings (621). In its supratemporality he goes with us, and causes us to go with him, our time being kept by him (623). In its posttemporality he will be there after us as the goal, as the future of all futures, as our absolute future (623ff.; for a further development of this entire theme cf. the section on "Jesus, Lord of Time" in Vol. III,2).

In a thought-provoking excursus Barth points out that the three forms must be held in balance without the one-sided emphases, particularly on pretemporality, which many theological schools display (631ff.). All the forms are "equally God's eternity and therefore the living God Himself," as Augustine remarked (638). God is not fixed in eternity. He lives eternally. Hence eternity has an irreversible direction as origin, goal, and the way from the one to the other. Nevertheless, since it is God who thus lives eternally, the distinctions do not imply disunity. Instead, one should speak of a perichoresis or circumincession of the three forms, of their mutual indwelling and interaction in analogy to the perichoresis of Father, Son, and Holy Spirit as the one God. In this distinction and unity God is eternal, Creator and Lord of time, the free and sovereign God (640).

Glory is the last of the counterbalancing perfections. In his eternity God is and has glory, his open manifestation as the one he is in his freedom to love, the radiant declaration of his divine perfections (641–643). Defining this more narrowly, Barth draws attention to four aspects of glory. First, the glory of God consists of the fulness of his being as God's being (646). Second, it consists of the light of this being in its reaching out to us (646). Third, it consists of his presence to us as the light of this being (647). Fourth, it consists of our illumination by this light in such a manner as to evoke our grateful recognition (647f.). Barth acknowledges his indebtedness to Mastricht for this fourfold understanding (649).

Probing more deeply, he asks what it is that is manifested and known in this light. In a striking and justly famous passage he turns to the concept of the beauty of God for his reply—a concept which he unhappily finds only in the pre-reformation tradition, for example, in Augustine or Pseudo-Dionysius. God enlightens and persuades us in the form of his beauty (650ff.). Beauty, of course, must be kept in context. It must not be allowed to take over as a leading concept (652). It arises in explanation of the glory of God. It plays little role of its own in scripture but rather is included in the very prominent biblical concept of the glory of God (653). In relation to God we are not to begin with a general idea of the beautiful, but with God in himself, who is beautiful as he is God, and who is thus "the basis and standard of everything that is beautiful and of all ideas of the beautiful" (656). In this connection Barth speaks eloquently of the related beauty of theology. Dealing with the beauty of God, theology has a corresponding beauty. This makes it a joy to the theologian, so that only the theologian who has joy in his work can be a real theologian. Reference is made to Anselm in support (656f.).

Considering the nature of the divine beauty, Barth points out that God is beautiful first in his being as perfections (657ff.), then in his triunity, his own being as Father, Son, and Holy Spirit (659–661), and finally in the incarnation. The peculiar beauty of the incarnation lies in its being the great act of divine love and freedom which means the suffering of the Son of God and the exaltation of the Son of Man in him (cf. Vol. IV). The face of Jesus represents at one and the same time the human suffering of the true God and the divine glory of the true man. This is why art can never capture this face and would do better not to try (666). (Barth has no liking for Christian art.)

Glory evokes glorifying. Centered on Jesus Christ, God's works are works of glory in which God, who is glory in himself, is glorified in man in an echoing and serving glorification (667ff.). This takes place in and by the Holy Spirit, for the creature can glorify God only as the Holy Spirit regenerates, enlightens, and sanctifies it for this as a new creature in Jesus Christ (669f.). Having made this clear, Barth concludes the subsection, the section, and the whole chapter with some incisive observations on the human glorifying of God which is enfolded in the divine glory.

First, and almost incidentally, he points out that God in his glory glorifies the creature, but only in so far as the creature is given a share in the glorifying of God (670). This leads to the decisive truth that our glorifying of God is not a possibility of our own but one that is given and permitted in Jesus Christ (671ff.). This permission can be exercised only in and with the restoration of man to the divine image which is man's destiny and the purpose of all creation and which reflects the divine glory (673). The outworking of the glorifying takes the form of following Jesus (673f.), of readiness to live to him (674), and of obedient self-offering (674f.). It is done in recollection of the perfect praise of the angels and the blessed (675). In its temporal limits it takes the specific form of proclamation, faith, confession, theology, and prayer (670f.). The import of this is that on earth the church is the provisional sphere of the glorifying of God. God is indeed glorified in all heaven and earth. In our life on earth, however, this is seen and known only by faith and in the church, which also knows and awaits its future manifestation. Thus Barth closes with the affirmation, with all that it implies in grace and judgment, that God is "the God who is glorious in His community, and for that reason and in that way in all the world" (677).

CHAPTER VII

The Election
of God

1. The Problem of the Doctrine (§32)

BARTH does not break off the doctrine of God with the presentation of his reality and perfections. He explores two further aspects in successive chapters on the election and the command of God. In these chapters he establishes in God the foundation of his later volumes about God's action and the corresponding action of man.

Beginning with God's election, he recognizes the difficulties that have arisen regarding this subject. He thus devotes a first section (§32) to the problem of the election of grace. In three subsections he discusses the orientation of the doctrine, its foundation, and finally its place in dogmatics.

Barth opens his subsection on orientation with a strong affirmation of his commitment to the witness of scripture. This is important, for he is going to diverge quite a bit from the reformers here, and can do this in good conscience only if he believes that scripture forces him to do so. From scripture he learns that election is the sum of the gospel (3ff.), for it is presented to us there as God's gracious covenant election in Jesus Christ (7ff.). As grace, election means the love of God, as election it means his freedom—a link with the presentation of God's reality in the preceding chapter. In grace God establishes fellowship with the other in Jesus Christ. In election he makes a self-election concerning this other, primarily the election of Jesus Christ (9ff.).

Rooted thus in God's love and freedom, election should not be understood as one form of predestination, with reprobation as the other form. To Barth the vital point is that an understanding of this kind obscures the fact that the election of grace is the sum of the gospel, or the gospel *in nuce* (13f.). In a historical excursus Barth recognizes that Augustine, Calvin, and Dort all want to protect the evangelical element in election. He feels, however, that their favoring of double predestination works against their good intentions (14–18).

All serious doctrines of election, Barth suggests, share and emphasize three points in relation to it: first, God's freedom in the election of grace (19), second, the mystery of God in his free decision (20f.), and third, God's righteousness in the mystery of his freedom (21f.). To understand these properly, he argues, we must set all three in the light of an evangelical understanding of the election of grace. He thus explores the meaning of the divine freedom, mystery, and righteousness from this standpoint, his aim being to show that in the last analysis each of them means blessing for the creature (27–34).

What, then, is the foundation or source of the doctrine? In his second subsection Barth considers first what he regards as unsatisfactory sources and finds four of these. First, traditional Augustinianism or Calvinism offers no proper basis, since it starts with an existing system and simply aims to restate and expound it (36f.). Second, the practical utility of the doctrine, real though it may be, can hardly serve as a foundation or source of knowledge, since utility is no necessary basis or guarantee of truth (37f.). Third, experience—the actual response of some and not of others—cannot serve as a foundation, although there are hints to this effect in Calvin, because it means starting with man and not with God (38–44). Finally, a general doctrine of divine sovereignty, which tends to see predestination as a branch of providence (Aquinas, Polanus, and cf. Boettner), certainly begins with God but with an abstract God instead of the specific electing God of holy scripture (44f.).

Positively, Barth locates the true foundation or source of the doctrine in the biblical witness to the electing God in Jesus Christ (51–54). This directs us, not to man in general as God's covenant partner in election, but to Israelite man, who finally, after a process of narrowing down, is again Jesus Christ as the one true Israelite (55–58). Hence Jesus Christ, according to scripture's witness, forms the proper basis of the doctrine as himself both electing God and elect man (58f.). Barth realizes that Christ has always been given a central place in election by the great teachers on the subject, for example, Augustine, Luther, and Calvin, but he does not think the christological reference has been adequately made by them (60–67). Similarly both Arminianism and the Synod of Dort take note of election in Christ but fail to bring out its true significance (67–70). Lutheran orthodoxy in its resistance to the absolute decree also points to Christ but makes the mistake of not beginning concretely with Christ but generally with God's good will to save (70–76).

In the third subsection, Barth locates the place of election in the dogmatic structure. For Barth, Jesus Christ is, as we have seen, the foundation of the doctrine. But Jesus Christ is God. Hence the proper location of the doctrine of election is in the doctrine of God. Barth defends this thesis in detail as follows. In himself God is the one who in his Son elects himself. It is in this self-election that he elects his people. In election God loves in freedom and is free in loving. Thus to know God, the one who loves in freedom, is to know the electing God. It is as the electing God that God initiates and executes all his dealings with us. The election, then, stands at the head of all other doctrines except for that of God himself. We cannot speak of God without speaking of the electing God (76f.).

In contrast to his own placing of the doctrine Barth considers and evaluates six other historical arrangements. First, election is put immediately after the doctrine of God, as in the Westminster Confession and also in many dogmaticians, for example, Polanus, Wollebius, and Turrettini (77–80). Second, it is put after creation and providence, as in Zwingli's *Fidei ratio* and J. Gerhard (80f.). Third, it is related to reconciliation, as elsewhere in Zwingli and in Calvin's *Institutes* of 1536 and *Catechism* of 1542 (82–84). Fourth, it comes immediately after christology, as in Calvin in 1537, Peter Martyr, and Witsius (84). Fifth, it is related to sin and precedes christology and soteriology, as in many Reformed confessions and in theologians such as Cocceius and the Lutherans Quenstedt and Hollaz (85f.). Finally, it forms the climax of the doctrine of reconciliation, as in Melanchthon, later editions of Calvin's *Institutes*, the Anglican and Rhaetican confessions, Bucanus, and the Lutheran Calov (85–93). Barth appreciates the positive elements in these possibilities but only with his own arrangement does he think that the doctrine can fulfil "the function proper to it in the biblical testimony to God and to the work and revelation of God" (91).

2. The Election of Jesus Christ (§33)

In the second section (§33), on the election of Christ, Barth immediately begins at the source and heart of the doctrine. This time he has two subsections arising directly out of the material. The first is on "Jesus Christ Electing and Elected," the second on "The Eternal Will of God in the Election of Jesus Christ." In the former he makes his central point and in the latter he works out its implications.

Barth sees Jesus Christ as the mediator between God and man, himself both God and man—God showing himself to man, man seeing and knowing God. As the mediator Jesus Christ, the Word of God, stands at the beginning of all God's ways and works with men. He is the beginning of God and as such the election of God, which is the election of God's free grace, both in the inner being of God and also in his outward operation (94f.). Barth supports all this with a careful and interesting exposition of John 1:1f. (95–99).

If the Word of God be thus understood as the election of God, this means that election is not to be regarded as an abstract exercise in freedom by an abstract subject. On the contrary, it is God's specific election of grace in the specific election of Jesus Christ as the one in whom God wills to be gracious. This election was at the very beginning and Jesus Christ was there at the beginning as both its subject and its object. He is thus the election of God in its specific orientation to man and to the divine covenant with him (100–103).

Election has, as we have seen, a twofold reference: first, to the elector as its subject and, second, to the elected as its object. Jesus Christ as the election of God may thus be viewed in two ways. Being both God and man he is at once both the electing God as the subject and elected man as the object. Barth has a look at both these aspects, beginning with Jesus Christ as the electing God (103).

Now it is true that, even as God, the Son is elected by the Father. Hence one might consider Jesus as the elected God. Nevertheless, the primary reference of his being elected is to his oneness with us as the Son of Man. One may say, then, that election in the passive sense of being elected is primarily a human determination of his existence, and election in the active sense of electing is its divine determination (103).

As Son of God, Jesus Christ is, with the Father and the Holy Spirit, the electing God not merely in a secondary sense as the executor of election, though he is this, but in the primary sense of himself being the subject of election, the divine freedom in operation, and the manifested decree of God that we know—not the one behind whom and whose work lies a speculative decree that we do not know (104ff.). In Jesus Christ we go back as far as there is to go in divine electing, for in him we go back to the electing God himself. Certainly it is in him that God executes the decision of grace in which we have our own election. But we also see in him the divine decision itself, revealed and not inscrutable, for he is the God who makes it.

In defence of this crucial point, Barth appeals to a variety of passages in John and appropriate verses in Matthew, Paul, and Hebrews. Historically, he takes issue with Aquinas, who speaks of Christ only as predestinate (108f.). On the other hand he can adduce Athanasius and Augustine in favor of his thesis (108–110). The reformers in their discussion disappoint him, but Polanus offers an important insight (111), and Cocceius with his covenant theology opens up interesting possibilities of a better understanding, although not without serious defects (114f.). If one might argue that Barth does not have too strong or extensive backing in either scripture or history, two things may be said on his behalf. First, there can be no doubt as to the electing ministry of Christ in relation to his disciples. Second, if Christ be truly God in the triunity of Father, Son, and Spirit, then even though election be specifically appropriated to the Father, the fact that all outward acts of God are acts of the whole Trinity leaves the common resistance to Barth on this issue with little theological justification.

If as Son of God Jesus Christ is electing God—the subject of election—as Son of Man he is also elected man—its object. He is this not merely as one elected man but as the one in whom all others are also elected (116f.). His is the all-inclusive election in which we see what election always is, the unmerited acceptance of man by grace (118). Augustine, Aquinas, and Calvin all express this truth (118–120).

Barth proceeds to work out three specific implications. First, the grace of the election of Jesus shows us that God is gracious at the beginning of all his ways and works with us. This grace is not just his benevolence but the overflowing of his inner glory in self-giving. For us who are elect in Christ grace means participation in the grace of the electing God, in his creatureliness, and in his sonship (120f.).

Second, the election of the man Jesus is specifically his election to vicarious obedience and suffering. This brings out again the undeserved and therefore gracious nature of our election. All that we merit is wrath, judgment, rejection. Jesus as the Lamb slain bears this rejection in fulfilment of election (122f.); he is elected to rejection. In this connection Barth portrays in vivid terms the vicarious, representative, substitutionary aspect of the election of Jesus Christ, and of all others in him (124f.).

Third, in virtue of the faithfulness of Jesus Christ to God and of God to him, the election of others in him means concretely their faith in him on the basis of his actualization of election on their behalf. Election may thus be described as election to believe in him, which is to see, honor, laud, and love in him the Son of God, the priest and victim, the divine justification, and the representative (125–127). Those who do this are the objects in him of the divine election of grace.

Barth ends the subsection with a lengthy and detailed discussion of the controversy between the supralapsarians (e.g., Beza, Gomarus) and the infralapsarians (e.g., Turrettini), and of the attempted compromise between them (Mastricht). He analyzes the arguments and counterarguments on both sides. After stating the common features, he then considers the advantages and disadvantages of each position. He finally shows how, in his view, supralapsarianism contains the greater promise for the future. It can fulfil this promise, however, only if it is reinterpreted christologically along the lines that Barth has attempted (127–145). Barth might be described, then, as a reconstructed supralapsarian.

Coming to his second subsection on God's eternal will in the election of Christ, Barth first argues epistemologically that if we know both the subject and object of election in Jesus Christ, then we also know the eternal will of God in it (146f.). God's predestinating decree cannot be the inscrutable decree of an unknown God concerning an unknown object (149f.). Its content cannot be a total mystery. We learn this, Barth thinks, from holy scripture. It is also brought to our attention in a striking article in the *Scots Confession* of 1560. It is finely stated, too, in a paper by Pierre Maury at the International Congress of Calvinist Theology held at Geneva in 1936 (154f.).

Barth acknowledges that the divine decree can be called the eternal and immutable beginning of all things. As his second point, however, he claims that it is wrong to describe the decree as obscure and absolute in the traditional sense (156). The decree is God's eternal will, and God's eternal will is Jesus Christ. It is known to us in the revelation of Jesus Christ (157). The decree has as its content one name and one person. The decree *is* Jesus Christ. For this very reason it is not the absolute decree of tradition (158).

Third, and materially, the eternal will of God in the election of Jesus Christ is the will of God to give himself in the incarnation of the Son (161ff.). This self-giving has both a negative and a positive side. Negatively, God elected himself to be man's covenant-partner and as such he suffered death, bearing man's merited rejection (163ff.). As Barth succinctly states, "he is rejected in order that we might not be rejected" (167). Here again Barth offers a powerful exposition of Christ's vicarious work whereby he was rejected for us, "suffering what man ought to have suffered" (167). Positively, the divine self-offering means that God elected man in Jesus Christ to be his covenant-partner and thus to be taken up into his glory as his witness and the bearer of his image (167ff.). Double predestination may thus be affirmed when election is equated with Jesus Christ, but in a radically new sense. It is not now that some are elected and others rejected, but that in Jesus Christ God elects himself for rejection and man for election. The rejection is, of course, teleologically oriented to the election, so that God's eternal will is affirmation, not reprobation (174f.).

Fourth, and finally, Barth learns from Christ's election that God's will is not a fixed and static predecision but a divine activity in the form of a history between God and man (175ff.). God initiates this activity in eternity (176). This eternal activity finds a counterpart in which God's election of man evokes faith and thus brings about man's election of God (177f.). Barth hastily adds that it is Jesus Christ who makes this response of a free election of God by man (178ff.). He does it in such a way that no rivalry exists between God's free election of man and man's free election of God (179). He does it on our behalf, so that in him we can attain the true freedom of participating in this election by a decision of faith and obedience (179f.).

From all this it may be seen that God's predestination is his will in action. It is neither an abstraction from this will nor a static result of it (181). God is no prisoner of his own will, nor is the creature. God has not deistically started a process and left it to run its course alone (182). Certainly his will and purpose will not change. Election has the force of a grammatical "perfect." Hence the word "decree" must be retained (183). Nevertheless, God's will cannot be understood as though he had once willed but now wills no longer. He still wills what he once willed. He still wills both the cause and the effect. His will is not the presupposition of his action (186ff.). His election is his free election in time which in the history and encounter between God and man entails new decisions in time, as seen in Jesus Christ, who is the event, history, encounter, and decision between God and man.

Barth concludes this important discussion with an acute excursus on The International Calvinist Congress of 1936, commenting on the dynamic interpretation of predestination advanced by Peter Barth, the reaction to it, and the possibility of working it out only if predestination is equated with the election of Jesus Christ. Barth has attempted to work it out along these lines. In so doing he has, he thinks, preserved God's sovereignty in his loving act. The decision of God is not conditioned by a complementary human decision and yet this decision, as the acceptance of man, includes and grounds the human decision. Apart from Jesus Christ all this would be an impossible abstraction. In Jesus Christ, however, it has and is being effected in such a way as to retain God's freedom, avoid synergism, and preserve a living relationship between God and man (188–194).

3. The Election of the Community (§34)

After the section on the election of Jesus Christ, Barth shifts his focus to the election of the community. The first of four subsections deals with the community in its twofold form as Israel and the church.

As Barth explains, the divine election is primarily that of Jesus Christ but his election includes the election of man (195). This does not just mean the election of individuals. Between Jesus Christ and individuals scripture teaches us to consider the election of the community, which in its mediate and mediating role mirrors the one Mediator, Jesus Christ. Naturally, the election of the community does not take place outside that of Jesus Christ. On the other hand, it is only by this mediating election, by inclusion in the elect community, that individuals are elected in and with Christ's election (196f.).

Scripture presents the community as one. Yet it has a twofold form which, according to Barth, corresponds to the double predestination of Jesus Christ. Jesus is both the crucified Messiah of Israel and also the risen Lord of the church. He is so in indissoluble unity. Similarly the community is both the Israel which resists its election and also the church which is called on the ground of its election. It is this in indissoluble unity. In this unity in differentiation an irreversible movement leads, as from the cross to the resurrection, so from Israel to the church. The unity and differentiation, however, can be known only as Jesus Christ and his election are believed and known. In them Israel and the church are the mediate and mediating object of election (201).

Throughout this section Barth supports the material of the subsections with a running commentary on Romans 9–11. The passage in 9:1–5 forms the biblical basis of the initial statement of the first subsection (202–205).

Next, Barth considers Israel and the church from the standpoint of the judgment and mercy of God. The elect community has a common task—that of serving the self-presentation of Jesus Christ (205). The common task breaks up into two specific forms of service corresponding to the double predestination of Jesus Christ and the twofold form of the community. Israel renders the specific service of reflecting the merited judgment from which God rescues man (206f.). It does this whether or not it is obedient to election (207). In fact, it does not obey but displays an enduring obduracy (208). This does not alter its election, Barth hastens to add, but only the manner in which it fulfils its appointed task (208f.). In contrast the church renders its specific service by reflecting the unmerited mercy of God (210). It reveals what God has chosen for man, his "whole selflessly self-giving love" and all the precious gifts that this includes (211). Lest the differentiation alone be stressed and the unity neglected, Barth issues a reminder that the church has a preexistent if hidden life in Israel too, just as the service of the church still includes within itself that of Israel. Thus the elect in Israel, culminating in Jesus as the one elect, reflect the mercy of God, and the existence of Jewish Christians keeps the Gentiles in mind that they are snatched from the same judgment and saved by the same mercy. A detailed exposition of Romans 9:6–29 follows in support of this understanding (213–233).

Looking at the situation from another angle, Barth in the third subsection describes it as the function of the one but differentiated community to serve the promise of God in Jesus Christ that awaits man's hearing and believing (233). Here Israel has the specific task of hearing the promise as God's Word to man (233). Hearing indispensably precedes believing. Believing has as its object the Word which God gives us to hear (234f.). Hence, if Israel as a whole does not move from hearing to believing, even in its failure to hear properly it is still the chosen people of Jesus Christ (236). The goal of hearing is believing. The church has the special function of believing the Word as God's Word and therewith of mediating it to the world (238f.). Here again the church preexists in Israel in the form of prefiguring believers and doers of the Word (239f.). Nevertheless, it is the church which, on the basis of the hearing of Israel, has the specific task of believing what it hears and of thus becoming a living testimony for the world and Israel (240). Barth takes Romans 9:30–10:21 as the biblical basis for this subsection and engages in a long and careful exegesis of the passage (240–259).

In the final subsection Barth looks at Israel and the church in terms of the passing man on the one side and the coming man on the other (259ff.). As the old man passes in Jesus Christ, and the new man comes, so the one differentiated community has a passing form and a coming form (259f.). Israel as the passing form renders the special service of praising God's mercy in the death of the old man and of showing what God elects for himself in electing fellowship with man, namely, the death of Jesus Christ with a view to his resurrection, in which Israel itself is dead with a view to its rising again (261ff.). It shows this by now living a futureless life among the nations because of its refusal to accept its crucifixion and renewal in Jesus Christ (262f.). In contrast, the church has the special task of bearing witness to the coming new man and of displaying what God elects for man in electing him to fellowship with himself (264f.). In this form, too, the church preexists in Israel. Thus Israel's election is confirmed as the ultimate meaning of God's dealings with it. Awakening to conversion, the church already exhibits the new man, yet the new man in unity with the old, the one man who "both passes and comes in the person of Him who has suffered death for all and brought life to light for all" (267). A lengthy exposition of Romans 11 supports and concludes the subsection (267–305).

Barth, who had worked so hard on Romans at the beginning of his theological revolution, attached great importance to the expositions of Romans 9–11 which accompany this whole section. If, for lack of space, they are simply mentioned and not summarized in this introduction, this does not mean that students can or should ignore them. When studying Barth's thinking on the issue of the community and the interrelations within it of the synagogue and the church, one should certainly wrestle with his detailed exegesis which underlies the section, offers many illuminating insights, and has general significance for his whole understanding of election.

4. *The Election of the Individual* (§35)

Having presented the election of Jesus Christ and the election of the community, Barth finally turns in §35 to the election of the individual. Lest one should think that this is unduly minimized in his thinking, it ought to be noted that he has written nearly two hundred pages on the topic, again divided into four subsections.

The first subsection concentrates on Jesus Christ, the promise, and its recipient. Barth begins by stating the obvious: the election of the individual has a valid place (306). He can even go so far as to say that methodologically it might well have been given the first place (309). Nevertheless, as Augustine, Aquinas, and Calvin at least intimated, it does not and should not hold the chief place (307–309). It falls within the election of Jesus Christ, which both relativizes and establishes it (310). This being so, individualism is excluded, but so too is a collectivism that erases and crushes the individual (311). Election recognizes the individual within humanity as a whole. God does not just elect humanity. Within it the one God through the one Son elects the one person (313f.).

What does individuality mean in this context? In itself it might simply refer to human particularity, but God's election, as an election of grace, does not relate to this alone. It addresses the autonomous individuality of the sinner who sets himself against God. It thus comes as the forgiveness that confers new and true individuality with the reception of the promise of grace and mercy in Jesus Christ (315ff.).

The gospel declares that the individual is already elected in Jesus Christ, who bore his merited rejection. This is the promise of grace (317ff.). The individual begins to live as elected by the event and decision of receiving this promise (320ff.). If he does not receive it, "he lives as one rejected in spite of his election" (321). If he does, "he now lives that which he is in Jesus Christ . . . by the fact that in Jesus Christ his rejection, too, is rejected, and his election consummated" (322). Hence individual election always takes the form of personal address: "Thou art the man" (323). The task of the community is to declare the election of the individual in this form, whether explicitly or implicitly (324f.).

Barth appends to the first subsection a long and important excursus on the Reformed doctrine of individual election (325–340). While critical of the general presentation, he finds a few intimations of his own interpretation: (1) the emphasis on faith in Jesus Christ (326ff.); (2) the stress on grace (328f.); (3) the insistence on perseverance (329ff.); and (4) the grounding of assurance in Christ (334ff.). The tragedy, as he sees it, lies in the failure to develop properly these authentic and central elements.

Next, Barth distinguishes between the elect and the rejected (340ff.). In this subsection, Barth first states that the elect are so by a distinction in God's relation to them in and with Christ's election as well as by way of the community (340f.). This derives from a free determination of God preceding and underlying their free self-determination (343f.). "Because and as God is God, they—the elect—are this or that person" (343). To this distinction of God's relation to them corresponds their own difference from others which is their calling by the Holy Spirit (345f.). In this calling the elect have a recollection and an expectation—these two important concepts recur at this point. The elect *recollect* that God's distinction of them is primarily the distinction of Jesus Christ, apart from whom they are rejected, but who in his own election bore their rejection (347). The elect *expect* for others that they will not finally be rejected, for despite their rejection in themselves they cannot overthrow their election in Jesus Christ and they are not excluded from the divine distinction "as by their lives they appear to be" (349).

On this ground Barth insists on seeing the elect and the rejected together. Certainly he finds two classes of people. Nevertheless, the one person of Jesus Christ manifests both what divides and what connects them. In him we see what an elect person truly is (351f.) and also what a rejected person truly is (351–354). Neither elect nor rejected must be seen apart from the one Jesus Christ.

Barth supports this from the Old Testament witness to Christ as he learned it from W. Vischer's book on the theme. He begins with the constant distinction of persons in the early chapters of Genesis (355ff.). He then considers from this angle of christological unity and distinction the rituals of Leviticus 14 and 16 (357–366). Next he discusses at length the relationship between Saul and David in its christological significance (366–393). Finally he engages in a fascinating exposition of the strange story of the two prophets in 1 Kings 13, in which he thinks the two double pictures and their interconnection offer us a prophecy that is fulfilled in Jesus Christ (393–409).

What is the determination of the elect man? For what purpose is he elected? Posing and answering this question in the third subsection, Barth first repeats his basic point that individual election takes place in Jesus Christ and with the community (410f.). Primarily it is election to be loved by God. It is thus a determination to eternal bliss (411). Nevertheless, eternal bliss is not a dead end. It embraces gratitude and this finds expression in a representation of God in his gracious work (413). Hence the determination of the elect may be described as a determination to witness and service in an official and not just a private calling by the Holy Spirit (414f.).

God, of course, elects. He does so in Jesus Christ. The elect cannot do what God does. All the same, there is something they can and should do, namely, bear witness to God's election and in this witness issue a call to election (415f.). As they do this, "the ongoing of the reconciling work of the living God in the world . . . takes place" (417). "The election of each individual involves the enlargement of the closed circle of the election of Jesus Christ and his community in relation to the world." God wills this by grace. He also controls it. Hence "we cannot venture the statement that it (the circle) must and will finally be coincident with the world of man as such." At this point Barth bluntly rejects any necessary universalism as "historical metaphysics." On the other hand, since all is by grace, he will not rule out the possibility of this final enlargement in Jesus Christ. Denial of it, he thinks, suffers from no less abstraction than its affirmation. The certain fact is that by God's grace and power individuals are elected. The circle does not remain stationary or fixed. It does enlarge and extend itself (417f.).

For support Barth turns to the witness to Christ in the New Testament. He opens by contrasting the ambivalence of the Old Testament with the clarity of the New (419f.). He then discusses passages on the scope of Christ's work (421–423). Next he examines the New Testament evidence for election as an election to witness and service (423ff.). A long and significant account of the apostolate brings the excursus to a close (431–449).

There remains only the question of the determination of the rejected. Barth defines the rejected individual as one who is against God and ungrateful to God even though God is for him and gracious to him. What purpose does God have for such a person (449)?

Barth begins his answer to this question with an insistence that God has only one will for man and not two wills. Hence the rejected is determined by the same will as the elect but in a different way

(450). This implies that he has no autonomous existence. He exists improperly and incidentally only as the elect exists properly and authentically (451). It also implies that only the elect knows the rejected, perceiving him supremely in Jesus Christ, who took the place of the rejected and bore his rejection (451). Having no existence except this existence with the elect, the rejected can only *have been* rejected. He can proclaim himself "only as one who has been but is no longer." He has been displaced by Jesus Christ even in his rejection. He can live only in a negative mode, that is, against the gospel (453). He can be only in relation to election, not independently in his rejection (454).

From this fact Barth derives the three specific functions of the rejected. First, he has the task of representing man in need of the gospel (455). Second, he has the determination of showing what is denied and overcome by the gospel (456f.). Third, he has the function of indirectly manifesting the purpose of the gospel, namely, to give to man without a future a future in the gospel. Herewith the final determination of the rejected is disclosed as a determination to hear and believe; to become—not a reluctant and indirect witness—but a willing and direct witness to the election of Jesus Christ and his community (457f.).

Barth bases his presentation on the person of Judas Iscariot. In a very detailed and intricate excursus (458–506) he examines the sin (459–465) and end (465–471) of Judas. He then sets Judas in antithesis with the other apostles and particularly with Jesus, who is *for* Judas even as Judas is *against* him (471–480). Finally, in the context of the New Testament use of the term "to hand over," Barth points out that Judas does in fact carry out his apostolic ministry by "betraying" ("handing over") Jesus. He does this in the wrong way, not the right way. Nevertheless, God uses the handing over by Judas in the fulfilment of his purpose in gracious election. Thus the rejected, too, must serve election. His divine determination, as may be seen in the elect, is to come to election on the basis of the election of Jesus Christ and the handing over of Jesus to rejection on his behalf.

Barth's doctrine of election has undoubted strength. The focus on Christ has attracted criticism but has also been found sound and helpful even by many who are not prepared to go all the way with Barth. It can hardly be dismissed as unscriptural. The refusal to accept a balanced double predestination accords with the best of the tradition and has also had a clarifying and correcting influence. Nor can much opposition be brought against Barth's stress on a living and dynamic decree instead of the static and almost deistic decree of past theologies. This reinterpretation leaves room for the ongoing activity of God in his dealings with man without forfeiting the eternal character of election. It links up with God's eternity as co- or supratemporality and posttemporality as well as pretemporality. The grounding of all God's work in his gracious electing will can hardly be faulted and if creation is understood as grace it does not have to mean the subsuming of creation under reconciliation that many fear. The bearing of rejection by Christ has a strange ring at first, but it links up well with the biblical account of his vicarious and victorious action on our behalf. A further asset in Barth's reconstruction is the attempt to do justice to the election of the community, not in isolation, but in integral relation both to Christ's election on the one hand and to that of the individual on the other.

Problems also arise. Many of them are problems of detail that hardly affect the doctrine as a whole. Thus the interrelating of Israel and the church, though thought-provoking, smacks of simplified systematization. The expositions of Romans 9–11, even admitting the difficult nature of the passage, are not always clear, are hard to follow in relation to the general theme, and do not in every case have the necessary cogency. The christological passages relating to individual election surely carry typology to excess, as in the matter of the Leviticus rituals, and if there is validity in the contrasting of Jesus and Judas, more weight seems to be placed on the biblical material than it can easily bear.

Behind the details looms the larger problem of the incipient universalism of the understanding. Barth undoubtedly views all people as elect in Jesus Christ, in whom their true reality is to be found. Now the church has commonly held to the universal scope of Christ's atoning work. It should also be said that Barth does not come out for the attainment of each individual to eternal bliss and voluntary service. Without difficulty he finds a place for man's electing of God within God's electing of man. He knows that the gospel has to be received, believed, and obeyed as well as heard. He rejects an abstract necessity of universalism in logical consequence of the election of all in Christ. He speaks of the ongoing life of those who "have been" and of the negative fulfilment of the divine determination. Nevertheless, it is not apparent why, in his view, the Holy Spirit in his ministry of calling should not positively fulfil in all individuals the one eternal will of the triune God. A gap arises here which Barth can finally fill only by an appeal to the divine freedom. He is no doubt on biblical grounds in making the appeal, but why not bring this out much earlier instead of leaving the initial impression that the relating of election to Christ removes all obscurity? The ambivalence at this decisive point—will all be saved or not, and if not, why not?—by no means outweighs the solid merits of Barth's presentation. Nevertheless, it undoubtedly casts something of a shadow over them, particularly in view of what seems to be the solid and consistent witness of scripture to eternal perdition as well as eternal salvation.

CHAPTER VIII

The Command
of God

1. Ethics and the Doctrine of God (§36)

THE covenant relation that God establishes with man has two sides.
On the one hand it implies election. God has elected himself to
be the God of his people. On the other hand it implies command. God
has elected his people to be his people. On this ground Barth deals
with the command as well as the election of God in his doctrine of
God. In so doing he lays a double foundation, not of dogmatics alone,
but also of ethics. He works out the ethical aspect in four subsections:
a first and general one on ethics as a task of the doctrine of God (§36),
a second on the command as the claim of God (§37), a third on the
command as his decision (§38), and the last on the command as his
judgment (§39).

In the introductory section Barth first establishes the relation between election and command in a subsection on the command of God
and the ethical problem. In his free loving and loving freedom God
in Jesus Christ has entered into covenant partnership with man (509).
This means that he wills something for man (election) and also wills
something from him (command) (510f.). According to Barth, this causes
no conflict with grace, for grace is ruling grace. Hence the one Word
of God is law as well as gospel, or law enclosed and implied in the
gospel (511f.). The indicative of God's work for us carries with it the
imperative as well as the future of our conformation to what God is.
In the covenant the electing God is thus the commanding God (512).

For Barth this means that ethics, having its root in the covenant,
belongs not only to dogmatics but more specifically to the doctrine of
God within dogmatics (512f.). If general ethics asks about the good in

human life, as various moralists show (513–515), theologically the doctrine of God answers this question, repeating the answer that is provided by God's electing grace with its sanctifying and claiming of men, putting them under the divine command (515f.). Naturally men in their systems attempt to give their own answers instead of simply *being* the answer by God's grace. They cannot succeed in these attempts, for they put the question in a vacuum as if it existed in itself and were not posed first of all by God (517ff.).

In face of human systems Barth considers three courses that theological ethics might be tempted to take but should at all costs avoid. First, it must not let itself be drawn into discussion. It must annex the ethical field by beginning with the answer. It should not feel any need to render an account to general ethics in the form of an apologetic dialogue as in Schleiermacher, De Wette, Hagenbach, or Herrmann (520f.). This type of apologetics can succeed only if it abandons its indispensable premise (521ff.). Theological ethics has a self-vindication from within (523f.).

Second, theological ethics must not accept an allocation of spheres in which it allows one area to philosophical ethics while reserving another for itself. Various theologians, including Mayer and Kirn as well as those previously mentioned, have taken this course (525). It has the unfortunate effect of imposing on theological ethics an arbitrary and impossible restriction.

Third, theological ethics must resist coordination with general ethics. Roman Catholic ethicists have often adopted this procedure. They have treated the two forms of ethics as two stories in the one building, or as superstructure and foundation (528f.). In Barth's view this means beginning at the wrong place, not with God in Jesus Christ, but with a metaphysics of being.This achieves only a surreptitious harmony and theological falsification ensues (530–532).

Theological ethics find its true point of departure in the reality of the command of God as the sum of the good (535f.). It cannot treat this reality as a mere possibility. It accepts the attestation and interpretation of this reality as its true task (536f.). It thus directs its attention to the Word and work of God which have taken place in Jesus Christ, and which are man's sanctification and the establishment and revelation of the divine law (538). In the last analysis Jesus Christ forms the basis and starting point of theological ethics, for in him God has done what is right with man, and in him man has done what is right with God (538ff.).

In conclusion, Barth considers the possibility of a non-theological ethics, that is, of a knowing and doing of the good apart from Jesus Christ. He concedes that thanks to God's patience and wisdom and man's inconsistency the good may in fact be known and done, at least in part, by non-Christians. Yet this forms no basis for an independent ethics. In principle this knowing and doing of the good is right only in so far as it is Christian. It will always need to be corrected by Christian ethics. Scientifically, then, theological ethics is the only ethics (540–542).

In a second subsection Barth deals more briefly with the nature of theological ethics. Negatively, it cannot build on general ethics (543) nor have a human orientation (544f.). Many ethicists take issue on these points (543, 544–546). Positively, it rests on the Word of God which declares God's goodness in his dealings with us and claims an obedient commitment by us in an obedience that is good because the Word, or God, is good (546). Ethics has the task of showing that God's good action means claim, decision, and judgment (547) in an event, a command directed to man (548f.). Barth concludes, then, that the Word as command will have a triple orientation to man, first as creature, then as reconciled sinner, and finally as heir of the kingdom (549). In correspondence with dogmatics, theological ethics will be further developed in relation to creation, reconciliation, and redemption (550).

2. The Command as the Claim of God (§37)

As yet, of course, Barth is simply laying the foundation for the ethics of creation, reconciliation, and redemption. He is doing this within the doctrine of God and has stated that the command of God, which in the covenant goes hand in hand with his election, is directed to man as his claim, his decision, and his judgment. He thus goes on to discuss each of these aspects in a carefully articulated statement in which each section is divided into three subsections. He begins with the divine claim under the three heads of its basis, content, and form.

What is the basis of God's claim? Barth rejects three possibilities: divine power considered merely as power (552f.); God's being as the essence of the good (554f.); and God's all-sufficiency for us constituting him the good without whom we cannot live (555f.). Instead Barth finds the proper basis in the gracious gift of God whereby he gives himself to us in Jesus Christ (557). This self-giving God is one in whom we may believe and who demands our obedience (559f.). "The grace of God in Jesus Christ is the proclamation and establishment of his authority over us" (560). Jesus as man exemplifies acceptance of the divine claim as the obedience of the free man to the free God (561). On this side, too, God has acted for us. His claim rests on what he has done, as the Old Testament legislation bears witness (562–564). When

God commands, he has fulfilled what he commands. Hence he has a right to claim (565).

If Jesus Christ constitutes the basis of the claim, he also rules its content (566). He does this, not haphazardly, but in accordance with grace. God's grace has teleological power; it aims at our restoration in the divine image (566f.). Jesus Christ is the form of this power. In his obedience he shows what God rightly wills and he impels us to love and obedience to himself (567–569), that is, to discipleship (569f.). The community of Jesus Christ can also be seen as the form of the teleological power of grace, for by grace this people bears the grace of God for all and with it the command of God on all (571). Looking more closely at the aim of God's grace and command, Barth develops it in terms of conformity with God's action (575f.). Conformity, of course, does not mean equality or identity, as though man could be a second Christ (577), or as though another community could stand beside the community of Christ (578). It means (1) acceptance of God's gracious action as right (579), (2) recognition that we do not belong to ourselves (580f.), and (3) acknowledgment of the rightness of God's mercy and righteousness (581f.).

The form of the divine claim, the manner in which it comes to us with its demand for hearing and obeying, differs from that of all other claims by being one of permission and liberation. At this point Barth again insists that God's freedom does not compete with man's. When God commands, he gives the freedom to fulfil the command (585f.). The command does not enslave; it liberates (586). Even in specific orders which harass the disobedient sinner, God's command has the form, not of a categorical imperative, but of a liberating Word: "Do this . . . because in this freedom you may do this, and can only do this" (587). This is why the command is for Barth a form of the gospel. He adduces passages from Matthew and John, and from James and Paul, in support of this hotly contested thesis (588–593). Naturally God does not command us to use the pseudo-freedom we have as sinners. His own authentic permission cancels our feeble permissiveness by unmasking its tyranny, deposing the self as lord of good and evil, and giving us the true freedom and joy (593ff.) that counteract fear and anxiety (587–602). As the Word of grace fulfilled in Jesus Christ, the command of God imposes obligation without legalism and gives permission without license (602). In this unity of permission and obligation the command is spiritual. That is to say, it is revealed and operative in the presence and work of the Holy Spirit (603ff.). It is also personal; it meets us in the person of Jesus Christ (607) and demands personal decision for him (609). Being personal, the decision required by the command is a joyous one (611) which is constantly repeated and confirmed (612). To underscore these points Barth ends the subsection with an extended and penetrating exposition of the story of the rich young ruler (613–630). The ultimate message of the story as he understands it is that the command "binds the man who hears it to the person of Jesus Christ" (630).

3. The Command as the Decision of God (§38)

The section on the command of God as the decision of God (§38) contains subsections on the sovereignty, the definiteness, and the goodness of the divine decision. Barth's initial point is that in issuing his command, God makes the decision of grace in Jesus Christ (631f.). This decision relates to the right use of our freedom, or, in different words, to the way in which God will have us. As a decision of this kind it is a sovereign decision. Again, however, Barth argues that the sovereignty of God's decision in no sense eliminates human decisions (634f.). It means that all our decisions relate to this decision (635). In our own decisions, then, we neither ignore God's decision on the one hand nor view it as ineluctable fate on the other; we have responsible regard to it (636). In this respect, Barth has an interesting excursus on the New Testament use of *dokimos* (636–641). As he sees it, the term "responsibility" best brings out the meaning of taking decisions with due regard to the divine decision (641ff.). We fulfil this responsibility by considering four aspects of the basic ethical question: "What shall I do?" First, we ask *what* we shall do (645–649), then what *shall* we do, or what *should* we do (649–653), then what shall *we* do (653–657), and finally what shall we *do* (657–661). At the very end Barth issues a reminder that the question is not properly addressed to us, for in its original setting in Acts 2:37f., it is addressed to God and his witnesses. We are directed, then, to address the question to holy scripture, for if Jesus Christ is the supreme criterion of all ethical reflection, he cannot be separated from the apostolic testimony to him. The answer given in Acts: "Repent and be baptized . . ." should also be kept in mind, for Barth sees in it the one answer that is constantly given in many different forms (661).

As regards the definiteness of the divine decision, Barth points out that the decision is total and yet specific, so that our responsibility to it must also be total and specific (661ff.). God does not just give us a general command that we have then to apply for ourselves (664f.). For this reason Barth objects to the categorical imperative of Kant, to generalized ideas of the good, and to an indefinite appeal to conscience (665–669). As his decision, God's command is definite, clear, and unconditional (669). Only disobedience can pretend that it is not

(669f.). God's law in scripture is always composed, not of general rules, but of concrete commands in concrete situations, as many examples from both the Old and the New Testament make abundantly plain (672ff.). Even summaries of the command that are designed for many people, the Ten Commandments for example (683–688), or the Sermon on the Mount (688ff.), are not to be detached from the more immediate or the more general biblical background in which God is the personal subject in all his commands (680–683). Barth attaches great importance to this point. He will no more tolerate a deistic command than he will a deistic election. The one who commands does not merge into his commands. If Barth cannot deny the existence of embracing commands both in the Old Testament and the New, he regards these as cables, so to speak, along which God transmits his specific commands to individuals. God does not speak apart from the cable, which summarizes his commands; but along this cable there is a specific wire through which he issues a specific command.

Having stressed the sovereignty and the definiteness of the divine decision, Barth sets it in its ethical context by drawing attention to the goodness of this decision. He defines goodness here as the sum of all that is right, friendly, and wholesome (708f.). Goodness as thus defined constitutes the unifying element in God's decision (709ff.). Barth develops this along three lines. First, the goodness of the specific commands of God shows that they all represent or express the one will of God. By way of illustration Barth uses more of his studies in Romans, specifically in chapters 12 and 13 (713–716). Second, the goodness of the divine decision unites the recipients of the command in spite of the diversity of its claims. It allows them freedom, but only the freedom of fellowship (717). This time Barth uses the entire passage of Romans 12–15 to support his point (716–726). Finally, the goodness of the divine decision unifies each believer in himself and thus makes him an instrument of harmony to others (726–728). Again Barth finds a basis for this view in Romans 12–15 (728–732). It may be noted that in the chapters on the election and the command of God, Barth works into the *Dogmatics* a revised version of the work on Romans which had been his first significant contribution to theology. Romans 9–11 were exegeted in §34, Romans 12–15 are exegeted here in §38, and even if they are not specifically exegeted, the early chapters from Romans on judgment and justification obviously underlie much of the discussion in §39.

4. The Command as the Judgment of God (§39)

The chapter concludes with a section (§39) on the command considered as God's judgment. Following the same structure as before, Barth deals with the topic in three subsections: the presupposition, the execution, and the purpose of the divine judgment. He begins by affirming the fact that God pronounces judgment in his claim and decision (733). There can be no disputing this. But on what presupposition does he do so?

Barth's answer is quite simple. The presupposition of judgment is that God wills to count man as his own. Essentially this has a positive thrust, but it works out negatively at first. Man is God's—that is the positive side. As God's, however, he is responsible—hence he comes under the judgment of God. This presupposition implies that God is just in his judgment (734f.). Here again, of course, we are not to think of God or his judgment abstractly. We are to think of them in relation to Jesus Christ. In him the will of God is decided, executed, and manifested (736ff.), not merely in the sense that God judges us in Jesus Christ, but also and supremely in the fact that Jesus Christ endures the judgment for us and in our place—a theme that Barth will work out in detail in the doctrine of reconciliation (IV,1). In him, therefore, the positive thrust of the presupposition of judgment is clarified, for he is our election and sanctification (738ff.). Even in his ethics Barth is thus led to the very heart of the gospel.

He works this out a little more fully in his next subsection on the execution of the divine judgment. For us confrontation with the command of God entails the disclosure of our own sin. We are "proved relentlessly and irrefutably to be its transgressors" (742ff.). We do not meet its claim nor are we the people we ought to be on the basis of its decision. We cannot stand against its sovereignty or pretend obedience in the face of its definiteness or specificity (744f.). Why not? Not because the judgment of the command awaits us but because it has been executed in Jesus Christ (746ff.). God demonstrates the total hopelessness of our position by executing judgment in the sin-bearing death of Jesus Christ (748ff.) and by bringing it home to us in and by the Holy Spirit (751f.). Since judgment has already been executed in Jesus Christ, we cannot argue about it, or hope for the best, or cover ourselves with excuses. We are totally wrong before God. Nevertheless, the judgment executed in Jesus Christ is vicarious judgment. Hence we are totally wrong before God only as we are totally right before him. Our knowledge of ourselves as sinners can only be penultimate knowledge in contrast to the ultimate knowledge of ourselves as justified sinners. We have this ultimate knowledge because in the very execution of his judgment God also justifies, accomplishing this justification in the raising of Jesus Christ from the dead (758ff.) and making it known to us by the Holy Spirit (762f.). At this point, too, Barth anticipates his development of the doctrine of reconciliation in chapter fourteen, which comprises the main part of the first part-volume of Volume IV.

Having made it clear that the command as the judgment of God discloses our justification as well as exposes our sin in the judgment, Barth ends the section and the chapter by expounding the purpose of the command from this angle. God wills man as his own: the pre-supposition. He justifies him: the execution. He wills to have him as the one who passes from the judgment: the purpose (764f.). In its ethical implication this means that we are directed to live by the grace of God. More precisely, it means that we are called to faith as acceptance of the rightness of God's right and as affirmation of his judgment on our being and action (766). In its origin and basic form this faith is repentance, the recognition of the forgiveness of sin as *sin* (768f.) and of sin as *forgiven* sin (770ff.). In penitent faith we see that the old man is dead and we are to live as new men on a new day. Thus the purpose of the command of God as his judgment might be described as our sanctification, our direction to eternal life (772ff.). Sanctification as the purpose of the command, of course, must be seen as a fulfilled sanctification. It may be ours as such, but only as we stand in a definite relationship to Jesus Christ in whom it is already a fact (775ff.). (To some degree Barth is anticipating here what he will work out as the second aspect of reconciliation in chapter fifteen, the second part-volume of Volume IV.)

From the ethical standpoint, the significance of what he says lies particularly in the explicit christological grounding of ethics. Ethics as the doctrine of God's command can be developed only as the knowledge of Jesus Christ who is both the holy God and sanctified man in one (777f.): "Jesus Christ is our sanctification because we are what we are only in relation to Him" (778). Faith confirms this in obedient response to the self-grounded witness of the fact (778f.). In this obedience of faith we receive the Holy Spirit whose gift and work in us is "that Jesus Christ should live in us by faith" and that "our obedience should be necessary and our disobedience excluded" (780). In this light—and this is Barth's final point—we realize that the required life in repentance and conversion consists of prayer; of prayer best summarized in the constant but joyous petition: "Come, Creator Spirit" (780f.).

The
Doctrine
of Creation

CHAPTER IX
Creation

1. *Faith in God the Creator (§40)*

BARTH originally planned to follow up his volume on the doctrine of God with six successive part-volumes on the doctrine of God the Creator, the Reconciler, and the Redeemer. After taking up the theme of creation in Volume III, however, he found that his four chapters were so lengthy that he needed four part-volumes, one for each chapter, instead of the previous two. He begins with a chapter on the work of creation (III,1), and divides this into three sections: faith in God the Creator (§40), creation and covenant (§41), and the Yes of God the Creator (§42).

As he explains in the preface (ixf.), Barth had feared that the treatment of creation would take him into many areas, particularly the area of science, in which he had neither competence nor understanding. Reflection on the specific task of theology relieved his fears. Christian faith, he concluded, does not endorse random scientific findings or hypotheses. It views the creature relative to the Creator. Its proper work concerns the Creator and his creative action considered in and of themselves. Hence it must not begin with an apologetic statement in face of scientific research, nor with the quest for a comprehensive world-view, but rather with a study of the implications of the confession of God as Creator. Faith in God the Creator, the theme of the first section, forms the proper starting point.

Barth begins the section—a third with no subsections—by asserting bluntly that like all other doctrines the doctrine of creation is an article of faith. This is stated plainly in Hebrews 11:3 and accepted by such diverse theologians as Theophilus of Antioch, Aquinas, Polanus, and Quenstedt (3f.). There are three reasons why it has to be so. First, the doctrine asserts that God does not exist alone but by his will and action there exists another distinct from him. Neither the negative nor the positive side of this assertion can be either demonstrated or contested (5f.). Second, the doctrine asserts that creation does not exist alone but does so only in virtue of God's will and action. Again neither the negative nor the positive side of this assertion can be either demonstrated or contested (7ff.). Third, we can make these assertions only in answer to the divine self-witness as this is brought before us explicitly and implicitly in scripture's testimony to Christ and its appeal for faith (11). Scripture teaches us (1) that the Creator God of scripture, the Father of Jesus Christ, is not the general God of, for example, Aristides (11–13), (2) that God created in a unique event or act of free grace which underlies the Creator/creature relation (13–15), (3) that the world created by God is and always will be a gift of God standing in a creaturely relation to him through his contingent act (15–17), and (4) that the object of God's creative act is heaven and earth in their unity and distinction, with man at the center (17–22).

Having given these reasons why the statement about creation must be an article of faith, Barth asks what it means that the doctrine of creation is knowledge and confession in reception of the divine self-witness and response to it. He advances two theses. The first is noetic. We know creation from scripture but from scripture as God's witness to himself, that is, to Jesus Christ (22f.). Finally, then, we know creation from Jesus Christ who is both God and man. From Jesus Christ as God we learn that God, although absolute in himself, has a partner outside himself (25f.). From Jesus Christ as man we learn that man is not alone, that he is not absolute in himself, and that he too has a partner (26ff.). From Jesus Christ as God and man we learn who God is as Creator, what he does, and what his creature is (27f.). With Jesus Christ as our point of reference we not only know the dogma but with absolute certainty we also know the truth of this knowledge (28).

The second thesis is ontic. Jesus is the Word by which we know creation because he is the Word by which God made, upholds, and rules creation (28). Barth does not expand on this, since his concern is with the noetic relation, but his point is that from every angle Jesus Christ is the key to the secret of creation. In a short excursus Barth expresses surprise that even such theologians as Aquinas, Luther, and Calvin make so little of the christological approach to creation in spite of their obvious awareness of creation as grace (29–31).

Since the knowledge of creation comes to us in and by Jesus Christ, it follows, Barth thinks, that this knowledge has to be a knowledge of faith. Faith involves an attitude, a decision, the recognition of God's creation of the world and his lordship over it (31f.). It means, then, a life in the Creator's presence, for it is as Creator that Jesus Christ is present for us, as quotations from Paul make plain (32–34). Faith as life in the Creator's presence carries with it the experience and recognition of his power over all things and all situations, he being not merely the ruler but also the origin of creation (34f.). It carries with it, too, an experience and recognition of his right over the creature, a right superior to every creaturely right by virtue of his original ownership of creation (36–38). Finally, it carries with it an experience and recognition of his goodness to the creature, for in spite of every appearance to the contrary, the Creator as known in Jesus Christ the Mediator is the God of benevolence and mercy, the eternal Father, whom we may also name as Father (39–41). With faith in Jesus Christ we know and apprehend creation as grace (41).

2. *Creation and Covenant* (§41)

In the next main section (§41) Barth investigates the biblical witness to creation in the Genesis stories. The clue to these, he believes, lies in the relation between creation and covenant. Theologically the two accounts depict two different aspects of this relation. He thus expounds the stories successively under the complementary titles of creation as the external basis of the covenant, and the covenant as the internal basis of creation.

Before this, however, in an introductory subsection, Barth raises the historical question under the heading of "Creation, History, and Creation History." By creation scripture means a divine work—the first such work—but it is in a series with other works spanning the history of the covenant which precedes it in intention, but for which it provides the necessary setting (42–44). Barth observes in this connection that the Christian confession necessarily drops away if the doctrine of the Creator is replaced by a concept such as the sense of absolute dependence (44f.). The uniqueness of creation as the work of the triune God can be understood only if it is related to the purposed work of covenanted grace that succeeds it. Judaism hints at this, Lactantius, Lipsius, Ritschl, and Troeltsch express it in a humanistic perversion, while theologians from Tertullian by way of Melanchthon and Calvin to Polanus and Quenstedt give it a more accurate formulation (46–48).

As the first work, creation is rightly appropriated to the Father, the source of the other modes of divine being (49). Yet, since the outward works of the Trinity cannot be divided, creation may be seen also as the work of the Son, who became creature, and of the Holy Spirit, the lifegiver (50ff.). Barth offers a collection of biblical references and theological quotations supporting creation by the Word (51ff.). He finds less support for creation by the Spirit but thinks the Nicene term "lifegiver" points in the right direction (57ff.).

Creation aims at history. The Creator is the triune God who acts in history—in covenant history—or salvation history as labeled by nineteenth-century theologians (59ff.). Aiming at history, creation belongs to history. Although unceasing, it has the character of an event fulfilling time (60f.). The creation stories, then, are neither meaningless (61) nor are they revealed metaphysical or scientific cosmology (61f.). They tell us about the event of creation (62). In our exegesis, then, we must neither fill them out with metaphysics, as Augustine and Aquinas did, nor detach them from the ensuing history of the covenant (64f.). They offer, in Barth's opinion, the prehistory of the people of Israel (65).

Creation as prehistory—not timeless truth—may be defined as a historical reality that took place in time as the basis of time (65ff.). Barth now takes up again the discussion of time begun in I,2. God created time with the execution of creation in time (67–69). Here Barth has to take issue with Augustine (69–71). The temporality of creation underlies the temporality of salvation history in which it has two counterparts: fallen time, in which flux has become flight (72), and the time of grace, its true sequel running alongside fallen time as the prototype of true time (74–76).

Creation history, while genuinely historical, has a distinctive and exceptional character as the beginning of history. The distinctive way in which it is known and told reflects this. This leads Barth to make an important statement on history as *Geschichte* and *Historie,* two terms which he seems to understand more in their ordinary senses— history as event and history as record—than in the specialized theological senses which have led to such confusion in modern debate. Creation actually occurred, but it did not take place in a creaturely context as all other events do. Hence it cannot be recorded or studied like other events. From this angle it may be called non-historicist, for creation occurred prior to human and natural history. Two different stories record it which are not easily *combined* if viewed as historicist accounts. The stories, however, are not to be regarded as less valuable or trustworthy because they do not and cannot have the historicist form which modern western scholars absurdly have set up as the criterion for judging the authenticity of history (76–81).

Barth proposes that the biblical creation narratives are properly termed saga. (Tale or story might be a better rendering in the English.)

Saga as he defines it is an intuitive and poetic account of a prehistorical reality truly enacted in time and space (81). It expresses immediacy to God. For this reason the Bible contains a good deal of it even in ordinary historical accounts and without prejudice to their historical truth or validity, as liberal theologians unfortunately have failed to perceive (82). Barth staunchly maintains that this genre has just as much place in scripture as have the many other genres—law, epic, lyric, proverb and so forth—which it also employs. Saga must not be confused with fairy tale or myth. In particular myth stands in direct contradiction to creation (86f.). Comparison with the Babylonian creation myths makes this clear, for these do not have creation as their true theme, whereas the Genesis accounts are genuine creation stories (87ff.). Parallels to the creation stories may be found, Barth thinks, throughout the scriptures. Prophecy offers a good example, for in it poetic imagination is interwoven with real events. This has to happen if scripture is to perform its essential task of being, not just the history of God's people, but witness to its encounter with God (89–92).

How can we know the difference between biblical saga and other forms? Only as we constantly relate creation to the covenant and its fulfilment in Jesus Christ. Only as we know in Jesus Christ the God to whom the biblical witness is given. Only as the Holy Spirit who spoke to the biblical authors speaks also to the hearers and readers. Only as he who is the object of the witness is also the self-disclosing subject. Barth concludes that within themselves the creation stories, like all human testimonies, are an inadequate medium. In content and credibility they live wholly by their object, that is, by the self-witness of the Holy Spirit. Their humanity can be freely recognized. They will not convince us by meeting our own arbitrarily imposed criteria. Nevertheless, this in no way destroys their true credibility. The relation to the object is their mystery and miracle (93f.).

Having clarified this, Barth offers in the second subsection a combined theological and exegetical exposition of the first creation story from the standpoint of creation as the external basis of the covenant. In creation God posits the indispensable and perfect presupposition for the realization of his purpose of love in relation to the creature (96). The purpose is touched on only at the end of the story with the creation of man and the sabbath rest of God (97). All else has to do with the forming of the necessary setting for the fulfilment of this purpose. It can be properly understood only in the light of the concluding reference (98f.).

In his exposition Barth divides the verses into ten groups. Three of these are introductory and cover only the first three verses. The other seven follow the sequence of the seven days. In each case a brief theological exposition is first given and a longer exegetical discussion follows, the details of which cannot be pursued in the present context.

1. *Genesis 1:1* The truth presented in the opening verse is simple. God, his will, and the execution of his will stand at the beginning, not the creature with its own will and act. Creation, then, is no accident. God fashions the cosmos of heaven and earth that is best adapted to be the theater of his covenant and its history (99; exegesis, 99–101).

2. *Genesis 1:2* In this verse Barth sees a reference to the divine decision whereby God excludes and banishes what he does not will. In his mercy God preserves his creation from what he denies and refutes. Hence it can be a peaceful and harmonious setting for his acts (101f.; exegesis and discussion of alternative interpretations, 102–110).

3. *Genesis 1:3a* Barth finds this verse important because it identifies God's creating with his speaking. This points to the personal nature of the Creator: he knows, wills, and speaks. The creature comes into being as the work of the Word, posited by God, not emanating from him. From the beginning it is thus related to the Word, in whom it has its Lord, in obedience to whom it finds its freedom, to whom God remains faithful even in its disobedience, and in whom covenant history begins and will be fulfilled, so that the creature may deny but cannot remove or abrogate the Word (110f.; exegesis, parallels, and insights from Augustine, Anselm, and Luther, 111–117).

4. *Genesis 1:3b–5* The first act of God or the Word is the creation of light, and also of darkness in virtue of its separation from light. Light declares life and the vanquishing of what God does not will. It is the sign of God's work and therefore of God's grace. Although God is Lord of darkness, he does not work in this sphere and it has its place only between evening and morning. Light has no intrinsic authority or dignity. Only by God's creation and judgment can it be called day. Yet God has called it day and as such, before anyone is there to see it, it carries the promise that nature will move forward to an encounter with the God of grace (117–119; exegesis, discussion of light in relation to the sun, moon, and stars, the question of evening and morning, and of evening and morning hymns, 119–133).

5. *Genesis 1:6–8* The establishment of order proclaimed by the creation of light finds fulfilment on the second day in the distinction of the upper and lower waters and the subsequent conservation of the earth as the theater of covenant history. Testimony is given in this way to the creation of the world, not for judgment but for grace and freedom, not for death-dealing law but for life-giving gospel (133–135; exegesis, 135–141).

6. *Genesis 1:9–13* Separation of the waters makes possible the establishment of land on the third day. This is marked off from the terrestrial waters that represent the averted threat of destruction. With the assurance of divine mercy, land bears fruit by the Word. While created for itself, the vegetable kingdom carries the promise of future forms of life and makes provision for them. It is the table that God has prepared and that man always needs even in his dominion, so that in the exercise of this dominion he is always thankful for it (144; exegesis and quotations from Basil, Ambrose, and Calvin, 144–156, with an important note on human usurpation, 152).

7. *Genesis 1:14–19* The fourth day brings the creation of the sun, moon, and stars as the bearers of light for creaturely eyes. These exist in heaven but function in and for the lower cosmos. Dispensable to God, they are indispensable to animals and men, and therefore to men as God's covenant partners, for whom he has designed them and to whom they give orientation to himself (156–158; exegesis, 158–168).

8. *Genesis 1:20–23* An orderly progression may be seen in the work of the fifth day, for this day corresponds to the second as the fourth does to the first. Autonomous living creatures—fishes and birds—now appear on the scene. These free-moving creatures prefigure man but in the alien elements of sea and air that are threatening to man. In their kinship to man they display God's mercy and lordship. They are assured of continuity by the blessing of procreation by which they also point ahead to the creature that as God's covenant-partner is ordained for fatherhood and sonship (168–171; exegesis and comments by Calvin, 171–176).

9. *Genesis 1:24–31* Here Barth finds another sequence, for the work of the sixth day corresponds to that of the third in juxtaposition and differentiation. Man is seen in his individuality yet also set in the kinship and company of animals, which, even if inferior, serve as a prefiguration and which as sacrifices will finally point him to the saving self-offering of the Son of Man (176–181). The work of this day also forms a climax, so that a solemn introductory formula is used with an inward rather than an outward reference (181–183). In contrast to all other creatures man is said to be made in the divine image, that is, in correspondence to a divine prototype (183f.). In amplification man is then said to be created male and female, in other words, with a counterpart in differentiated unity (184–187). We then learn that man is given dominion, but not unrestricted lordship, over the earthly kingdom, although this is not equated directly with the divine image (187f.). Finally, under the divine blessing, man is to multiply, not just as animals do, but, according to Barth, with a view to the true image in Jesus Christ and the church (188–191; exegetical discussion of the

divine image, 191–206). The use of plants as food for man and beast is viewed as involving dissolution but not the taking of life. After the fall the taking of animal life will be allowed, not as a concession to human degeneration, but as a positive and prophetic sign of God's acceptance of a vicarious life for the forfeited life of man (207–210; exegesis, 210–212). Pronouncement of creation as good denotes concretely its recognition as perfectly adapted to God's will and purpose (212f.).

10. *Genesis 2:1–3* Creation is finished but the story ends with God's resting on the seventh day. God does not have to recuperate after hard work. He has reached his goal. Hence his rest manifests his freedom and the specificity of his love. Since this rest is also event, God accepts his work, and does not deistically abandon it. He accepts it with the creation of man, so that covenant history begins on the seventh day. Man, on this his first day, shares with all creation in the divine rest. If his own working week will also end with the sabbath, he thus learns from the outset that he stands on God's gracious work and not his own. Creation forms the external basis of the covenant in which the love of God moves to its fulfilment (213–219; exegesis, discussion of the six-day schema of the fathers, and of the sabbath in Aquinas, Calvin, and Irenaeus, 219–227).

Note should be taken of three significant and hotly contested theses in Barth's exposition. First comes his interpretation of 1:2, which lays a foundation for his later teaching on evil. But does the verse actually mean what he understands it to mean? Second, we have his close relating of the image of God to man's being as male and female, which will play a vital role in his doctrine of man and his ethical teaching. Can the parallelism be pressed as hard as Barth presses it here? Finally we have the christological and covenantal understanding which controls his whole exegesis. Is this a valid interpretation in the total context of scripture, or is Barth with his rich and fertile mind seeing things that are not actually there? Whatever answer may be given to these questions, at least we are indebted to Barth for a stimulating presentation, for much useful historical information, and for several individual insights from which every reader can profit.

Turning to the second creation story in the last subsection, Barth first points out that in spite of the unity of theme we have here a new and independent account, not antithetical to the first, but given from a different angle. Creation has meaning. God gives it this by making it the witness to his own intention, plan, and order. The meaning at the heart of creation, its material presupposition and inner basis, is the divine covenant. This is the new angle from which creation is now viewed. This is why, instead of giving a comprehensive and connected account, the second story focuses on certain themes in which the covenant is uniquely significant and which lead on to covenant history (228–232).

1. *Genesis 2:4b–7* Though Barth does not think it appropriate to break up this account into small units, he finds three broad divisions in the material. The first division, vv. 4b–7, includes three essential points: first, God bears now the covenant name of Yahweh; second, he is the Creator of earth and heaven, the focus now being on earth; and third, although man is taken from the dust and will return to it, he is directly animated and called by God in intimation of the movement from death to life, and of the perfecting of earth through Israel, and finally through Jesus Christ (234–238; exegesis, comparisons, and commentary on Ezekiel 37, 239–249).

2. *Genesis 2:8–17* On earth the spotlight now falls on the fruitful garden with its rivers, its two special trees, and man as its keeper. After the manner of saga this represents a definite but unique place that is only partly identifiable. The stress lies, not on man's work, but on God's provision, as denoted by the tree of life. The tree of knowledge implies a possibility of judging good and evil in usurpation of the divine prerogative. Hence the first word of God to man grants free permission to eat of all the trees with the exception of this tree, the fruit of which will mean death and destruction. God does not make the eating of it physically impossible but offers man the freedom, not to choose, but to obey. In these different aspects the story looks forward to the life and destiny of Israel in the land of promise and definitively to the person of the crucified and risen Christ in whom real fellowship is established between God and man (249–276; exegesis, with references to Augustine, Luther, and Calvin, 276–288).

3. *Genesis 2:18–25* For Barth the second story reaches its climax in the creation of man, not as male alone, but as male *and female* (cf. 1:26). The divine Word initiates the provision of a helpmeet or partner who can be freely hailed as such. The animals do not fulfil the need and their naming brings this to light. Consequently God fashions woman from man, so that she is part of himself but not his creation. If man suffers loss with the making of woman, he becomes whole in virtue of it. While seeing a part of himself in her, he also sees an autonomous being with its own nature and structure. Bringing woman to man, God gives man the freedom to recognize her, as he does in v. 23. The name he gives her brings out the truth that woman is secondary in order but of equal humanity and dignity, completing man's own creation. Hence love and marriage take the corresponding form of unity (or totality) in distinction. Marriage may also be seen as the goal of the recognition of woman as helpmeet. In it is achieved the

openness in which is none of the shame and disruption that arise with man's perverted usurpation of the judgment of good and evil. In this connection Barth points out that no mention is made of children, who are so important elsewhere because of the fall and expectation of the promised Savior. As in the Song of Songs we have here a pure covenant of man and wife with an eschatological reference to its fulfilment in the covenant of grace between Yahweh and Israel and Christ and the church (288–324; brief exegesis, 324–329).

The exposition of the final verses develops from another angle Barth's understanding of the relation of the divine image to man's being as male and female. By creation male and female belong together in ordered unity. Neither can be truly human without the other. If creation establishes an order, this embraces differentiated equality and indispensability. Marriage conforms to this created reality of humanity. The interlude of sin gives new and central importance to the Son but in its ultimate significance marriage prefigures the final fellowship between God and man, so that here, too, the connection with the divine image should not be overlooked. Barth will have more to say about this in his anthropology (III,2) and his ethics of creation (III,4). He now lays the foundation for what follows.

3. The Yes of God the Creator (§42)

Having finished the expositions which are the core of the chapter, Barth ends it with a shorter section on God's acceptance of his work. He deals with this in three subsections on creation as benefit, actualization, and justification.

From the outset, Barth suggests, creation has the definite character of benefit. It expresses God's benevolence and beneficence. God affirms what he has done, for it is well done (330f.). We must affirm it too, for we know it to be well done from our knowledge of the Creator God and his covenant (331f.). To snap the link between creation and covenant is to lose sight of the fact that creation is benefit (332ff.). Marcion does this with his malevolent and maleficent creator and his bad creation; he looks exclusively to the covenant (334ff.). Schopenhauer does the same with his pessimistic view of phenomena; he looks exclusively at creation (335ff.). Neither world-less God nor God-less world will lead to creation as benefit. No world-view, only revelation, can show it to be such (341–343). For this reason—and Barth advances a familiar thesis here—the doctrine of creation must not become a world-view, base itself on a world-view, guarantee a world-view, or come to terms with a world-view (343f.). Instead it must claim its own source of knowledge and pursue its own task of apprehending and reproducing the Creator's own self-witness in revelation and scripture (344).

Approving creation, God has given it reality. Through its Creator the creature may be, and is. Affirmation means actualization. The creature is because God is its Creator. Because God is, and is its Creator, it may say "I am" also (344f.).

Actualization, too, may be known only from revelation, not from autonomous awareness of either God or self (345). We know it because we are told it. We affirm that we are because we are authorized and compelled to do so (346). Awareness of creaturely reality rests on God's self-communication in revelation. It is a response, an echo. Doubt is ontically excluded, for God is, and is not not. It is noetically excluded too, for God is not hidden but revealed (350). To illustrate his point Barth engages in a critical analysis of Descartes, whom he sees to be right in principle but totally wrong in execution, since he does not put his question seriously enough and therefore cannot give an ultimately serious answer (350–363). Giving greater precision to his own answer, Barth adds that we know creation as actualization because in Jesus Christ we know the God who is, and has revealed himself to be, the God of the covenant (363ff.). "The gracious God is, and the creature which receives his grace is. For the God of grace discloses Himself to the creature as the One He is, and in so doing discloses the fact that the creature also is" (364). This closes the door on Cartesian theology and also on all abstract Christian theology.

Affirmation of creation by God means its justification as well as its actualization, in other words, its goodness as well as its reality. Existence is neither bad nor neutral but good. It is right in God's eyes. In its own order it could not be better. In actualizing it, God justifies it (366).

This, too, may be known and said, not in the light of our own ideas, but only by God's self-revelation as the God of grace in Jesus Christ (368–370). We do not know it from the brighter side of creation, although creation's Yes confirms God's (370f.). We need not doubt it because of the darker side of creation, for God's Yes is not compromised by creation's No but echoes and underlines it (372f.). In relation to both these aspects of creaturely being, revelation does three things. (1) In transcending and relativizing them, it confirms them. (2) In confirming them, it transcends them. (3) In confirming and transcending them, it discloses the perfection of creaturely being (375–378). The crucial question is how it can do this.

Revelation can do it because it shows that God in Jesus Christ endures the contradiction of the two aspects in Jesus Christ (379f.). He thus affirms his Yes by setting a Nevertheless against his No. God's real goodness is revealed in his not allowing the creature's contradiction to remain alien to himself (380f.). From all eternity he made the creature's cause his own in Jesus Christ. He solved our problem even before it was our problem, or we knew it to be a problem (381). He solved it for us, bearing the contradiction on our behalf, so that by the life and death and resurrection of the Son we live (382).

Does this mean that the contradiction exists eternally and is thus a final word even though it is overcome? Barth thinks not, for in Christ the Yes and No have different emphases and give evidence of a definite direction. Jesus shares the creature's pain and death transiently and teleologically; he is raised again eternally and definitively. The No is spoken for the sake of the Yes (383f.). Hence creaturely being has the justification, not of a static perfection, but of the overcoming of its imperfection by God's intervention for it (385).

The Christian, then, will neither yield to optimism nor defy pessimism when he utters his own Yes. He will echo God's Yes. Finding joy and assurance here, he will see that it contains a No that God spoke in offering his Son. In faith, however, he will realize that the No is penultimate, the Yes ultimate. He will thus recognize the justification of creation. Confirming and transcending the two aspects, and thereby disclosing perfection, revelation gives secure and binding knowledge, for we are not neutral but caught up in it, so that beyond optimism and pessimism, under the constraint of God's victorious love, we have to accept the divine pronouncement and bear witness to it (387f.).

Barth ends the subsection, section, and chapter with a brilliant and, in places, almost hilarious discussion of eighteenth-century optimism. He begins at the top of the ladder with a sober analysis of Leibniz (388–393). He moves down a rung to the popularizer Wolff (393–396). He comes down another step to the redoubtable Lesser and his *Insecto-Theology,* from which Barth culls some choice examples (396–399). Down another rung he meets the pedestrian and complacent Brockes, who, in the comfort of his study, can find consolation in every unhappy circumstance (399–402). At the bottom of the ladder Barth finds a Swiss poem, which, edited by Kyburtz, can be sung to *Nun danket,* and which traces God's hands in the practical utility of the Swiss mountains (402–403).

Barth does not want to make fun of optimism. Its basis is sound. Its overthrow does not prove it wrong (404f.). It declined because it took the darker side of creation too lightly (406f.), found too little joy in the brighter side (407f.), was too anthropocentric (408–411), lacked true authority (411f.), and above all, apart from a single reference at the end of Leibniz' *Theodicy,* did not put Jesus Christ at the center

(412f.). If it had seen that God's choice of this world as the best relates to Christ as Member and Head of creation, as well as Lord, Savior, and Hope of the world, it could have withstood the Lisbon earthquake and Enlightenment criticism (413). Substitution of the two books of nature and grace for the one book of revelation was its basic error. Knowledge of the justification of creation, Barth concludes, can be securely achieved only as knowledge of him to whom all power is given in heaven and on earth (414).

CHAPTER X
The Creature

1. Man as a Problem of Dogmatics (§43)

FROM the work of creation Barth moves on to the creature. He has five sections on this theme, the first being a preliminary study of anthropology in a dogmatic context. He divides this section into a first subsection on man in the cosmos and a second on man as the object of theological knowledge.

Definition constitutes Barth's primary task. By the creature he means man (III,2,3). Why not the cosmos, in which man is set and which must obviously be included in the discussion? Because, Barth replies, scripture has no cosmology. He makes five important points in this regard: (1) Scripture uses various cosmologies but adopts none (6f.). (2) It takes this course because its theme is man in the cosmos, not the cosmos itself (8). (3) It is free and noncommittal and can even be disloyal in relation to specific cosmologies (8f.). (4) Our own commitment to a cosmology can mean defection from faith (9f.). (5) Faith will always be in some contradiction with the cosmologies with which it associates (10f.).

Creation forms a theme of scripture only in relation to the covenant. Hence it constitutes a cosmological border, heaven being the invisible limit reminding us of the divine horizon, earth the visible reality forming the sphere of human activity. Only when God's Word is not heard will the cosmos be a sphere of independent theological concern as a kind of third force between God and man (11f.).

Barth comments here on the methodological closeness of dogmatics, not to philosophy, but to exact science. Neither is tied to a world-view. Each observes, classifies, and understands what is there.

Each does so anthropocentrically, or, in the case of theology, theoanthropocentrically. Each recognizes a sphere both within and beyond the range of human observation (12f.).

If man in the cosmos is the theme of dogmatics, his resemblance to the cosmos may be accepted but not to the point of seeing in him a microcosm, although certain fathers (e.g., Augustine), some of the orthodox (e.g., Bucanus), and moderns like Dorner have done interesting research along this line. Man is both more and less than the cosmos. Furthermore, God's relation to the cosmos, except as it is known through man, remains a mystery to us. The most one can say is that the relation is illumined by the knowledge of man and God's purpose for him revealed in his Word (13ff.).

What is this knowledge of man? Barth discusses this in the second subsection. He first lays down the twofold thesis (1) that theology presents man in his revealed relation to God and (2) that in so doing it expounds the truth about him (18–20). The question of other anthropologies arises here. Barth sees these falling into two classes, speculative and scientific, the former being hostile to faith, the latter neutral (23f.). Both classes differ from theological anthropology, since this deals with the disclosed reality of man in his relation to God, whereas even scientific anthropologies can deal only with the phenomenon of man, or man in himself (25f.).

Knowledge of real man confronts a serious problem even when we look at the revelation of man in scripture. The man we find here is sinful, corrupt, and perverted. How can we move from man's inhumanity to his true humanity? Certainly man in his corruption remains God's human creature. Nevertheless, the distortion is serious and we share it as knowers even when we try to know man from God's Word (30). How, then, can we know man? Barth has two suggestions to make.

First, we may know man as the object of divine grace. This indicates that sinful man is not real man. Sin, having no creative force, has not constituted a new man. Man still belongs to God, not to Satan, nor to himself, nor to anyone else. Barth takes up here a point he will develop more extensively in Volume IV, namely, that only in the light of grace can sin be truly seen and known (31–34).

Second, God himself knows the truth about real man beyond his sin. God can and does impart this knowledge to us by disclosing his ongoing attitude to us in continuity with his purpose in creation. This attitude may be seen in his attitude to the man Jesus, who is God's revealing Word, the source of our knowledge of man as God created him. Stated simply, this means that "this man is man" (43). Both noetically and ontically, anthropology rests on christology. We do not first

know man and then understand Jesus relative to this general knowledge. We first know the man Jesus and then understand all men relative to this special knowledge (38–46).

Difficulties arise here. If Jesus is man as we are men, human
nature is surely one thing in us and another in him. For as man Jesus
is also God (49). As man he is sinless (51). He reveals human nature
"in its original form" (52). This rules out a direct equation of christology and anthropology. Nevertheless Barth rejects a constitutive difference along Manichean or Marcionite lines. The man Jesus is
genuinely of one nature with us. We may thus infer our human nature
from his, knowing ourselves in him. Only as we start with the man
Jesus, Barth believes, can we reach knowledge of true man.

2. Man as the Creature of God (§44)

Starting with the man Jesus, Barth devotes a section to the study of
man as the creature of God. He begins with a look at Jesus in a first
subsection on "Jesus, Man for God." He then has a subsection on
other anthropologies under the heading of "Phenomena of the Human." He reaches his goal in the third subsection with an exposition
of real man.

Asking how the nature of man may be seen in the man Jesus,
Barth replies that we should see him in the continuity of his history.
He appears there as the bearer of an office, acting in a specific and
constant direction. He is real man in this; "the real man is the working
Jesus" (58). Naturally he is a person as we are, yet not in the neutral
sense of sharing in humanity but in the concrete sense of being the
one in whose humanity we must share. His exclusiveness lies in his
history; he does not merely have a history, he is his history (55–60).

How can we say this? Because his work in this history is his work
as the Savior. His history cannot be separated from his person, nor
can his work be separated from the work of God. "God acts as Jesus
acts" (62). He does only one work and in doing it he is one with God
and in this oneness he has his own being (60–63). Barth finds im-
pressive support for this presentation in Johannine christology (64–
68).

What does it all amount to? Barth summarizes his thinking as
follows. First, we see Jesus as the man related to God. Second, we see
him as the man who is thus related to his work as Savior. Third, we
see him as the man in whom God's sovereignty is not infringed but
demonstrated. Fourth, we see him as the man who is real man in and
by the sovereign being of God. Fifth, we see him, not as an instrument
of God's action, but as the action itself, he himself being his own

history. Sixth, we see him as the man for God, this being the true distinctiveness of this creature (68–72). (Incidentally Barth discerns the truth of the *enhypostasis* in his fourth point.)

Barth opens the second subsection by drawing from his study of Jesus six criteria which may be used in understanding real man. Allowing for the differences between Jesus and us, we may yet affirm that real man is to be seen as conditioned by his relation to God, his deliverance by God, his determination to God's glory, his standing under God's lordship, his being in history and freedom, and his service of God and being for him (73f.).

Barth uses these criteria to evaluate other anthropologies. He first states the principle that no anthropology based on self-observation alone can lead to real man, since such an anthropology necessarily moves in a vicious circle. Polanus offers an instructive example (75–77). Barth proceeds to examine the four main anthropological approaches of the modern period and finds that they are obviously defective when seen in the light of his criteria.

First, he looks at naturalism. But this runs into the immediate problem of being unable to establish man's distinctiveness in relation to other creatures. The suggestions made by Zöckler, Otto, Titius, and the more scientific Portmann can at best point only to human phenomena (80–87). They cannot establish authentic human reality.

Second, he considers idealism. Some progress appears to have been made here because of the concentration on the spheres of will, freedom, and purpose, but idealism still operates in the field of self-knowledge. The phenomena do not stand the test of the criteria of the relation to God and his action, glory, lordship, and service, nor is the freedom at issue a genuine freedom for God but only the shadowy freedom of estranged, enslaved man. Fichte offers an example. Analysis of his thinking on doubt, freedom, and knowledge leads to the devastating conclusion that when all is said "Fichte's god is Fichte's man and Fichte's man is Fichte's god" (97–109).

Third, existentialism appears even more promising. Deriving knowledge of man from questions of existence, it shatters the self-contained aspect, poses a need for existential self-transcendence, and, as in Jaspers, lays emphasis on the element of history (109ff.). Nevertheless, Barth asks some incisive questions. Why are some situations particularly significant? Why cannot the response to them include sheer indifference? What is the transcendence they are supposed to bear? Does it not lie finally in man himself? Are we not left without any clear view of man engaged in the movement toward transcendence (114–120)? Brief notes on Jaspers (113, 114, 120) provide illustrative material for the discussion.

Finally, Barth looks at theistic anthropology, which comes closest to his own interpretation. This anthropology presupposes an authentic and dynamic relation to a transcendent other. It renounces autonomy. Building on rationality and responsibility, it finds a place for freedom in historical decision. It thus meets some of the criteria. Yet in Barth's view it suffers from three vital weaknesses: (1) It does not need the God of self-revelation as the transcendent other. (2) It finds the reality of man in freedom of choice, not freedom for obedience. (3) It can offer only potentiality, not actuality. Brunner's anthropology in his *Man in Revolt* provides Barth with his example of this last approach, which again leaves us only with phenomena of the human, not with authentic man (128–132).

To understand authentic man, we must begin with the man Jesus (132). Barth works out the implications of this in the last subsection. He first points out our likeness to Jesus: "every man as such is the fellow-man of Jesus" (133f.). Yet Jesus also confronts us as the divine Other, not abstractly but as this man (134f.). Thus "to be a man is to be with God" (135). Being without God is ontologically impossible. Our true humanity excludes sin, for sin contradicts it (136). Man perhaps represents all other creatures in this being with God, but it does not appear that other creatures can sin as man does, so we should not talk too glibly about fallen creation. One cannot speak absolutely, of course, in this area (137–139).

What does being with God mean? Formally it means being created by him. Materially it means (1) being elected in God's elect and (2) hearing the Word, that is, Jesus, as the sum of God's address (140ff.). To be created is to be in the sphere where God's Word is spoken and heard in Jesus and to be summoned by this Word (149f.). Who am I really? I am in the Word (150). Barth concludes with a detailed discussion of creation out of nothing in its anthropological dimension (152–157).

If to be man with God is to come from God in the sense of election and summons, Barth feels that on the basis of the incarnation he can go on to call man's being a history, not a state or a succession of states. In man's sphere the history of the relation to God occurs, as we see from Jesus, in whom "the Creator is creature and the creature Creator" (159). Derivation, then, does not mean causal dependence nor does election imply contingency, for these would rule out a true history that has its prototype in God. Similarly, hearing the Word does not denote potentiality but the actual calling of the man Jesus in whom man has specific being as a creature in genuine history with God (163).

Four features of the Word ought to be noted. It is gracious, for to man alone does God speak in the existence of one of his own kind. It is sovereign, for it transcends the limits of man's own possibilities. It is imperative, not just passing on information but calling, claiming, and conferring the humanity in which man can answer. It involves gratitude, the proper response to grace, so that man's true being is a being in gratitude (164–166).

What is implied by being in gratitude? First, gratitude is merited by God alone (169). Second, gratitude alone is what is to be rendered to God. Third, man's true being is fulfilled in gratitude. Fourth, only man owes gratitude to God, although Barth does not rule out a certain solidarity with all creation in this respect (170–174).

Gratitude reminds us that receiving grace means returning to God in a new openness which may be called responsibility. This has the form of word but as word it is also act and has as such some inner marks by which the being of man as history may be known. These are the marks of knowledge of God (176–179), obedience to God (179–182, with a discussion of Calvin's *Catechism*, 182–186), invocation of God (186–192), and divinely imparted freedom (193ff.). In this man is not just object but divinely posited subject in responsible hearing, obeying, and seeking (194ff.). He is kept by God both in ability not to sin and inability to sin, sin being the negation of this true freedom in responsibility (197).

Barth concludes the section by showing how the phenomena of the human, if not given the status of world-views, can be valid indications of real man as known in the man Jesus. Naturalism puts man in his creaturely setting. Idealism pinpoints his distinctiveness. Existentialism portrays him in his openness to a transcendental other. Theism understands him theonomously as a rational being responsible before God in historical decision. None of these leads us directly to real man but on the presupposition that real man is known they all offer genuine information about him. No conflict exists, then, between these anthropologies and theological anthropology so long as they do not pretend to present real man but are content to offer symptomatic human phenomena (200–202).

3. Man in his Determination as the Covenant-Partner of God (§45)

Thus far Barth has looked at real man only in his relation to God. There are three additional relations: to others, self, and time. These four relations will play an important role later both in the ethics of creation (III,4) and also in the doctrine of sin (IV,1,2,3). Here they are areas in which real man is christologically known. Barth takes up the three remaining relations in the next three sections, beginning in §45 with the relation to others. His underlying theme is that in correspondence with the being of God the being of real man is a being in covenant.

The christological subsection discusses Jesus from this standpoint under the heading "Jesus, Man for Other Men." The humanity of man stands in indissoluble correspondence to his being as God's covenant-partner even though sin brings in an element of contradiction (203–206). One may see this in Jesus, for if his divinity implies that he is man for God, his humanity implies that he is man for men, man in *fellow-humanity* (207f.). In doing God's work of salvation he does it for his fellows (208–210).

This being of Jesus for others has an ontological side. He saves us in a history of which he is the free subject but this does not mean that he might not have been man for us. He is himself and properly God's Word to men. Hence his orientation to them is "primary, internal, and necessary" (210). The solidarity with which he binds himself to them is wholly real, as his compassion reveals (211f.). It involves comprehensive and radical identification: (1) he is determined by others and their needs; (2) he is determined by his obedience to God; and (3) he is determined in freedom by the inner relation in God reflected in his outer relation to the creature (214–219).

Barth finds in the third of these points the true meaning of the image of God. Jesus' humanity does not just repeat and reflect his deity: "It is the repetition and reflection of God Himself, no more and no less. It is the image of God" (219). As such it is not identical with God. There is disparity between the relation of God and man and the prior relation of Father and Son. Yet there is parity too, that of relationship, not being. The eternal love of Father and Son is also the love addressed to man. The inner being takes outer form in Jesus' humanity, and "in this form, for all the disparity of sphere and object, remains true to itself and therefore reflects itself" (220).

On this foundation Barth can consider in a second subsection what he calls the basic form of humanity. That Jesus is for others implies that their form of humanity is like his (222ff.). Learning from him, we find that this humanity of theirs cannot be an isolated one in abstraction from others. Sinful man certainly tries to be human in isolation. It is even difficult for him to recognize the rights and dignity of others. In fact, isolated humanity is a contradiction of humanity; it is inhumanity. Man acts against his true being when he comes out with a solitary "I am" (226–231). In a brilliant excursus Barth cites Nietzsche as his chief example (231–242).

Since humanity is a divine determination—a being with others— the "I am" in real humanity takes on new significance, resting ultimately on the "I am" of Jesus. Barth sums up this new significance in three ways: (1) the "I am" now implies a Thou (244); (2) "I am" means "I am in encounter" (245–247); (3) encounter must be described in the formula "I am as Thou art" (248).

Barth then suggests four constant elements in encounter which can be seen as categories of the distinctively human. The first is looking the other in the eye (250ff.). In this connection Barth includes criticism of impersonal bureaucracy (252). The second is speaking and listening to the other in the giving and receiving of address (252–260). Here Barth warns against the devaluation of words, but rightly points out that behind empty words stand empty people (260). The third is rendering mutual assistance (260–265). In this respect Barth comments on the ease with which we make an imposing and lofty thing out of something so realistically simple (264f.). The last element is doing all these things gladly, for if encounter is inescapable, true encounter occurs in the inner determination which is true freedom and involves neither absorption nor manipulation of the other (265–270). The secret of humanity lies in this free and glad being with others (273).

In a concluding excursus Barth issues a reminder that he is speaking here of created humanity. Hence he does not refer to Christian love. He refers to what belongs to humanity by nature, to what may be present and known, in part at least, outside Christian revelation. Grace does not have to be magnified, he thinks, by an undue disparagement of created nature. (Many commentators on Barth seem not to have read this.) From this angle eros has a certain validity for all the justifiable antithesis between it and agape. Humanity in the sense of a glad being with the other is neither eros nor agape, yet it contains the element of gladness which eros reflects and agape should never lack if Christian love is to be authentic love. In a surprising turn, which all Barth readers should examine closely, he thus finds an element of humanity common to non-Christian and Christian alike and recognizable in each by the other for all the strangeness of agape to the one and eros to the other (274–285).

In the third subsection Barth looks more deeply into the nature of fellow-humanity. On the basis of III,1, he finds this to be posited from the outset in sexual differentiation. One cannot even say "man" without saying "male and female" (285f.). Barth does not attempt here a physiological or psychological distinction, and he warns indeed against facile generalization in these fields (287). He also explains that he has more in mind than sexual love and marriage, since the male-female encounter occurs in a wider as well as a narrower circle (288f.). His simple point is that no one exists outside or above this differentiation. Genesis 2 and the Song of Songs are decisively important in this regard. Nor does Galatians 3:26f. bear contrary witness, for not even christologically does it suggest unisex. While ruling out discrimination or hostility in virtue of the common being of Christians as God's children by grace, it does not abolish the natural distinction that is of the essence of humanity (294–296).

Pursuing the thought of humanity as likeness, Barth discerns in the male-female relation a reflection of the basic covenant or marriage relation between God and man (297ff.). Initiated in Yahweh and Israel, and reaching its goal in Christ and the community, this relation is the first and proper object of the divine will and by it we know the dignity, brokenness, and promise of the sex relation (299ff.). In this light, and with a wealth and depth of insight, Barth discusses in detail the Pauline texts referring to man and woman, particularly 2 Corinthians 11:2f., Romans 7:1f., 1 Corinthians 6:12–20; 7; 11:1–16, and Ephesians 5:22ff. (301–316). No one concerned about the biblical teaching on man as male and female should fail to work carefully through these packed lines of exegesis.

As Paul reminds us, humanity is a great mystery that faith alone understands by understanding its content and reality in Christ and the community (316f.). Man as God's covenant-partner by nature is created to be his covenant-partner by grace (319). He thus inescapably bears the likeness of what he is destined to be. He does so in hope. Bearing witness to the orientation, the likeness forms the ground on which one may hope for the fulfilment (319ff.). Ultimately, of course, the likeness of man's being as male and female is not merely to the covenant relation of God and man but to the very being of God. God has created man in correspondence to himself, in his own image and likeness. As God exists in the essential relation of Father, Son, and Spirit, so he has created man in that of male and female. In this sense the image neither is nor can be lost. What is more important, however, is that what man is in this image, he is in hope, namely, hope of the being and action of God as the original in the relation (322f.).

4. Man as Soul and Body (§46)

The relation to self forms the topic of the next section (§46). Here Barth looks at man as soul and body. Again beginning with Jesus Christ, he sees him in the first subsection as "Whole Man." Man is normally described as soul and body, but on what basis and in what sense? In Jesus Barth finds, not a union of soul and body, but a whole man, embodied soul and besouled body (325–327), a totality in his life, work, death, and resurrection. New Testament passages, and the general combination of word and work in his ministry, are adduced in support (328–331).

This totality, Barth suggests, is an ordered one that is structured from within, Jesus being his own law and living his own life (332). The special relation to the Holy Spirit calls for notice here, for while the Spirit does not make Jesus the Messiah, it is as the perfect bearer of the Spirit that he has the fulness of perfect life in an ordered and harmonious unity of soul and body (332–340).

Jesus as true man in this ordered relation stands in a twofold analogy. We see first a likeness to his own being as both Son of God and Son of Man (340f.). We then see a likeness to the relation of himself as Head to the community as his body (341f.). More distant analogies also suggest themselves. Thus one might discern a resemblance (1) to heaven and earth in creation, (2) to law and gospel in the Word, and (3) to faith and works in man's response to God (343). The main analogies, however, suffice to show how the knowledge of man as soul and body brings us close to the center of all Christian knowledge.

Moving from Jesus to us, Barth looks first at the Spirit as the basis of soul and body, the theme of the second subsection. Man exists as he has Spirit. He is creature, not God, and yet he is not without God, but constituted by him. There can thus be no understanding of man apart from God (344–347). In free grace the living God constitutes him as the soul of his body, part of the physical world as body, yet living as soul and thus belonging also to the invisible world, besouled body and bodily soul (349–351). That man is body is a grace, for unbodily soul would be in bondage (351f.). That man has life is also of God, for body without soul would be a disintegrating material thing with no part in the covenant (353). Either way, man has his being, not without God, but only with and from him.

This is why Barth says that man exists as he has Spirit. He does not think it biblically correct to say that man is spirit (354f.), for Spirit implies God's operation on creatures and particularly his movement to man (356). In the present context Spirit means God in his outward action as the principle of creaturely reality without which man cannot live (356–359). Yet in this outward action of God, Spirit must also be seen biblically as the principle of man's existence in the covenant—the principle which encloses the first one as its presupposition and promise (360–362).

Pulling the threads together Barth notes that having Spirit means four things. (1) God is there for man, not giving man a share in his own essence, but graciously assuring man of his being (362f.). (2) Man is determined as the soul of his body, the Spirit being the principle and power of the life of the whole man (363f.). (3) The Spirit is present in but not identical with man, constituting him a human subject but not being the subject (364f.). (4) The Spirit has a special and direct relation to the soul, and through the soul an indirect relation to the body, so that in the ordered relationship of soul and body the soul is over the body (366). It might be observed that in the English translation it would have been better to have consistently capitalized Spirit since Barth rejects trichotomy and seems always to be referring to the Spirit of God.

The third, fourth, and fifth subsections deal with soul and body successively in their interconnection, particularity, and order. In regard to interconnection, Barth points out that soul and body, representing man's life and nature, do not have the same distinction as Creator and creature, although they reflect this (367–369). It is grace that the distinction here is merely relative, for because of it man enjoys a unity in which he may be a subject before God, who, even if in a different way, is also subject (371).

The unity of soul and body means negatively that soul is not Spirit and positively that soul can be only as soul of a body (372f.), just as body can be only as body of a soul (373). Soul represents the independent life and action of a subject. Hence one cannot speak of the soul of inanimate things, or even of plants and animals, unless there be a special plant or animal soul beyond our ken. Nevertheless, the life and action of the independent subject come to expression in bodily acts, for, even if I am not my body, I do not exist without it. I know myself only in the common act of soul and body. Hence I am, not as abstract life, but as life in the spatio-material world of body (374–376). Along this line man's body is properly called organic body *(Leib)* rather than material body *(Körper)*. To drive home his point Barth has a short excursus on the Hebrew and Greek words for "soul" in scripture (378f.).

Three delimitations close the subsection. (1) Dualism, which severs soul and body, must be avoided; it may be detected in the medieval and orthodox slogan that human nature consists of soul and body (380–382). (2) One must also steer clear of an abstract materialistic monism which swallows up soul in body (382f.; examples up to and including Marx, 383–390). (3) Also to be resisted is an abstract monistic idealism which makes soul the one substratum of reality and treats body as garment, symbol, or even obstacle (390f.). Materialism, denying soul, leaves man subjectless; idealism, denying body, leaves him objectless (392). All these errors miss the interconnection of soul and body because they miss the point of connection—that man is as he has Spirit (393f.).

Interconnection does not exclude particularity, the essential distinction being that soul animates and body is animated (394f.). What this means can again be seen only from the having of Spirit, for it is in virtue of this that man is in relation to God and his Word in distinction and responsibility. At its core, relation to God is being-as-subject, as soul, while on the periphery it is taking the corresponding action, as body, not in isolation of being and action but certainly in differentiation (396–398). "Not without his body, but as soul and not as body, man is the subject of his own decision," and "not without his soul, but as body and not as soul, man must execute his decisions" (398).

In the meeting with God, two presuppositions emerge. We have perception of God and his distinction from us in awareness and thought and we have activity in relation to God as desire and will (399–406; supporting biblical analysis, which demands detailed study, 402–406 and 409–416). Perception and activity correspond to man's twofold but total being as soul and body. From them we learn three things: (1) soul and body have distinctive functions; (2) they have these in indissoluble but irreversible relation; (3) the soul has primacy in the relation, its dignity being to precede, that of body to follow, but in such a way that man's being the soul of his *body* is no less indispensable than his being the body of his *soul* (417f.).

The closing paragraph of the fourth subsection opens the way to the fifth on the order of soul and body. The basic thought here is that man is rational because, having Spirit, he is ruling soul and serving body. Rationality in this sense applies to both soul and body, for body as well as soul stands in and under the meaningful order of rule and service (418f.).

Can this also be said in relation to animals? Barth does not think one can know this. Indeed, we can say it of ourselves only because, even if imperfectly, we do in fact act as rational beings in this sense, constantly giving evidence of the unity and distinction of soul and body in the ruling superordination of the one and the serving subordination of the other (420f.). Our rationality consists of our being addressed by God; indeed, of our being created for this address, so that we are under a categorical demand to understand and conduct ourselves as rational beings (423; cf. Zwingli's concept of the divine image in his *Clarity and Certainty of the Word of God*).

That God addresses us as ruling and serving beings has three implications. First, we cannot see ourselves as pure souls—as purely thinking and ruling subjects—for even though our souls rule over our bodies (or we would not be men), we think and rule in the sphere of our bodies (424f.). Second, we cannot see ourselves as pure bodies—

as purely sensing and serving subjects—for even though our bodies serve our souls (or we would not be men), we sense and serve in the sphere of our souls (426). Third, we cannot see ourselves as dual but only as single subjects—souls with bodies and bodies with souls—for the one divine address encounters the one man "who can rule himself as soul and serve himself as body" (427).

For this relation of soul and body Barth finds three analogies, that of the fellowship of God and man, that of the relation of Christ and his community, and that of the relation of man and woman (427). Death alone can destroy the order by alienating soul and body but with the divine deliverance from death the order has the last word (428). Having established it, God upholds it (427f.). Barth concludes with an excursus, first on theories of the parallelism and interaction of soul and body (428–433), and then on the biblical evidence for his own understanding (433–436).

5. Man in his Time (§47)

In the final section of the chapter (§47) Barth considers man in the fourth relation, namely, the setting of human life. In consonance with his particular interest in time, Barth has specifically in mind the temporality of human life. He begins christologically with an important subsection "Jesus, Lord of Time" and follows this up with four shorter subsections on given, allotted, beginning, and ending time.

Barth opens his christological exposition with the simple truth—or truism—that "man lives in his time." He defines this time as created or co-created time, as the succession of past, present, and future (437). Man's constitution as soul of his body "presupposes his temporality" (438).

Jesus, too, lives in his time. As God's representative to men he does so both with God and to God, and as men's representative to God he does so both with men and for men (439). He lives in his time as judge as well as representative, vindicating God's right in men's eyes and men's in God's (439). Since he lives for God and men, his time ceases to be his alone. It is also time for God and men, so that he is the contemporary of all men, his time having the character of God's time—of eternity—of the simultaneity of past, present, and future. He is the Lord of time (440).

Jesus has a lifetime, a fixed span from birth to death. But his history does not end at death. He has a second history, the central Easter history of the forty days (440f.). Here we see him as the Lord of time, for the Easter event is presented in the New Testament as an event in time and history. He was among the apostles, not timelessly, but in the time of the forty days (442). In a critically important excursus Barth defends the historicity of the Easter event against Bultmann's demythologizing (442–447), contesting in particular the five dogmatic presuppositions about history and scientific thinking which underlie the misinterpretation (445–447).

Five implications of this subsequent time of Jesus are developed next. (1) Jesus obviously moved among the disciples as true man (448). (2) No less obviously he appeared in this time in the mode of God (449f.). (3) His unveiled manifestation formed the ground of the Easter faith of the apostles, so that they had to call him Lord (449f.). (4) He manifested his eternal glory in his real and physical resurrection from the dead. In this regard Barth allows that the resurrection stories do not belong to the same genre as modern historical writing but stands firmly committed to the historical reality of the appearances (451f.), the empty tomb, and the ascension which marks the limits of the Easter happening (452–454). (5) The Easter time reveals the mystery of the preceding time of the man Jesus, showing it to be the time when God was man—eternal time (455f.). Barth finds a reference to this time in Titus 1:3, discerns types of it in the jubilee and the sabbath (456f.), discusses the significance of the Christian adoption of the Lord's Day (458), expounds the concept of the fulness of time in Galatians 4:1f., Ephesians 1:9f., and Mark 1:14f., and points to the equation of this with the last time which is also the beginning of the new time as seen in 1 Peter 1:20 and Hebrews 1:1 (456–462).

The next step is to advance three distinctions between the time of the man Jesus and our time. Our time begins, has duration, and ends. His time begins but exists before its beginning, has duration but in such a way that his present includes his past and future, and ends but in such a way that the time after its end is that of his renewed presence. His time, then, is eternal time—he is the Lord of time, as Revelation 1:8 and Hebrews 13:8 indicate (463–466).

Barth closes the subsection with a more extended exposition of the meaning of the present, past, and future of Jesus in the light of Revelation 1:8. His present denotes absolute temporal presence in which his yesterday is still today and his tomorrow is already today, even though the past is not cancelled and the future is still expected (466–468). Extensive New Testament support is offered, particularly from the stories of Paul's conversion and that of the Emmaus walk (468–474).

The past of Jesus embraces not only his earthly life but Israel's history, creation, and ultimately his eternal being with the Father in his pretemporal counsel. This does not conflict with his being in the present as the one he is nor his being in the future as the one who is to come. "As the one who never was 'not yet,' he cannot possibly be 'no longer' but will always be for ever" (475–477). The stories of the transfiguration, baptism, and infancy support this (478–481) and the interpretation of the Old Testament by the New adds confirmation (481–485).

Finally the future of Jesus covers not merely his impact on world history but his resurrection, coming again, and kingdom. It is not divorced from his past and present. He who comes is he who was and is, so that his future is already in his past and present. His tomorrow is no more a "not yet" than his yesterday. The future to which we look forward from his present is, like the present and the preceding past, the time of Jesus, the Lord of time. Barth seeks an exegetical basis for this understanding in 2 Peter 1:16ff., Acts 3:19f., and 1 Peter 1:10–12 as well as in John 14:18 which relates Easter, Ascension, Parousia, and Pentecost. Additional exegetical support is found in some synoptic sayings, and finally in the parables of Matthew 25 and their presentation of the community as that of the last time with the resurrection behind it and the parousia ahead (493–511). More detailed study of this expository excursus is recommended.

Turning from Jesus and his time to us and ours, Barth initially views our time as given time. He begins with the very different nature of our past, present, and future. Our past is the time we leave and are in no longer (513f.). Our future is the time we do not have but may have (514f.). Our present is the fleeting step from the "no longer" of the past to the "not yet" of the future, a flight which is also a chase (515).

Negatively, this points to God's judgment. Our being thus in time is the being in time of sinners. This is why attempts to interpret or amend it fail. Yet we know ourselves as sinners in time only in virtue of the manifestation of time in the real being of Jesus Christ for us in time. This is what unmasks and sobers us (517).

Positively, the being of Jesus Christ in time for us, while displaying God's judgment, serves also as a guarantee that our being in time will not perish. The time we have is the time that God has created and given. With our true nature our true time has not been forfeited, thanks to God's free grace in Jesus Christ (519–521).

One may thus say that humanity is temporality. We know God in time and history (520f.). This does not mean that we possess time. We did not create it and cannot evade or reverse it. We have it only as God has given it. Even if unwittingly and unwillingly, to say man or time is to say God (525). Temporality differs from eternity. In the truly prevenient grace of God it is the form or dimension of existence that God has willed, created, and given to us (526f.).

What does this imply for our present, past, and future? For the fleeting present, which slips from us even as we come to it, the implication is that it is secure as we are creatures under and with God. Since the present of God, the Creator of time, is the secret of our present, we have a real Now (529–532). The same security is implied for the vanished past for, while we cannot secure our own past, for example, by memory, we always have a genuine Then in God's eternity in which he loved us and willed to give us time and gave it (532–540). For the future, too, the implication is a similar security. In myself I am not the one I shall be; indeed, I may not be at all. Neither optimism nor pessimism can help here. But under and with God the problem disappears, for as God's eternity is past and present it is also future. With God we can find comfort and even joy in relation to our future (541–552).

The eternal God who thus guarantees our present, past, and future is not, of course, an empty word or abstract concept. He is the God made known by the name of Jesus, the Lord of time, who was, and is, and is to come, the eternal God. On this ground one can say that man has real time, that his time is related to God's eternity, and that this eternity is eternity for us. This might seem to be mere speculation; if not, it is in virtue of the divine being for us in Jesus Christ (551–553).

Time must be described as allotted as well as given. What Barth has in mind is that to each is given a limited span for life (553f.). But why? Does not life's fulfilment demand indefinite time? In the short subsection Barth gives six replies to this question.

(1) The distinction between God and the creature has to be considered. God's time, eternity, differs from endless time. To us as creatures belongs created time, not eternity. The proper dimension of creaturely life is created and limited time (558f.).

(2) Unlimited time would not serve man, for neither length nor even infinity can guarantee fulfilment. Unrestricted time means only unrestricted opportunity and allotted time does not of itself entail final loss (560f.).

(3) Infinite time would bring with it the pain of endless and restless aspiring. Even in our restricted span we continually yearn for more and in unrestricted time the yearning would be perpetual. "Could there be any better picture of hell than unending life in unending time?" (562).

(4) Allotted life does not have to be viewed as restrictive once it is related to God. In this time of his creation God is around us and with us. We are defined, but by him and for him, as those whom he encounters in this time and who may look to him in it (562–566).

(5) God has allotted us all the time we need to fulfil our destiny. God gives us the destiny as well as the time. This destiny is fellowship with him. We can achieve it in our limited time because he comes to us in this time (566f.).

(6) We can achieve it because God means Jesus Christ. In Jesus Christ God graciously comes to us and receives us in our time. If he limits time, he is present not only in its duration but very clearly at its beginning and its end. By its very nature, our creaturely human being in allotted time is referred and bound to the gracious God who is outside us but wholly and utterly for us. Why should we sinfully resist this divine ordering of our being for grace when it is so plainly set before us in the very allotment of our time (567–572)?

Allotted time means specifically beginning and ending time, and Barth discusses these in turn in a short fourth and a longer fifth subsection. The problem of beginning time is that of the Whence: Where do I come from? The urgency of the problem arises from the thought that if I am but was not, perhaps I shall not be (572ff.). In this respect locating the beginning makes little difference. Emanationism eliminates the problem but also eliminates creation. Pre-existence, traducianism, and creationism all leave us with the same problem of beginning from non-being. The only true solution is that, while we certainly come from non-being, we do not come from nothing but from God, who guarantees not only the duration of allotted time but also its beginning and end (576).

There was a time when we were not. But even then God was. Where do we come from? We come from God's preceding being, speech, and act. As the gracious God even before we were, God was not without us but for us. Our beginning does not hang over the abyss. It is preceded and held by God in the context of the time before our time. Thus life in allotted time stands under a promise. The light of the beginning shines on its course and end. It assures us that we move to and toward a good and reliable goal (577). In a supporting biblical excursus Barth looks at the role of the fathers and of blessing in Israel and then at that of Jesus Christ in the church as the end of Israel's history and the beginning of its own. He draws attention to the radical change of focus here and sharply criticizes the tendency of the church to regard its own history as a continuation and repetition of that of Israel, as though it were not the community that came from the goal of all history (578–587).

Finally, we face the problem of ending time. This is the problem of the Whither: Where am I going? (587). Genuine urgency arises here: I am, but as I was not, so I shall not be (588). Death lies at the end, as the Old Testament vividly shows (588–593). Can this truly be

God's good determination? It might seem that this is so, for intrinsically, ending is no more menacing than beginning. Nevertheless, there is no escaping the fact that historically death stands in a special relation to judgment. It thus has the aspect of an evil that God has suspended over us, a regression to non-being fulfilling the divine rejection (594–596).

Death is undoubtedly a sign of judgment and cannot be regarded as an inherent part of human nature as God created it (597). We cannot evade this. We fear death because in our guilt we rightly see it as judgment. If the Old Testament makes this plain, the New makes it even plainer, particularly in its account of Jesus' death for us (598–607). "The finitude of human life stands in the shadow of its guilt" (607).

Nevertheless, at the end God awaits us as well as death. At a first glance this might seem to make our end even more terrifying, for God, the Lord of death, is to be feared far more than death, which he himself has appointed to its office. The Lord of death, however, is the gracious God (609ff.), who is for us even as we are against him, so that to fear him is to find the comfort of knowing that even when we die he still lives and will be for us (609ff.).

All this becomes concrete in Jesus Christ. In him God is the boundary of the death that binds us because he put death behind us when he bore our death in his. Even in and beyond it we may expect everything from him—our hope, victory, future, resurrection, and life (614f.). The Old Testament forms the starting point of this assurance with its plain testimony to God's sovereignty over death (616–620). The New Testament gives it a solid basis and content with its witness to the vicarious death and resurrection of Jesus Christ, who abolished guilt and death, will come again as he rose again, and gives us by faith in him new and eternal life in God (620–625).

From his discussion Barth draws three simple but weighty conclusions. (1) The death of the sinner coincides with judgment—the second death—but in Jesus Christ, even judgment is a freely accepted end (628). (2) Because of the vicarious death of Jesus Christ, the first death—the end of life—no longer coincides with judgment, although it still serves as its sign (629). (3) Since death is robbed of its sting by the death and resurrection of Jesus Christ, we may still fear it as the sign of judgment but we need not fear it as real judgment. We can see it again as the good and natural end of human life which has a true *beyond* in God, in whom our being in time will be manifested in its glory and may thus be eternal life in God (632f.). Scripture bears witness to this in Enoch, Moses, and Elijah, in the distinction of the two deaths, in the catching up of believers to meet their Lord, and in the description of their death as a falling asleep with a view to rising again at the resurrection (633–640). In this light death may be preferred, yet we are not to desire it. We are to desire the life bounded by it as the earthly sphere of service. Affirming Jesus Christ as our beyond, we understand our life here and now as a life that is affirmed by his beyond (640).

CHAPTER XI

The Creator and His Creature

1. The Doctrine of Providence (§48)

IN chapter eleven (Volume III,3) Barth carries his scrutiny of creation a stage further, and investigates the relation of Creator and creature in the form of what is traditionally known as providence. He divides his study into four sections, the first on the doctrine as such, the second on God the Father as Lord of his creation (§49), the third on nothingness or evil (§50), and the fourth on the kingdom of heaven (§51).

The general introduction on the doctrine of providence consists of three subsections dealing with the concept, the belief, and then the doctrine itself. Barth rightly begins with a definition. As derived from Genesis 22:14, providence provides as well as foresees (III,3, 3). Providence must be distinguished from predestination, with which Lombard, Bonaventura, and Aquinas confuse it. Predestination is God's eternal decree, providence has to do with its execution. Guaranteeing and confirming creation, providence constitutes the external basis of covenant history as creation constitutes the external basis of the covenant (5–7). As the break in Genesis 2:4 indicates, it must not be viewed as continuous creation but as the continuation of creation, distinct from it, yet related to it (7–9).

The relation is important, for providence could mean little if the Curator were not the Creator and the Creator would not be the true Creator if he were a mere manufacturer who no longer cared for his products once they were made. In this connection both Calvin and Gerhard rightly inveigh against Epicurean deism and Heidanus acutely perceives that Aristotle with his prime mover has no real Creator.

141

Deistic trends are noted in Augustine and Aquinas but even the flippant remark of D. F. Strauss that a deistic God should be applauded as the inventor of perpetual motion does not counterbalance the obvious error of deism (10–12). As Barth views the matter, God's providence simply means his coexistence with the creature. Mere foreseeing does not meet the bill. God also provides. As Zwingli pointed out, he would not be God if he could not act as well as see, or if he would not do so. Indeed, he would be a demon. God is God precisely in his will and action as the sovereign and loving Lord of the creature (13f.).

Understood thus, providence is believed. In a short subsection Barth analyzes this belief. First, it is faith in the strict sense, not an idea, postulate, conclusion, or value-judgment, but faith as a hearing and receiving of God's Word (15–18). Second, it is faith in God, not in the creature, a cosmic process, or a system (18–21). Hence it must not be equated with a philosophy of history, which may or may not be useful (21–23). It stands closest to the prophetic view of history which sees God as the Lord and Ruler of history (23–26). Finally, belief in providence is faith in Christ. It knows God, not as a general God of providence, but as the God of fatherly providence, the Father of Jesus Christ (26f.). It parts company here not only with pantheism and polytheism but also with Judaism (27f.). Unfortunately the reformers and their successors do not make the relation to Christ sufficiently explicit, so that belief in providence could collapse under the impact of the Lisbon earthquake or be filled out demonically by National Socialism (30ff.). "The Christian belief in providence is Christian and . . . must not be . . . an extract from what Jews, Turks, pagans and Christians may believe in concert" (33).

Looking more specifically at the doctrine, Barth first lays down the principle that we know God's purpose from revelation and not from history. God has revealed and is revealing himself in Christ, as the ascension and session remind us (33–36). The execution of his purpose in salvation history offers the key to an understanding of world history. The latter exists for the sake of the former, while the former is embedded in the latter (36f.). We can be sure of this because overruling all things is Christ, the one God being the God of both world history and covenant history, the God who coordinates and integrates the two (39–43). Confusion may often be seen in creaturely events but faith can pronounce a confident "Nevertheless" in view of the presence and action of the God whose lordship may be seen in the covenant of grace (43–45).

In providence God allows the creature a meaningful role as the subject of the history which forms the external basis of covenant history. Four features mark this creaturely history. (1) It has a servant role (46). (2) It exists so God may work for and through and on it as a necessary theater of his action (47f.). (3) It constitutes a likeness or reflection of covenant history (49–51). (4) All this may be said of it, not in virtue of intrinsic qualities, but only as it takes place under God's providential sway (51–53).

Barth concludes with four important inferences. (1) God's free love alone, not its own goodness, can give creation its function, *telos*, and character (53). (2) Creaturely history has meaning as the external basis of covenant history only as it receives this meaning (54). (3) Although we may inquire into this meaning without faith, we cannot know and expound it without faith, for world rule cannot be known apart from the world Ruler (55). (4) A static world-view—even a supposedly Christian one—is ruled out, since faith is constantly given by the Holy Spirit and its freedom follows God's freedom in his providential overruling (55–57).

2. God the Father as Lord of His Creature (§49)

God the Father, then, is Lord of his creature. What does this mean? Barth's answer to this question forms the heart of his understanding of providence. He develops it in four subsections, the first three on God's preserving, accompanying, and ruling, and the fourth on the Christian under God's universal lordship.

Looking at preservation first, Barth at once strikes a christological note. In providence, that is, his fatherly lordship, God preserves the creature for the sake of his covenant purpose and because of the advocacy of Jesus Christ at his right hand. Thus to say that all things are from God and are preserved by him is to say that they are preserved, not by a supreme being, but by the God of Israel who is the Father of the incarnate Son.

Preservation might properly be described as conservation. Unlike Heidanus, Barth likes the twofold "service" implied by the term, not along the lines of creaturely cooperation, but in the correspondence of the eternal preserving to the serving of redemptive grace in Christ (60f.). Preserving or conserving has four facets. (1) God gives the creature a limited continuation so that it may play its role and have a share in the history of grace that leads to eternal life in fellowship with God (61–63). (2) God grants this conservation as a free act but does it indirectly through the creature as a means, not directly as in covenant history in which his people witnesses to grace but is not its means. On this point Barth cites Augustine and Gerhard but criticizes Lipsius for equating indirect preservation with the uniformity that rules in all things (63–67). (3) God confirms rather than continues creation in its preservation. Goethe's observations are considered and rejected here. As Aquinas correctly notes, God does not have to preserve the creature. His faithfulness to creation rests on his faithfulness to election. He preserves the creature in grace. For the sake of the Son he will not allow it to perish (68ff.). (4) God in his conserving meets the need of the creature as it stands under the threat of nothingness. By nothingness Barth does not mean metaphysical evil, as Augustine and later Burmann and Heidegger seem to do. He means that which lies under the divine non-willing and rejecting. From this only God in his positive willing and election can grant conservation (77ff.).

The last point leads Barth back to the idea behind conservation. We are assured of conservation by preservation, by Christ's coming to save (82ff.). But what exactly is conservation? It implies four things for the creature. (1) It may continue in being. (2) It may continue within its limits. (3) It may be actual within these limits. (4) It may continue before God eternally. Since even the smallest creature serves the covenant of grace, the end of its existence does not mean the end of the divine faithfulness underlying its preservation; thus it has a constant preservation in the divine eternity. This preservation, which belongs to providence, should not be confused with the resurrection, which belongs to reconciliation and redemption. Commentators can easily make fools of themselves by jumping to a hasty, illogical, and totally unfounded conclusion at this point.

Providence embraces God's accompanying as well as his preserving. Preservation in actuality means preservation in activity. But God does not abandon the creature to this activity. He accompanies it in its activity in the threefold sense of surrounding it with his own activity, affirming it in its autonomous activity, and going with it as Lord (91–94).

Known in older dogmatics as concursus, this accompanying raises the hard question of the relation of divine and human causality, of the first cause and secondary or particular causes. Activity means causing. Barth does not quarrel with the term. It can be used properly, however, only if it is not used impersonally, apart from Jesus Christ, as though it were a concept above both God and man. It should be given its content from biblical instead of philosophical concepts. Barth is unhappy with the older orthodoxy for its failure at this crucial point (94–107).

The truth behind the concept of cause lies in the supremacy of God's operation even in cooperation with the creature (107ff.). Yet this is no abstract supremacy but the revealed supremacy of eternal self-giving (107–109). In the concursus the will of the God of love and freedom is done, and it cannot be conditioned by the activity of the creature (110ff.). God concurs with the creature, not the creature with God. The reformers and their successors saw this, but did not see as clearly that the God of the concursus is the triune God, that his will is the fatherly decree of grace, and that his work is the historical execution of the decree in the sacrifice of the Son and the ensuing ministry of the Holy Spirit (115–119). This insight alone rescues the divine sovereignty from being viewed as despotism and the creature as a mere effect.

Concursus includes precursus, the preceding of the creature's activity by God's. Precursus means not only foreseeing but also omnipotent foreordaining, not along the lines of a causal nexus equal to the sum of cosmic forces or laws to which the creature is subject, but with a personal reference to the ordaining God whose ordination stands before and above all others but whose freedom establishes the authentic freedom of the creature (119–131).

Strictly speaking, concursus is acompanying. "Going with" does not differ in content from "going before," but it has reference to the creature's present. It is the simultaneous concursus in which God's foreordination comes into force and the divine and human activity may be seen as one, as Aquinas and Quenstedt rightly observed (132–134). How can this be so? Ultimately, as Cocceius said, the "how" remains a mystery. Yet we can still say what we know about it (135). Negatively, the union of the two activities is neither causalistic nor by infusion, and positively it entails richness and not monotony (135–139). It is effected by the Word and Spirit, in whose activity in creation history, as in covenant history, is accomplished the activity of the Father. This activity gives God's supremacy its full due while not suppressing but vindicating the dignity of the creature, for the God of this activity is no tyrant but the Father who allows it its own sphere and work in its own integrity (145–150).

Concursus finally embraces succursus, God's following of the creature's activity in the form of helping to bring it to effect. As God in his eternity was before the creature and is with it, so he is also after it. Hence the accompanying of God very naturally has this third aspect as well. All acts aim at goals, but the creature cannot control the effects of its acts or guarantee the attainment of goals. Once acts are finished they have their own history in their own freedom. This history and freedom are apart from those of the creature, but not from the history and freedom of God. God decides the form, compass, meaning, and range of the completed act. He follows it where the creature cannot go and arranges its result, so that nothing will be in vain but everything will fit in according to his original precursus. Here the divine concursus obviously merges into the divine ruling, but in such a way that the distinctiveness of effects may still be perceived (151–154).

The divine ruling, expounded in the third subsection, expresses the purposefulness of the divine preserving and accompanying. It may thus be described as the divine governance *(gubernatio)* or, in New Testament terms, the kingdom *(basileia)* of God (154–157).

God alone rules. He is himself the goal of his glory and blessings (158–160). He is neither one necessity among others nor the sum of such necessities. He is above them all and yet in them all to the exclusion of fate on the one side (cf. the Reformed) and chance on the other (cf. the Lutherans) (160–164). God in his rule transcends the cosmic antithesis of necessity and freedom (164).

The divine ruling breaks down into four components. God actively orders creaturely occurrence (164). He comprehensively controls it, both in its execution and its results (165–167). He directs it to a common goal, without invalidating its individual features and aims (167–169). He coordinates it, mutually conditioning the individual moments and actions to the individual and corporate praise of God (169f.). In an excursus Barth insists that God relates directly to every creature, so that the horizontal relativization does not mean that anything, however small, can be simply the means to fulfil the end of the created whole or of more important creatures (171–175).

Coming to the heart of the matter, Barth focuses on the God who rules. Who is this God? It is vitally important here to see and say that the God of providence is not just a supramundane being (Aquinas) but the God of the covenant, the King of Israel, the great "I am," the incarnate Word (175–182). According to Barth, the rule of God has its controlling center in the actualized "I am" of the covenant of grace. The special events are the internal basis of the general, the general the external basis of the special (183f.). The older distinction between general and special providence might be reinterpreted along these lines so long as the former is understood in the light of the latter and not *vice versa* (184f.).

Having shown who the ruling God is, Barth reexamines three things he said earlier about the divine ruling. God alone rules, because he is gracious in his freedom and free in his grace (186f.). He is the goal, because he, as Son of the Father and Father of the Son, is love (187). He transcends necessity and freedom, because he is almighty in his mercy and merciful in his almightiness, turning to the creature in his own free and self-conditioned reality (187f.).

From the same angle he reexamines the four characteristics of the divine rule. God orders events as the King of Israel who is plan and planner in one. He controls and directs events in the freedom of his grace and therein validates the creature and its activity not in tension but in a calm, clear, and positive relation. He coordinates all creatures and events into a community which rules out both collectivism on the one side and individualism on the other. He is no faceless monad but the revealed God with a revealed purpose that gives form and unity to events even as yet it is hidden in them (188ff.).

Barth closes the subsection by pointing to four constant elements that serve as signs of the divine rule in world history. (1) The first is holy scripture in its origin, transmission, exegesis, and influence (200–204). (2) Then comes the history of the church, a result of scripture, with its remarkable claim, ability to resist, and capacity for renewal (204–210). (3) Next comes the history of the Jews in their survival, identity, and persistence as a people, wherein may be seen our own sin and God's electing grace (210–224). (4) In an abrupt switch Barth finds the fourth in the limitation of human life in its universality and particularity as the once-for-all place of personal history and personal opportunity to hear God's Word (226–238). At the very end he mentions an additional sign that is more important than all the others and indeed embraces them all. He alludes to the existence and function of angels (236–238). He will discuss angels later but introduces them here with the warning that if we miss, ignore, deny, or banish them we shall probably end up missing the other elements and even the living God himself, for "where God is, there the angels of God are," and "where there are no angels, there is no God" (238).

In the last subsection Barth examines Christians under God's fatherly lordship. Christians know God's providence, seeing what others do not, accepting their creatureliness, and renouncing self-assertion and self-glorying (239f.). They can thus participate in God's lordship from within. They do not understand all that happens, and will often be astonished at events. But they know the Father from whom all things come, and even if they do not see how it is achieved they know his goal and purpose. They look, then, for the positive side of whatever comes and cooperate with it (241–243).

How do they have this decisive and distinctive knowledge? They have it, Barth suggests, in the threefold Christian attitude of faith, obedience, and prayer, all of which must go together if the attitude is to be authentically Christian.

Faith means receiving God's Word as such. It comes first and thus has a primacy of order. It must be seen, not as a magically imparted quality, nor as submission, nor as self-attained conviction, but as wholly God's work and wholly man's. As participation in Jesus Christ, the Word received, it may be participation in God's fatherly lordship. It is this as enslavement which is emancipation, as the acquiring of a

Lord who liberates him from the self as lord. It necessarily embraces obedience and prayer (246–253).

Obedience means doing God's Word. It must not be understood as meritorious achievement or the mere fulfilment of a code. It is a work of the Holy Spirit bound to the direction of the Word. Like faith, it involves participation in Jesus Christ and therefore in God's fatherly rule, not just in the religious sphere, but more specifically in the secular. Obedience is free achieving under the strictest authority. It necessarily includes faith (as its root) and prayer in order to be the first and most effective form of action (253–265).

Prayer is the basic form of both faith and obedience. It consists of the sequence of praise and thanksgiving, confession and penitence, petition and intercession, and again praise and thanksgiving. At its heart it is asking as petition and intercession. This asking rests on prior hearing by Jesus Christ. It is grounded in his vicarious intercession, whose first target is the asking community of which each individual Christian is a member. It can only be the prayer of faith and is the basic act of obedience. Participating in Christ, it, too, participates in God's universal lordship. It is not just a high form of edifying self-dialogue but something by which God allows himself to be determined (265–286).

Barth is thus brought to a striking conclusion. In faith, obedience, and prayer Christians are set with Christ at God's right hand. In this threefold creaturely movement "there moves the finger and hand and sceptre of the God who rules the world . . . the heart of God" (288). We cannot rate this attitude too highly, for in it we are "at the seat of government, the very heart of the mystery and purpose of all occurrence. The subjective element conceals, contains, and actualizes the most objective of all things, the lordship of the One who as King of Israel and King of the kingdom of grace holds all things in His own hands" (288).

3. God and Nothingness (§50)

What about the opposing and alien element from which God keeps us? How does this affect God's providence? Barth examines what is usually called evil under the heading of *Das Nichtige* (*nihil*, nothingness, what is not), first stating the problem, then disposing of a misconception, and concluding with subsections on the knowledge and reality of it.

The problem arises because although God overrules nothingness, neither he nor the creature can be regarded as its author, so that God does not will or even permit it (292). A further problem is that nothingness may either be regarded as too strong, as though God had not overcome it, or as too weak, as though we could overcome it ourselves (293). Its theological presentation causes a final problem. Its presence and action mean a break in the relation of Creator and creature. Theology knows its object only in the shadow of this break. Hence it can speak of it only brokenly, particularly, and exemplarily where the break is at issue. Rigorous logic should be applied but a unified system cannot be expected (294f.).

The misconception dealt with in the second subsection is the equation of nothingness with what Barth calls the negative side of creation. This equation slanders creation. As is so beautifully brought out in Mozart's music—Barth pays his famous and astonishing tribute to Mozart here (297–299)—creation in both its light and darkness is God's good creation. Hiding behind this negative side, nothingness makes itself seem harmless and innocuous (299f.), contradicts God's self-manifestation in the incarnate Christ, brings itself into an apparently positive relation to God, and cannot be recognized as the true enemy it is (300–302).

How, then, is true nothingness known? In the third subsection Barth argues that even here one must start christologically. It is known from Jesus Christ as the enemy that he has defeated (302–305). Its concrete form is human sin, although Barth issues the caution that one cannot know it directly from knowledge of our own sin (305f.), since sin may be properly known only when it is not seen as aberration but as disobedience to God or, more specifically, as the repudiation of his grace and command (308). The God against whom we sin is known to us in Jesus Christ; this is why he is "the objective ground of knowledge of sin and nothingness" (309).

In Jesus Christ we learn that nothingness includes sin but also exceeds it. With real sin there is also real evil, real death, a real devil, and a real hell (310). Nothingness cannot be confined to the moral sphere but constitutes a comprehensive totality. We know this because Jesus Christ defeated this totality as the total Savior who not only secures remission of sins but conquers physical ills in his miracles and vanquishes death as himself the resurrection and the life (311f.).

Barth appends to this subsection a long excursus in which he successively examines and evaluates the contributions to this subject of Müller, Leibniz, Schleiermacher, Heidegger, and Sartre (312–349). No account can be given of what amount almost to independent essays on these figures. With his customary verve, penetration, and insight, Barth appreciates the positive aspects of their teachings but goes to the core of their theological inadequacies in a way which brings to light not only his opposition to Leibnizian optimism and

Schleiermacherian liberalism, but also to existentialism. All serious students of theology should work through this excursus carefully and reflectively.

From the noetic side—the knowledge—Barth moves on to the ontic—the reality. He has seven points to make here, of which the first is a reply to the question: What do we mean when we say that nothingness "is"? It "is," he says, neither as Creator nor creature is. Yet it is not nothing. It "is," therefore, improperly in a third way of its own (349).

Second, he argues that nothingness cannot be negatively defined relative to what it is not. God is not creature, but there is no nothingness in him. It belongs to his perfection not to be creature, and to the creature's perfection not to be God. The creature's "not" forms a frontier, for beyond what it is by God's will lies what God does not will it to be. It is at this frontier that nothingness gains entry into the creaturely world, but the mere fact that the creature is not something does not mean that nothingness is intrinsic to it (349f.).

Third, nothingness in its distinctive mode of being stands in no relation to the creature by which the latter may know it of itself. It is a reality for the creature, but it cannot be the object of creaturely knowledge. The creature knows its reality only as it knows God in his attitude to this enemy (350f.).

Fourth, the ontic context in which nothingness has its own reality is that of God's election of grace which is also rejection and judgment. Nothingness "is" as that which God rejects. Only under God's No to what he does not elect can one say that it "is," "but on this basis it actually 'is' " (351). It "is" paradoxically as what Barth calls "impossible possibility." What God rejects is not just nothing but has its perverse reality grounded not in itself but in the divine non-willing (351–353).

Fifth, nothingness, as what God does not will, cannot be grouped with either God or creature. As negated negation of grace it is intrinsically evil, alien to God, hostile to him and his creation, chaotic, disordered, subject to God's opposition, and destined to defeat (353f.).

Sixth, defeat of nothingness is primarily God's affair. The creature alone cannot overcome it. Although man did not have by nature a capacity for sin, he opened the door to nothingness by thinking, willing, and acting contrary to grace. In response to our human plight, God takes up our cause and fights nothingness for our sake. In Christ he defeats it as man, the incarnate Word. He enables man to have a part in the conflict, for in taking action for man he empowers him, not self-sufficiently but under the wings of the divine mercy, to range himself with God (354–360).

Seventh, nothingness has no perpetuity. Being neither God nor creature, it is from the very first what is past. It does not continue on the basis of a supposed logical necessity whereby God must always hate if he loves. God does not have to concern himself with it eternally. He has definitively overcome it at the cross, where it met a victim it could not master. Nothingness can no longer "nihilate" because it has been destroyed. We treat it with full seriousness in the light of this victory, but with the seriousness of joyful assurance, not of anxious trepidation (360–364).

To conclude the section Barth draws from what he has said an alternative theodicy. The usual way of stating the problem of theodicy—how can God be omnipotent and good, or the creature good and imperfect?—suffers at the very outset from a fatal abstraction. Instead, one should approach the matter in retrospect of the refutation of nothingness at the cross and the manifestation of this refutation at the *parousia*. In this light one sees that nothingness has no ultimate power or actuality but only that of an echo or shadow. Indeed, it has this semblance of validity only in God's hand and under his decree. Involuntarily, then, it is forced to serve God until its day is done. It is a strange servant, driving us to seek refuge in him who defeated it. "Good care is taken by this One that even nothingness should be one of the things of which it is said that they must work together for good to them that love Him" (365–368).

4. The Kingdom of Heaven (§51)

To complete his doctrine of providence Barth adds a final and counterbalancing section (§51) on the kingdom of heaven, God's ambassadors, and their opponents. He opens with a subsection on the limits of angelology in which he admits that the field is difficult, partly because it is difficult to ask the right questions and give the right answers, and partly because no fruitful results seem to accrue (370). Angels exist on the very boundary of Christian knowledge, since their name denotes a reality distinct from both God and man. It is easy to transgress the limits, as Origen, Augustine, and Calvin all observe (369f.). But this is for Barth a good reason why the boundary should be explored and something should be said about the divine relation and ministry of angels (371).

By way of introduction Barth makes five important methodological clarifications. (1) We must strictly adhere to what holy scripture teaches us and not indulge in abstract speculation; that is, we should view the angels of scripture as we view the God and man of scripture (371ff.; cf. Calvin and Quenstedt).

(2) Angelology demands explanation as well as belief if credibility is not to be threatened, and although accounts of angels have an imaginative quality because angels exist in another dimension, this does not negate their facticity, nor allow us to remove them from the particular history in which they appear, as in so many artistic representations (373–378).

(3) The doctrine of angels must be genuinely theological and follow the maxim of faith seeking understanding. It should not start with a general idea of what they might or must be, which has produced a good deal of speculative ballast and the corresponding reaction of altogether denying or ignoring angels. In a long excursus Barth offers examples of the approaches to be avoided: the apologists and fathers (381–385), Pseudo-Dionysius (385–390), and Aquinas (390–401).

(4) One must not try to follow the double track of an understanding based on faith confirmed by an understanding on another basis. In such an attempt "our philosophy will spoil our theology and our theology our philosophy." Here, as elsewhere, theology can be truly free only when it dares to keep both eyes on scripture alone. The risk in this is simply that of obedient trust in the promise of the Holy Spirit. Among those who have erred here are orthodox dogmaticians such as Quenstedt and Bauer (401-404), supranaturalists such as Reinhard (405), rationalists such as Bretschneider (405f.), idealists such as Rothe, Dorner, and Martensen (406–408), and early twentieth-century theologians such as Schlatter and Troeltsch (408–410).

(5) The last clarification tends to be a summary of the preceding four. Theology must not become philosophy. It must allow the Bible to speak for itself, accepting its form, respecting its silence, recognizing that angels do not occur independently, and relating what it says to our own world. Exclusive commitment to the scripture principle controls angelology and enjoins a serious angelology (410–413). Barth concludes with some examples of theologians who do not take angels seriously: Strauss, de Wette, Lipsius, Kaftan, Kirn, Haering, Nitzsch, Seeberg, and Stephan (413–418).

The kingdom of heaven is the theme of the second subsection. To say God is to say heaven as well as earth (418ff.). Within the cosmos of heaven and earth God is indeed nearer heaven than earth and heaven is thus superior to earth (423). It exists as the inalienable counterpart of earth before which there are earthly happenings (424f.). As such it exists as the invisible sphere bordering earth (424f.).

Barth turns next to something concrete. Heaven, like earth, stands related to the covenant God. God's gracious work is presented to us as a movement (429f.). As such it is a movement in the creaturely world (430f.). The movement is to man and thus earth is the *terminus ad quem.* The movement is from God and thus heaven is the *terminus a quo* (431ff.). God speaks and works from heaven. The coming kingdom of God is the kingdom of heaven (433). In this connection Barth has a long analysis of the use of the word "heaven" in scripture, particularly in the New Testament (433–441).

To call heaven the *terminus a quo* means that heaven is not a vacuum; something is done there (443f.). Since heaven is God's place, this something is God's will (444f.). The will of God that is done there has earth as its aim and it thus takes the form of a harmonious differentiated movement corresponding to the multiplicity and mobility of earthly and human existence (447ff.). Heaven may be seen as an order embracing units, elements, individuals, or members engaged in its service (450f.). We are thus led to angels as the heavenly host or entourage accompanying, surrounding, and following the coming kingdom (451f.). Barth adduces several biblical references to angels in support (452–459).

The subsection closes with two observations on this angelic service. Negatively, angels do not do what God alone can do, for example, speak his Word, save, redeem, liberate, create, reconcile, judge (460). Positively, they bear responsive testimony to what God does: obeying, declaring, giving thanks, and serving as God's primary, constant, inflexible, and infallible witnesses. Barth backs up this understanding with a striking exposition of Revelation 4–5 (463–476).

In the third subsection Barth deals more directly with angels and their opponents. Angels are where God is (477). Hence there can be no experience of angels without God just as there can be no experience of God without angels (477f.). Angels do not rival God but they surround, serve, and attest him and therefore they are always linked to him (478f.). Where angels appear, one may be confident that God appears to speak and act. To perceive angels is to perceive God and in this sense they offer pure witness in a liturgy of service (480–486). The bearing of this on the phrase "angel of the Lord" is discussed in an interesting excursus (486–493) which closes with a sharp attack on the inanity of the usual artistic or poetic depiction of angels.

In what precise relation do angels stand to God? First, they do God's will exactly, without deviation, addition, or omission (493). Second, they do it indirectly, not as mediators, but more loosely by being there when God mediates himself (494f.). Third, they do not cooperate with God but serve to distinguish his words and acts from others. In this sense they can be said to work with God and to have a mediating ministry (496ff.).

What is their witness? It is the witness of those who are there when God's will is done (497). More profoundly, it is the witness that confirms God's Word and work to earthly creatures. Even here they prepare and follow, rather than replace, the witness of the prophets and apostles, of the community, and finally of all the lower creation. Nevertheless, theirs is a primary and indispensable witness constituting "the atmosphere in which there can be a witness of men and earthly creatures" (498f.). Barth looks for illustration to the christological role of angels in the gospel stories, particularly at the beginning and the end (499–511).

What about their name? In view of their function Barth thinks it is a good one. It describes their activity as that of carrying messages (511f.). "Ambassadors" as used in diplomatic circles conveys the idea. They act as God's plenipotentiaries in whose words and acts we have direct dealings with God (512–514). Angels cannot be abstracted from God as general hypostases or intermediaries. God's angels are the only angels (514f.).

Do angels act in general history as well as covenant history? For Barth this question is stated incorrectly. General history cannot be isolated from covenant history, in which lies its meaning and center. Acting in the latter, angels act in the former too. Where God's kingdom is, there angels are (515–517). Along these lines one may properly speak of national angels. In contrast Barth sees no solid support for the idea of guardian angels. The individual does not need a special angel, since all the angels have a protective function in relation to him (517–519).

Barth concludes with a quick glance at the opponents of God's ambassadors. He will not accept the common origin of angels and demons. Confusion arises if good and bad angels are lumped together. Demons might be called "angels," just as nonsense is a type of "sense," but they are related to true angels only as chaos is to creation or myth to kerygma (519f.).

Demons oppose God and his angels. But they have been defeated and we are not to respect them or spend much time with them. They are indeed a proper subject for demythologizing, not in the sense of throwing them out as part of a discarded world-view, but in the sense of not giving them a place in the real world of God's creating. They belong to nothingness (522f.).

These opponents resemble angels but only by pretending to be what they are not. This is not to deny that they have their own reality. Facile rejection of the devil can result only in subjection to the devil. On the other hand, nothingness must not be granted the reality of God's world, for this will ensure its power as well (526).

The power of demons is like their reality. They are mere imitations but they have all the power of falsehood. Anything other or less than the truth is no match for them. Nevertheless, their power is false power. God's truth unmasks and dispels it. When demons are shown in their true colors, they are disarmed and rendered impotent. Jesus Christ defeated them. In faith, obedience, and hearing and proclaiming his Word, we are summoned to follow him in this triumph, the angels participating as counterwitnesses to the lying messengers of the kingdom of falsehood (529f.).

Regarding an angelic fall, Barth examines the relevant texts but does not find them clear enough to affect the insights underlying his presentation. The devil, he argues, was never an angel. He was a liar from the first. Angels do not fall. They have freedom, but do not need what is called free will, that is, "the freedom to become fools." Barth does not expunge the verses that hint at a fall of angels. He simply objects to the way they are expounded. Unfortunately he does not back up the objection with any direct biblical material. His interpretation stands, then, under the shadow cast by these verses. They do indeed suggest an "angelic catastrophe," as Augustine put it. Nor would it seem that Barth's understanding is totally compromised if this be their meaning. Yet he takes a firm stand on the issue and in so doing lays himself open to criticism at a vital point: Is he really obeying scripture as the criterion of dogmatic purity and truth (530f.)? When he has done so much to restore angels (and demons) as a theme of serious theological enquiry, it is a pity that the whole discussion should end with so questionable a thesis and procedure.

CHAPTER XII

The Ethics of Creation

1. Ethics as a Task of the Doctrine of Creation (§52)

SINCE ethics falls within dogmatics in Barth's view, the doctrine of creation includes an ethics of creation. For this reason Barth has a special section on the divine command as the command of God the Creator in which he takes up the problems of ethics in this specific context (III,4). The chapter has particular interest because although Barth wrote a draft of the corresponding chapter on the ethics of reconciliation, he died before completing it and never reached the ethics of redemption. Here, then, we have his final ethical statement in the *Church Dogmatics,* though readers must be warned to keep it in the total context.

Barth divides the chapter into five sections. He first discusses in §52 the nature of theological ethics in relation to creation. He then expounds the command of God as Creator as a command of freedom in the four anthropological areas advanced in III,2: freedom before God (§53), freedom in fellowship (§54), freedom for life (§55), and freedom in limitation (§56). The first section has two subsections, the others have three.

Addressing the theme of ethics in relation to creation, Barth first looks at special ethics. He forges a link with the ethical chapter at the end of I,2 by pointing out that dogmatics as investigation of the true God and his action involves ethics as investigation of true man and his action. Theological ethics views God's Word as God's command. It does this as general ethics (cf. II,2) in which the command is seen as God's claim, decision, and judgment. It also does it as special ethics in which the command comes to man in his concrete situation, this time as creature of God (3–5).

Special ethics must not be confused with casuistry. This, too, deals with specific cases, but in the form of expounding and applying a biblical text, natural law, or ecclesiastical ruling. The Penitentiaries (Aquinas, Wollebius) and the works of Perkins and Ames on conscience ought to be noted here (6–8). Casuistry has the qualities of concreteness and communal concern, but it errs by making man the judge, freezing God's commands as rules, and eliminating both God's total claim and man's free self-giving (8–15).

What alternative is there? We obviously do not have an endless series of revealed commands and individual decisions. Vertical commands are given but in a horizontal context in which God's command and man's act have continuity and constancy. The context must be sought from God in his Word. Brunner, Bonhoeffer, and Soe fall short here, although their concepts of orders, mandates, and universal problems show awareness both of the problem and of the lines of its solution (16–23).

Barth's own solution rests on knowledge of the partners in the ethical event. The God who commands, as known from the Word, is Creator, Reconciler, and Redeemer. All his commands will be commands of this God. The man who acts, as also known from the Word, is the creature of God reconciled and redeemed by him. All his actions will be those of this man (23–26). The constant in all ethical events is the history between these two in which we have an articulate and differentiated action of God and response by man. Definite spheres may be seen in which God commands and man obeys or disobeys. By considering these spheres, special ethics establishes approximations and directives of command and conduct (27–31).

Taking up creation in the second subsection, Barth looks at the command as that of God the Creator, the relationship of Creator and creature being the first sphere in the history of the commanding God and acting man (32). As Creator, God is also Reconciler and Redeemer but by appropriation the Creator is the Father. Similarly the command is the one whole command of God and yet it has here the special form of the command of the Creator (35f.).

Three presuppositions, the first a principal and the others subordinate, underlie all that is to be said in this sphere. First, the God who meets man as Creator is he who is gracious to him in Jesus Christ. Second, the one command of God is also that of the Creator. Third, the command is already the sanctification of what man does or does not do (35f.).

How do we know this? Brunner's appeal to an undefined "reality" will not do, since it abstracts from the Word, introduces the unhelpful concept of order, and ventures into a supposed area of truth accessible apart from revelation and faith (36–38). The right answer is easy to find. The subordinate presuppositions flow from the first. God's grace in Jesus Christ includes creation and its command both noetically and ontically. The one command is also that of the Creator in the comprehensive reality of God's grace (40f.). This command already sanctifies the creature because it is for man who in Jesus Christ—true man—knows the one who is elected by God, in encounter with others, subject of a material organism, and set in temporal limitation (41–44). Thus the ethics of creation investigates God's command and man's sanctification in the four relations to God, fellowman, self, and time.

2. Freedom before God (§53)

Taking up the four relations, Barth begins with the relation to God under the heading of "Freedom before God." He has here three subsections on the holy day, confession, and prayer. In each his aim is to deal with the specific within the general. Thus every act is one of freedom and responsibility before God but there are also specific acts of this freedom and responsibility (47f.). Brunner and Ritschl are criticized here, for they do not allow for duties to God apart from those to neighbor (48f.).

What Barth had in view may be seen at once in relation to the holy day. All time belongs to God and yet God has chosen the special time of the Lord's Day (49f.). This day tells us that man's work is best understood in light of rest from work, that is, of readiness for the gospel (50f.). The holy day serves as a covenant sign at the beginning of our own work, pointing to the salvation history embedded in world history (52ff.). It serves also as an eschatological sign at the end of all man's work, pointing to the ultimate consummation of covenant and salvation history (56ff.). Trust in work is totally excluded, and renunciation and committal are enjoined (57f.). Our mortification and renewal are thus commanded (58f.).

Two benefits derive from this. Both may be described as freedom, for the command of the holy day brings liberation, not bondage. Negatively this freedom is freedom from the care of work, positively it is freedom for God's work and service (60). Nevertheless, these benefits are not the reason for the command. One might plead for freedom from the care of work on humanitarian grounds and all it might mean would be boring inactivity. One might plead for it on religious grounds and churchgoing might become a human work (60ff.). The benefits are not ends in themselves. They serve the true end of faith that trusts in God and renounces self (63f.). This is why it is important that the holy day be an interruption, a not doing of what is done on other days, a doing of what is not done on other days, reflecting the great interruption of the everyday of world history by Easter Day (65).

Rules cannot be given, for God speaks his command directly to each individual. Nevertheless, a disposition, an attitude, and the corresponding action are undoubtedly enjoined (66f.). Hence criteria may be advanced for the fashioning and correcting of the activity of the holy day. (1) The day is God's, not man's (67f.). (2) It is a festal day, a day of celebration, not of imposed religious duties. (3) It is a day of fellowship, not of isolation nor merely of family gatherings, but of assembly with God's people (68–71). (4) It should verify itself in the week that follows, giving meaning and joy to all other days. If, says Barth, the human service of these other days is found wanting, there is good reason "to take the divine service of Sunday far more seriously" (71f.).

Confession occupies Barth next. He accepts the truth that all Christian life should be confession of God. Yet express confession should also be made in the witness of praise (73–75). Barth again suggests criteria by which to measure the authenticity of specific confession. (1) It will have no ulterior motive but take place simply to God's honor (77f.). (2) It will have the form of a positive protestation of faith in face of questioning or attack (78–82). (3) It will be a public confession of the biblical and christological faith of the community, not just an individual confession of personal beliefs or experiences (82–84). (4) It will be a free activity, not governed by set acts or words, nor dominated by anxiety or fear. In the act of confession the believer "steps into the freedom of God in which he, too, may be free" (85f.).

In the last subsection Barth returns to the topic of prayer. All life should be prayer, but in this orientation to God and on the basis of the knowledge and summons of God specific prayer is enjoined (87f.). Like confession this will take the form, not of mood only, but of definite speech, outward as well as inward (89f.). This time Barth suggests five criteria. (1) Prayer, even as asking, will be grounded, not on need, but on the divine permission which is the divine command (91–97). (2) Prayer will be decisively petition which embraces thanksgiving, penitence, and praise (97–100). (3) Prayer is the asking, not of the isolated I, but of the We, the community, taking up God's cause (the first three petitions of the Lord's Prayer), and asking him to take up ours (the last three petitions) (101–106). (4) Prayer has the assurance of being heard on the basis of union with Christ and in his name, so that the miserable anthropomorphism of an immovable God is dispelled (106–110). (5) Prayer stands under the order of obedience and discipline, so that (in divine service at least) it will be vocal (112) and preferably short (112), it will be regular (including grace at meals) (113), it will be formed, yet it will also be free and spontaneous, since the obedience required is not to a rule but to God (113f.). Barth closes with a brief discussion of free and liturgical forms in congregational prayer, his tendency being to prefer the carefully prepared prayer of the minister which enables him to lead the congregation afresh each Sunday in the one agelong prayer (114f.).

3. Freedom in Fellowship (§54)

From the relation to God Barth moves on to the relation to others—perhaps the largest sphere of the command of God the Creator. He still has freedom in mind and discusses it in three forms of the relation: man and woman, parents and children, near and distant neighbors. He gives the most space (116–140) to the first of these forms in a particularly painstaking and stimulating discussion.

Building on what he said about man and woman in §41 (III,1) and §45 (III,2), Barth begins this first subsection with a reminder that the male-female relation rests on a structural distinction in unity (116–118). It is this relation that the command of God rules, relativizes, and directs to freedom (120f.). The threefold action of the command excludes certain views of the relation, particularly in marriage. Barth considers these views in detail: the concept of Romantic love in Schleiermacher (121f.), the sacramental concept of the Roman and Eastern Orthodox churches (122–125), the fusion of religion and eroticism in Schubart (125–127), the understanding of marriage as "primary experience" in Bovet (127f.), and its divinization in Leenhardt (128f.).

Since God's command claims the whole man, Barth warns against overemphasis on the man-woman relation and especially on sex within the relation. Thus sexuality in the narrow sense must be put in the context of sexuality in the broader sense, that is, man's humanity as male and female (130–134). As Barth succinctly states, "coitus without co-existence is demonic" (133). In an appendix Barth considers the significance of Genesis 2:24 in the light of 1 Corinthians 6:16 and Ephesians 5:31 and then in relation to the thinking of Schwarz, Bovet, van de Velde, and Strasser (134–139).

If the male-female relation covers more than sex, it also covers more than marriage. Marriage may be its telos, but the unmarried do not stand outside the relation. In defiance of a good deal of evangelical sentiment, Barth points out that celibacy has to be regarded as a valid option, as Paul makes so clear, both on negative and also on positive grounds, in 1 Corinthians 7 (140–148).

What, then, does God's command require? It requires that man be fully male and female in the differentiated relation and therefore in true encounter. This does not mean following a human phenomenology or typology such as one finds in Bovet (149f.) or Brunner (152f.). On the other hand it rules out exchange of roles, sexlessness, or abstract humanity. In relation to the exchange of roles Barth asks some difficult questions of women's liberation movements and endorses Paul's stand for the true dignity of women in 1 Corinthians 11 (156). Regarding sexlessness he takes issue with Berdyaev and Beauvoir (159–162).

Requiring faithfulness to sex, the divine command rules out a self-contained male or female life. The differentiation lies within the relation even though the relation be ordered differently on the two sides. Both man and woman are directed to freedom in fellowship. Attempts at segregation are disobedience and are associated with feelings symptomatic of homosexuality, which is at root a denial of humanity, avenging itself in an attempted substitute for it (163–166).

What is the mutual orientation of the sexes? In a general way Barth describes it as a considering, listening, and answering that leads to action in responsibility (167f.). A specific order of preceding and following controls the relation. This does not mean inequality nor alter the mutual bond and obligation. Neither exploitation nor revolt should disrupt the order. Each needs the other and each should help the other to true dignity and fulfilment in the order (168–172). Barth supports this from the New Testament, particularly Ephesians 5 and 1 Corinthians 11 (172–176). Order should not be allowed to degenerate into hierarchy with tyranny on the one side and mere compliance on the other. It carries with it the responsibility of mutual service (176–181).

Barth now looks at marriage as a specific form of the general relation (181ff.) and concludes:

(1) Marriage should not be seen as a self-evident state but as a distinctive calling and direction to a special fellowship that is wholly subject to the divine command. This foundation sets its seriousness in focus, as in Matthew 19 (183–187).

(2) Marriage cannot be regarded as just a matter of sex and family. It involves a task of life-fellowship which, even though it includes many other things, constitutes an end in itself and takes precedence of every individual component (187–189).

(3) This life-fellowship is full, total, and all-embracing. If it does not amount to an equation of partners, it certainly means "mutual

totality" in which each partner is together with the other in tested and demonstrated freedom (Ephesians 5) (189–195). Schleiermacher and Bovet need correction here, but Barth finds encouraging signs in Roman Catholic thought.

(4) Marriage as thus understood will be exclusive, not on a social basis, but on the basis of the element of choice in love and of the nature of marriage as a life-fellowship. This twofold basis could not sustain monogamy if it did not rest on the command of the God who freely elects in his grace. Marriage stands under the imperative that it be monogamous when it is set in the light of the covenant (195–199). In an appendix Barth discusses polygamy in the Old Testament (199f.), evaluates the teaching of Brunner and others (200–202), and judiciously considers polygamous societies and the command of monogamy in missionary situations (203).

(5) Resting on God's gracious covenant, marriage will be permanent. "To enter on marriage is to renounce the possibility of leaving it." Were this not so, there could be neither true love nor true marriage. The phrase "what God has joined . . ." expresses this. Does it mean that every marriage is indissoluble? Barth thinks not, for God may not always have joined those who enter into marriage. Thus a possibility of divorce arises. For Christians this will be an absolutely last resort, an "extreme case which is possible though not very probable," undertaken only after very serious questioning. Nevertheless, one cannot discount the possibility of dissolution so long as it takes place in the freedom of faith (203–213).

(6) Marriage requires mutual love as its basis, as one learns from the covenant, from Genesis 2:18ff., and from the Song of Songs. This love, which comprises understanding, self-giving, and desire, may correctly be called eros (Barth has no absolute antithesis of eros and agape). It goes beyond affection and rules out trifling and flirtation. Involving mutual agreement, it rests on agape, and if it is to be true love requires both faith and unity in faith (213–224).

(7) Marriage has a public or institutional aspect in relation to both act and status. If a wedding does not make marriage, marriage should still be publicly declared and recognized. This has a family side, for the family is broadened by it. It has a legal side, for the state has a valid responsibility in this area. Finally, it has an ecclesiastical side, for responsibility before the community arises with responsibility before God. Barth does not agree that omission in these areas ethically nullifies marriage but such omission will increase the inner obligation and will remove or decrease the responsibility to society (224–229).

Barth ends by considering what true observance of the command entails in this whole sphere. He makes three points: (1) It means acknowledging the validity of the command (231f.). (2) It then means recognizing one's failure in relation to it (232–236). (3) It means allowing oneself to be raised up and directed to a willing and doing of what is commanded. Thus the final word can be one of confidence. He who commands not only judges but also forgives, heals, and helps, so that "even where man does not keep the command, the command keeps man" (236–240).

In Barth's presentation the relation of parents and children forms the second area of freedom in fellowship. Parents stand in a special relation to children and children to parents. The relation broadens out, of course, to include grandparents and other relatives, but Barth thinks it best to stay with the primary form. He does not care to employ the word "family" in this connection and he objects to the reformers' use of the fifth commandment both to establish parental authority as a right and also to validate human authority in general (240–243).

Since all people are children, but not all parents, Barth looks first at the relation of children to parents. Children should be subordinate to parents in the sense of receiving direction from those who, having responsibility for them, serve as their guides and teachers. At this level parents are the primary and natural representatives of God to their children, and in this responsibility lies the basis of the respect owed them (243–245).

Parents can be no more than God's representatives—and this is the solid ground of their authority—because God is the only true Father (245f.), because the past they transmit is finally their beginning in God (246), and because the decision for which they are responsible is primarily and properly God's action (247). This entails on the one side a limitation of parental authority (cf. Luke 2:41–51) (247–250), and yet its firm establishment on the other (cf. Mark 7:6–13) (250f.).

The command requires obedience to parents. This will be free—though not capricious—and differentiated according to the childhood, adolescence, or adulthood of the children (251–255). It will not depend on the worth of the parents or their success or failure in the parental office (255–258). The child's obedience has been perfectly fulfilled only in Jesus Christ, but in him for us and in such a way that we must honor parents in obedience to him as the Lord and Master to whom we must answer (258–261). In an excursus Barth discusses the biblical situation in which obedience to Jesus Christ demands, not opposition to or disregard for the parent-child relation, but independence of it (261–264). He adds that those called to this independence should seriously test their call and never seek it (265).

What about the relation of parents to children? Barth points out first that parenthood is not indispensable in life or even in marriage.

He cannot agree with Brunner that the childless marriage is incomplete (266f.). An element of free responsibility arises in respect of parenthood. If one cannot choose to be a parent, one can choose not to be. Birth control and its options are discussed here. Three criteria are suggested: (1) the decision for birth control must be taken in faith; (2) it must be by mutual agreement; (3) the husband should not leave the bulk of the burden to his wife (268–276).

When husband and wife become parents, the relation to their children implies both honor and obligation. As God's representatives they live for their children, not in the sense of shielding them or finding fulfilment in them, but in that of witnessing to them that their lives are in God's hands (275ff.). They also exercise authority over their children, disciplining them and leading them to the point where they become disciples of God (277–281). What discipline means forms the topic of an excursus in which Barth focuses on Hebrews 12, Colossians 3:21, and Ephesians 6:4 (281–283).

In conclusion Barth reminds us that parental witness lies under a fourfold limitation. Limitation by time needs little discussion. Limitation by other influences should not be forgotten. Limitation of scope— of what one can do—calls for notice too. Finally limitation by the claim and kingdom of Jesus Christ must be looked at from this angle as well. Good parents will be ready for this fourth limitation, recognizing that God's will, not the relationship, is the basis of their responsibility on which alone it can be accepted as a good work (283–285).

Widening his horizon in the third subsection, Barth examines freedom in fellowship in the sphere of near and distant neighbors. In particular he has in mind the relation to one's own people and to others. What should be the form and content of these relations from the standpoint of the divine command (285f.)? Two factors govern the discussion: first, the indisputable existence of this context of near and distant neighbors, and second, the application of God's summoning and sanctifying command to this context, since here too God as Creator and Lord is also Judge and Deliverer, claiming us for his service (287f.).

As the command does not come in a vacuum but in the relation of man and woman or parent and child, so it comes in the relation to near and distant neighbors. These are distinguished by language (289–291), geography (291–294), and history (294–298). Barth has some sage observations on each of these distinctions and also on the endorsing but relativizing of the distinctive determinations by the divine command.

Before proceeding Barth raises a couple of questions. Do we have in near and distant neighbors only one sphere, or two independent spheres? Only one, he thinks (298f.). But do we really have here a special form of fellow-humanity and an independent form of the divine command? No, he suggests, for unlike that of man and woman or parent and child this relation is reversible (299), fluid (300f.), and transitory (301f.), so that one cannot describe it as either original or final (302f.). Thus there can be no specific command or obedience in this sphere, nor should a substitute be found in a supposed order of nationality (303–305). Barth closes the subsection with a long excursus in which he first analyzes and opposes the theological nationalism of National Socialism (305–309) and then studies the role of the nations in scripture in the light of the scattering of the peoples at Babel, the subsequent orientation to Israel as the covenant people, and the reversal of Babel at Pentecost (309–323).

3. Freedom for Life (§55)

The third area in which the command of God the Creator comes to us is that of the relation to self. Adding to his first two freedoms, Barth speaks of this in terms of freedom for life. His three subsections deal with respect for life, the protection of life, and the active life.

In the relation to self, God's command comes very simply as the command, and therefore the freedom, to be or to live. This form of the command must not be isolated from the first two forms, as in utilitarianism and naturalism. Nevertheless, it has its own validity (324–326).

What is this life which is to be lived? Too easily we think we know life, but secure knowledge, Barth thinks, rests on seven necessary premises. (1) In addressing us, God acknowledges our life (327f.). (2) He acknowledges it in its unity, distinction, and order (328). (3) He acknowledges it as this specific life (328f.). (4) He acknowledges it as a constant if mutable life in which we are always ourselves as subjects (329). (5) He acknowledges it in its independence and spontaneity (329f.). (6) He acknowledges it in its determination for freedom before himself (330f.). (7) He acknowledges it in its determination for freedom in fellowship (331f.). In a short excursus Barth considers an eighth premise: God acknowledges it in its unity with the rest of creation, but Barth rejects this as inadequately grounded and speculative (332f.).

Is not the command to live implied in the first two commands? Barth sees merit in the question but makes three points in reply. (1) Living has its own independence and therefore the command has also an independent form as the command to live. (2) Living, and with it the command to live, has its own content. (3) The command to live cannot be unconditional, since the Lord who commands is the Lord of death as well as life (333–335).

Very generally Barth defines the freedom to live as the freedom to treat life as a loan, both the life of others with ours and also that of ours with others. He has six things to say about this general definition: (1) It involves command and obedience. (2) It covers co-existence with others. (3) It implies a divine decree. (4) It denotes a divine benefit. (5) It points to an unmerited gift. (6) It involves the right treatment of the blessing (335f.).

When life is handled as a loan from God, the command requires that it be treated with respect, not because life as such demands this, but because God has given life a particular distinction, as seen in the incarnation (338ff.). Respect implies three things: (1) distance (340f.); (2) affirmation (341); (3) awareness of creaturely and eschatological limitation (342). The relativization implied in limitation offers no release from the respect commanded (343f.).

Positively, respect for life means living it to the full as human life. Exploring the ramifications of this, Barth suggests that a proper place must be found for impulses, but in a human way which avoids either excess or asceticism (344–348). A responsible attitude to plants and animals is required in this regard, for, although we cannot build here on an all-embracing concept of life, we still have to remember that the earth is the Lord's and not ours. Plants may be used for food and animals domesticated. On the other hand the irresponsible slaughter of animals is wrong in view of the eschatological hope of Romans 8:18f., although some killing for legitimate purposes may be allowed if it is not done as a right but on the basis of the divine authorization (348–356).

The will to live includes the will to be healthy. Many problems arise here: valid and invalid concern for health, health in sickness, psychosomatic health and sickness, hygiene, the medical profession, imaginary sickness, the reality of sickness as the precursor of death, the conquest of sickness, the struggle with it in Christ's name (Blumhardt), and the finitude of life as a divine blessing to be embraced with joy (356–374).

Mention of joy leads Barth to another aspect of the will to live which respect for life enjoins. This is the will for joy, delight, happiness, and exultation. Joy is here defined as a subjective arrest of the movement of striving and desire. One should always be ready for it and yet it cannot be contrived, for example, by arranging festive occasions. It is a social matter; we have it only as we give it. It is sovereign, not tied to specific modes, coming as material or aesthetic joy, as joy in nature or fellowship, in rest or even in everyday activity. It does not cut us loose from other responsibilities; one cannot be joyful at the expense of health, work, conscience, or other people. It is supremely joy in God, who gives it at the very point of suffering and judgment, so that its present fulfilment can be no more than a provisional anticipation of the eternal joy that is its goal (374–385).

Since joy means orientation to God, the will to live as the will to be oneself entails the surrender of the I and its regaining in the Thou. Self-affirmation as affirmation of the Thou-I is thus obedience and not claim, responsibility and not rebellion. Fulfilled in this way it fashions and confirms personal character (385f.). Character is God's work on man. It is the molding and disciplining of man's nature from the center of the Thou addressed by God. It is always open, since the divine address which is its source is a living event. It does not constitute an end in itself but "can only be the character of a particular service" (387–390).

Barth finds the final form of the will to live in the will for power, not as unqualified power, but as determination to use one's capacities. Four criteria distinguish authentic from inauthentic power: (1) Authentic power is given by God with the loan of life. (2) It is individual power known and decided by God. (3) It is necessary power as distinct from much of the power made available by technology. (4) It lies always under the decision of God, who with the power of achievement may give the power of apparent impotence, as in the power of Jesus Christ—the power of the Lamb as well as the Lion, of the cross as well as the resurrection. "The commanded will for power can always be the confident will for the kind of power which is now assigned to us" (390–397).

In the second subsection Barth deals with the protection of life. His primary thesis is that, since life is a loan from God, it must be protected from willful and wanton destruction. The protection cannot be absolute, for life is not absolute. Nevertheless, the command enjoins protection and only where the command permits it, as in exceptional cases, may life be terminated (397–400, with both Old and New Testament references).

Does this leave room for suicide? It does not rule out exposure to risk, although one has to consider whether the cause is worth the cost. Suicide in the strict sense has nothing to commend it. If it is not the unforgivable sin, it is a usurped decision, an act of unbelief, a failure to see life as grace. The biblical examples make this plain. A possible exception is the case of Samson (cf. St. Pelagia in the early church). One must remember, however, that the possibility of the exception is God's, not ours (401–413).

What about homicide? By created nature we know that this is

wrong, by corrupted nature we are capable of committing it. Because of our corruption we need to take God's command against homicide with the utmost seriousness even if obedience to the command may sometimes demand it. Various issues receive separate discussion in this connection.

(1) *Abortion* Barth insists that this is real killing. The fetus is no mere thing, nor a part of the mother, but in its own way a real human being. Its extinction, then, is extinction of life. Abortion is sin, murder, transgression. It is forgivable in view of God's saving work, but for this very reason all the more seriously under God's inexorable opposition. Only in the exceptional case, as when a choice must be made between the life of the fetus and that of the mother, may it be commanded. The criteria of legitimate abortion are life for life, scrupulous calculation in responsibility before God, and action in faith (415–423).

(2) *Euthanasia* Against the background of National Socialism Barth unhesitatingly denounces this as murder. Even on humanitarian grounds neither patient, relative, nor doctor can take responsibility for shortening human life without a clear-cut divine command. A possible exception arises with the artificial prolongation of life when medical duty becomes fanaticism, reason becomes folly, and the required assisting of human life a forbidden torturing of it (423–427).

(3) *Self-Defence* Initially, killing in self-defence seems to lie within the command. But one has to ask what emergency justifies this extreme measure. Except on the outermost margin this killing, too, is murder, as the New Testament makes plain. In Barth's view, the command allows killing in defence, not when one's own life or property is in danger, but when an assailant must be killed to protect a neighbor or to preserve law and order (427–437).

(4) *Capital Punishment* Barth defines capital punishment as self-defence delegated to society, although ultimately it is an individual who must convict and execute. Does the delegation absolve the individual? Does it automatically eliminate the command? He thinks not. Theories of punishment such as prevention, retribution, and correction provide no basis for evasion of the command. Only the command itself, aiming at the protection of life, can justify the death sentence. Extreme cases when this might be so are when a traitor or a tyrant brings the state and society under mortal threat. If it seems that the last hour is striking for the social order, perhaps "certain men must kill according to the command of God and in the service of the whole" (437–450), that is, either by public execution or by assassination.

(5) *War* War poses the most serious question regarding killing. Although the modern age has protested against war, it has raged more violently than ever before during this period. Barth begins with three

delimitations. War can no longer be regarded as just for soldiers. It can no longer be presented as a matter of ideals and moral values. One can no longer pretend that the goal of neutralizing the enemy does not involve large-scale killing. What all this means is that war is plainly against the command, that it is not a normal state, and that the church should always be working for a just peace in preservation of peace. As a last resort Barth can allow the possibility of a just war when the survival of one's country, or of an allied country, is threatened by brutal aggression—he himself did military service in Switzerland during the Hitler crisis—but even here he champions the right of serious conscientious objection and demands that the church do its duty by those who take this course (450–470).

The active life forms the theme of the third subsection of §55. Barth begins by assuming that human life in freedom will be an active one in the obedient fulfilment of a divinely given task with its own goals, directions, and achievements (470f.). The active life includes work, although in antithesis to the work ethic of the west Barth points out that in scripture work is not restricted to everyday labor (472f.). The heart of activity is that it correspond to God's saving and sanctifying activity and that it be an activity of service (476f.).

Service rests on God's call. The God who calls to service himself serves as active man in Jesus Christ. His call is a call to be active in his own service. This activity means true exaltation for man yet also a resultant subordination to God's will and work (477–483). As one may see from Jesus and the disciples, service is rendered in the community (483–488). This rests on four assumptions about the church, namely, that it is a particular, living, commissioned, and united people (488–490).

What does all this amount to in practice? Barth sums it up under three heads, anticipating much of what he will develop more fully in Volume IV. (1) The activity of the church means its constant and expanding presence (490–493). (2) It means its inner upbuilding with particular concern for unity, life, the word that sustains it, and the love that binds it (493–502). (3) It means outreach to the world, being for the world, calling people out of it, preaching the gospel to it, and exercising a prophetic ministry toward it (502ff.).

What about work? As the church's activity corresponds to God's saving action, work corresponds to his providential rule. The point of required work is that man should exist as man in order to be a Christian. Hence work is not done for its own sake. It is a *parergon* of the true *ergon,* its aim being to preserve human life for the *ergon* (516ff.). If this imposes a restriction, it also confers authentic dignity. This dignity necessarily distinguishes good work from that which is rapacious, harmful, or superfluous (525–527). Barth suggests five criteria by which serious and beneficial work may be known.

(1) True work involves the setting of goals and strenuous efforts to attain them (527ff.). (2) It promotes the needed universal and individual conditions of human existence. In this regard mere classification of occupations is not enough, for what is done within the classification also counts (529–534). (3) Motivation plays a part too. Here Barth pleads strongly for humanity in work, that it not be done in isolation or abstraction, that it not be competitive or exploitative, that it not entail a thoughtless disregard for others, that against every pressure an effort be made to maintain the element of brotherliness (534–545). (4) In true work there should be reflection. Barth does not see why in even purely mechanical labor there has to be inward vegetating, nor does he see why inner activity must always have an external form (545–550). (5) True work has freedom as its goal and falls therefore under the limitation of divinely commanded relaxation. The frantic pace of modern life—Barth cites diplomacy and church work as two examples!—leads only too often to "industrious irrationality." Since God has commanded rest, this is perhaps the most important criterion of all. Christians should join the struggle for free Sundays and proper holidays and they should also set an example by resting from daily work. Rest in this sense means self-contemplation which as an attitude of rest forms a transition to the hearing of God's Word and therefore to the finding of true rest in God, not as himself an object of contemplation, but as the gracious and active Subject of eternal rest (550–564).

5. Freedom in Limitation (§56)

Barth ends his ethics of creation with a section (§56) on freedom in limitation, the application of the command of God to men for whom a term is set. The theme of the first subsection, that of the unique opportunity, arises naturally out of the temporal relation. God himself sets the limits of birth and death. Between these the one opportunity of life in the freedom of obedience is given (565–570).

Can one speak of true freedom in limitation? Barth believes so for four reasons. (1) God gives to uniqueness the stamp of particularity. (2) He himself accepted a unique life in Jesus Christ. (3) He treats this unique span as meaningful. (4) He thus endows it with his own richness (571f.). In his limited span man is in the cosmos which is oriented to the covenant and of which Jesus Christ is the ultimate center and meaning (572–577). The command, then, is that we take our place and grasp our chance, knowing that God is our frontier. As the New Testament reminds us, our time is ruled and limited by him. It is also short. Yet it is of unknown duration. Thus the command comes with urgency. We must take ourselves seriously in our limitation. We are to become free and to be free in the one opportunity that is given (579–584).

Barth closes the subsection with three criteria of obedience to God's command from this angle. (1) We are to accept our place as right (585f.). (2) We are to claim and occupy it in work and service (586–588). (3) We are to recognize death but not to fear it, for God is our hope and fear is defeated in this hope (589–594).

Since the unique opportunity involves a special place, the command embraces both God's calling to this place and also man's response to this calling in his own decision and act. Introducing the concept of calling in the second subsection, Barth does not have in view the call to be a Christian. He will deal with this later under "Vocation" in IV,3. In the context of creation he has in mind what is often described as the choice of vocation or career, except that the choice will have reference to the knowing and doing of God's special will (595–598). Barth includes here—in anticipation of IV,3—a valuable excursus on the use of calling in the New Testament, the sense it acquired in the Middle Ages, the problems inherent in the reformation reinterpretation, the proper understanding of the Pauline exhortation to remain in one's calling, the role of God in calling, and the significance of his calling us to freedom (600–607).

In his customary fashion Barth proceeds by advancing criteria of true obedience to God's command in vocation or calling. (1) It should relate to the stage we have reached in life's journey (607–609). Specific suggestions are made in respect of youth, maturity, and old age (608ff.). (2) It should relate to our particular historical situation, not as an iron determination, but as an allotted place to be occupied both positively and critically (618–623). (3) It should relate to personal aptitudes as an obedience with all our known (and unknown) abilities (623–630). (4) It should relate to the everyday activity which, within limits and under God's providence, we have chosen and are pursuing in responsible answer to three crucial questions: Is this the right choice in view of our outer need and inner ability? Are we obedient in this sphere, both faithful and also open to God's renewing? Do we accept the possibility of receiving and obeying a divine command to transfer to another sphere when it unmistakably comes to us as God's command and does not arise in our own imagination through caprice or cupidity (630–647)?

Barth concludes the section and the chapter with a short subsection on honor. What he has in mind is that even in limitation freedom is a conferred honor reflecting God's honor. The God who commands is the God of grace. Hence his command is not law but gospel. It does not enslave but frees. It brings exaltation and not abasement (647–649). Sinners may reject and obscure the honor but since they cannot cease to be human, they cannot lose this honor which is God's and which reflects God's. Man can be "godless" but God is never "manless." Calling man to his service, he restores the honor with which he endowed him at creation (650–654).

What does honor mean? In a couple of paragraphs Barth describes it as distinction, distinction as derived from uniqueness and particularity. It implies value in one's own eyes and in those of others. Honor must not be construed as intrinsic quality or worth. It is ours as we are creatures from God and before God (655f.).

How does honor work out in life? Barth suggests four criteria of honorable action. (1) It will be action in service at the appointed place as the place of honor (656–662). (2) It will be action performed with modesty, which, as Barth sees it, includes gratitude, humility, and humor (662–668). (3) It will be action done with joy in God, whether or not human honor is given (cf. Joseph and Daniel), and even if human dishonor might result (cf. Jeremiah and Jesus) (668–675). It will be action in defence of honor so long as this is not a personal concern but deals with the cause, involves service, finds demonstration in action, and entails recognition of the honor of others (678–685).

Bringing the discussion into final focus, Barth points out that honor is from God, without whose honor there can be no human honor. Our true honor is to have Jesus Christ—the honor of God—as our brother. It is the honor of being the brothers and sisters of Jesus Christ and as such the reconciled children of God (685).

The
Doctrine
of Reconciliation

CHAPTER XIII

The Problems of the Doctrine of Reconciliation

1. The Work of God the Reconciler (§57)

MOST theologians and theological confessions put the doctrine of the fall and sin of man between the doctrine of creation and the doctrine of reconciliation. Barth follows a different course, moving directly from God the Creator to God the Reconciler. He has reasons for this. (1) Theology deals primarily with God and obviously one cannot describe the fall as God's work. (2) He has laid the groundwork for the fall in II,2 on election, particularly in the section on nothingness in III,3. (3) He believes that the fall can be properly understood and presented only in the light of the divine work of reconciliation. Hence he has no separate volume on the fall, sin, and plight of man.

In his approach to reconciliation Barth has an introductory chapter on the theme and problems of the doctrine. In it he offers a general characterization of God's reconciling work and then surveys the three aspects or forms which he will develop in the three succeeding chapters. He opens, then, with a section "The Work of God the Reconciler (§57) and divides this into subsections on "God with Us," "The Covenant as the Presupposition of Reconciliation," and "The Fulfilment of the Broken Covenant."

Barth explains in the preface to this volume that he is quietly contesting and correcting the existentialist subjectivism of Bultmann. He thus points out at the outset that the atonement, as God's work, is central to the Christian life (IV,1, 3f.). Reduced to its simplest form, reconciliation means Emmanuel, God with us. This is primarily a statement about God, then about believers and those to whom they are commissioned to carry the message (4f.). A brief discussion of the name Emmanuel in Isaiah 7–8 and Matthew 1 backs up the preliminary thesis (5f.).

What does "God with us" mean? Barth lists seven successive implications which provide critical clues to the understanding of reconciliation. (1) It means God's being in his act on which our being reposes (6f.). (2) It means God's act aimed at a specific and central goal (7f.). (3) It means an act dealing with man's salvation (8f.). (4) It means an act grounded in God's eternal purpose and taking precedence even to the work of creation (9f.). (5) It means an act on behalf of those who have forfeited their creaturely existence and have no claim to salvation, that is, of undeserving sinners (10–12). (6) It means God's personal identification with us and therefore not just a restoration but rather the very coming of salvation (12–14). (7) It means our being with God ("we with God") as we are lifted up, given a place, awakened to our true being, and made free for God in virtue of his being with us (14–16). Nor is all this a mere idea. It is a history that finds its fulfilment in the name of Jesus Christ, not as a sign or symbol, but as an authentic reality.

In the next subsection Barth strengthens the link between creation and reconciliation by pointing out that the covenanted fellowship between God and man, which was the inner basis of creation, forms the presupposition of the atonement (22). In a lengthy biblical excursus on the covenant (22–34) he makes the following general points: (1) It is a gracious covenant. (2) It is an event and thus takes the form of covenants. (3) It is sovereign. He then makes three more specific points: (1) It is with the whole race. (2) It involves the mission of Israel. (3) It undergoes a change of form into the new covenant. Barth sees in Jesus Christ the execution of the covenant as God's work and Word overcoming the contradiction of man (35–37). In Jesus Christ we realize that God is not initially neutral. He has pledged himself from the very beginning to be our God. This is the presupposition of reconciliation (37f.). It implies the pardon and beneficence of God and our own engagement to gratitude as the proper response to grace (39–43).

Barth stresses that none of this can be known by natural theology. It is revealed only in Jesus Christ and his saving work (43–46). In him, and in what he has done, we see God's reply to the episode of human sin (46), the fulfilment of God's original purpose (47), the divine necessity of reconciliation (48), its nature as an actualization of God's will and not an evolutionary achievement (49), its fulfilling of God's Word and not of an immanent cosmic telos (50f.). The Jesus Christ in whom atonement is made is, of course, the incarnate Word, not an abstract extracarnate Word (52). Nevertheless, he is the first and eternal Word who is with God and is God from all eternity. For this reason reconciliation precedes creation. Jesus Christ is "the content of the eternal will of God, the eternal covenant between God and man" (54), the primal and primary basis of atonement which distinguishes it from all of God's other acts.

Barth rounds off the subsection with a valuable historical survey of covenant theology (54–66). He first discusses the significance and problem of this theology. He then briefly notes Zwingli's contribution and the close tying of the covenant to election. He then criticizes the concept of two covenants—one of works and one of grace—as this seems to have been introduced by Ursinus, perhaps in development of the relating of the covenant to natural law by Musculus. Finally he analyzes the more detailed covenant theology of Cocceius, who posited five abrogations of the original covenant of works: sin, the compact of Father and Son, the covenant of grace, mortification, and final redemption, and who in so doing gave impetus to the influential but dangerous concept of an intratrinitarian contract. To this Barth opposes both the unity of the covenant and the unity of the Triune God, which renders unnecessary any particular pact within the Godhead.

The final subsection briefly examines the fulfilment of the broken covenant. The fulfilment of the covenant has the character of reconciliation because man broke the covenant by his sin and fall (67f.). God's faithfulness is greater than man's unfaithfulness. An even more glorious fulfilment—though this does not justify the idea of man's "happy fault"—has been freely and graciously effected by God in his reconciling work in Jesus Christ. To describe this Barth offers an interesting exposition of the two great atonement verses, John 3:16 and 2 Corinthians 5:19ff. Regarding the former, he points out that the word "loved" denotes an event, that "so" has the force of both "in such a way" and "so much," that "gave" in this context means "gave up," and that the second "that" has both final and consecutive significance, denoting both effect and purpose (70–73). Regarding the latter, he again finds the depiction of an event, sees emphasis in the fact that it is God who reconciles, discerns in reconciliation the original sense of exchange, and thinks it important that the reconciled are set in service, so that witness may be borne to reconciliation as that of the world (73–78).

2. Survey of the Doctrine (§58)

Barth planned his treatment of the doctrine of reconciliation on an ambitious scale. He thought it would be helpful, then, to clarify his thinking and approach by first offering, in a special section (§58), a survey of the material as he proposed to handle it. This time he had four subsections, three corresponding to the three basic themes, and the fourth displaying the architectonic structure of the total presentation.

The first and short subsection on God's grace in Jesus Christ opens with the insight that in fulfilling the covenant in reconciliation God acts to maintain his glory (79) but that he does so freely and not under any constraint except that of his own nature (80). In particular he does not lie under any dialectical-triadic necessity (80f.). Our thinking, then, must begin with the act itself with which God in Jesus Christ crosses the frontier to man (82), namely, the frontier of his own glory and man's sin (82). Everything hinges on God's own merciful and effective act wherein his grace is his free turning to man. Barth contrasts grace in this sense with the Roman Catholic view of grace expressed in its elaborate subdivision into increate and created grace, internal and external grace, grace of sanctification and grace of office, actual and habitual grace, medicinal and elevating, prevenient and concomitant, operating and cooperating, sufficient and efficacious, supernatural and natural grace (84–88). In grace God is everything. Yet to say "God is everything and man nothing" is "complete nonsense," for although man without God is indeed nothing—a prey to nothingness—the whole point of grace is that he may not be nothing but may be newly grounded as a subject (89). This newly grounded subject is reconciled man, God's man, the man in Christ (90–92). In this respect Barth dispels the common notion that in his theology God's utter transcendence annihilates humanity and human freedom. The truth is the very opposite. God's grace in Jesus Christ reconstitutes man in his authentic humanity and freedom.

The meaning of reconciliation for us is the theme of the second and longer subsection on man's being in Jesus Christ. The Christian is the one who both knows and exemplifies the new and true being of reconciled man. Becoming a new man in Christ occurs as three things happen. First, a verdict of God on man is executed and revealed whereby man is both rejected and accepted in the substitutionary work of Jesus Christ (93ff.), this being his justification and involving faith (96ff.). Second, a direction of God to man is also executed and revealed in which he is pointed to freedom in the house and kingdom of God (99ff.), this being his sanctification and involving love (101ff.). Third, the promise of God is executed and revealed in which man is given his destiny (108ff.), this being his vocation and involving hope, namely, hope in Jesus Christ as both the ultimate and penultimate expectation (111ff.).

In the third and very short subsection Barth looks at the one in whom this verdict, direction, and promise are given. There is at every point one who stands between the reconciling God and reconciled man, Jesus Christ the Mediator, in whom reconciliation is effected (122). In relation to Jesus Christ, Barth makes two important decisions which control his whole handling of the doctrine (123ff.). One cannot, he thinks, separate Christ's person and work. So closely are the two united that even methodologically, let alone materially, we dare not run the risk of isolating the one from the other (127ff.). Nor, he believes, should one divide the united person and work by viewing the two states of exinanition (humiliation) and exaltation chronologically. Jesus Christ is always the one subject of his work and his work is always the work of this subject. As Barth states, "It is in the particular fact and the particular way that Jesus Christ is very God, very man and very God-man that He works, and He works in the fact, and only in the fact, that He is this One and not another. His being in this One is His history, and His history is this His being" (128). Christology will thus be present from the first in reconciliation as its "necessary beginning," and "it will work itself out in the whole." One can see why Barth has reserved the full discussion of christology for this volume.

Putting the pieces together in the fourth subsection, Barth presents the three counterbalancing forms of the doctrine which will be developed in the next three chapters. Heading each chapter is the truth about Christ: he is God, Man, and God-Man. Relative to his work he acts, and is made known to us, as the Lord as servant, the servant as Lord, and the true Witness, or, to adopt the concept of the threefold office, as priest, king, and prophet. The fulfilment of the work carries with it the verdict of the Father, the direction of the Son, and the promise of the Spirit. In relation to the sinner, it exposes the threefold essence of sin as pride, sloth, and falsehood. Over against sin, however, it posits man's justification, sanctification, and vocation. Worked out by the Holy Spirit relative to the community, these take the form of its gathering, upbuilding, and sending. Worked out by the Holy Spirit relative to the individual, they mean faith, love, and hope.

Barth does not believe in systematization but here, as elsewhere in his *Church Dogmatics,* he obviously has no objection to systematizing. He makes no single doctrine the center. He focuses constantly on the trinitarian work that comes to expression in the person and work of Christ. Nevertheless, he elaborately integrates the many and varied elements in reconciliation in such a way as to see and understand it as an interrelated and comprehensive whole.

CHAPTER XIV
The Son of God

1. The Obedience of the Son of God (§59)

HAVING introduced the theme of reconciliation in chapter thirteen, Barth devotes chapter fourteen, which comprises the rest of Volume IV,1 (IV,1, 157–779), to a presentation of the first aspect of the doctrine under the title "The Lord as Servant." The sequence in this case is Very God, the Lord as servant, Jesus Christ as priest, the verdict of the Father, sin as pride, justification, the gathering of the community, and faith. Barth does not precisely arrange the material in this way, but combines the first four elements in a single section entitled "The Obedience of the Son of God" (§59). He then has a section for each of the other four (§60–§63).

The first section opens with a subsection on the downward movement of the Word in reconciliation. Barth entitles this "The Way of the Son of God into the Far Country." This title carries a plain allusion to the parable of the prodigal son. Barth finally explains the allusion in the parallel subsection in IV,2, but no great perspicacity is needed to discern a christological understanding of the parable.

The first point made in the subsection is that reconciliation is history. Noetically it is the history *about* Jesus Christ, ontically the history *of* Jesus Christ (157f.). Primarily this history is that of God's gracious condescension (158f.). Fully and authentically man, Jesus is the Lord, not by evaluation or ascription, but intrinsically and objectively (161ff.). This Lord is obedient. In his obedience he became flesh (164), Jewish flesh (166), the one true Israelite (170), in solidarity with sinful humanity, accepting its guilt and merited rejection (171ff.).

Incarnation, then, means obedience and self-humbling (177). Yet

180

it does not imply loss of deity, for it is a free divine act (179f.). Whatever *kenosis* (self-emptying) may mean, it does not mean Christ ceasing to be himself. In this regard Barth has an informative excursus on the *kenosis* debate of the seventeenth century and the later *kenosis* teaching of Thomasius and Gess in the nineteenth century (180–183). While Jesus Christ as God enters into the human contradiction, he is not God against God in absolute paradox (184ff.). He is Lord of the contradiction, for there is no paradox in God, nor is he properly defined by such abstractions as the Wholly Other—a concept which Barth trenchantly, and a little mischievously, describes as "quite untenable, and corrupt and pagan" (186).

In spite of all our ideas, God acts in the divine freedom of his love. He shows that in this freedom he can be God as man (186ff.). This is the mystery of Christ's deity (cf. Philippians 2) (188–192). In this freedom the Son of God goes into the far country. He can and does do this in obedience. This may be a mystery to us but it is no mystery to him. For obedience is not alien to the Son. Barth suggests that even in his eternal deity as the Son, Christ is obedient to the Father. Nor does this imply either subordinationism or modalism. To understand this, three presuppositions must be maintained: (1) Jesus Christ as God is the acting subject of reconciliation; (2) he is also the acting subject of reconciliation as an effective event in history; and (3) as the reconciler he is the lowly and obedient Jesus of Nazareth (197–199). In their different ways subordinationism and modalism are wrong because they attempt to evade the cross as God's own self-humiliation and are thus forced to juggle away the christological mystery. In Jesus the Reconciler we have to accept that the Triune God is not an absolute unit, nor a superior and inferior, but a first and a second in equal deity, so that his obedience as the incarnate Son points to his obedience as the eternal Son in which it has its ground (205ff.). It is precisely in his obedience that Jesus manifests himself as the Son, although without the limitation that the term "son" necessarily has for us (209f.).

What precisely did Jesus do in his solidarity with humanity as the obedient and incarnate Son? Barth takes up this central question of the atonement in the second subsection under the heading of "The Judge Judged in our Place." He first points out that the Son took his way into the far country for a purpose: the revelation of God's glory by his coming for us men and for our salvation (211–213). Salvation, of course, is grace. God is under no obligation to save. It may be known only by the fact of it, not by deduction from something else (213f.). But in what way is God "for us"? This brings us to the heart of the matter.

God is for us by making our situation his own, by meeting and overcoming our temptation (215). But why did he do this and what precisely did he accomplish? He came to save us. But to save us he came as Judge: "If He were not the Judge, He would not be the Saviour" (217). As Judge he upholds the right. He thus sentences us and, as the divine Judge, does so definitively (217–219). This sentence is inevitably one of rejection. Yet God in his freedom does not have to execute this sentence on man. He can save him even in his rejection.

God saves man in his rejection as the Judge judges by himself, being judged for man in the once-for-all event of the ministry, death, and resurrection of Jesus recorded in the gospels (222–228). Nor does the "for us" have here only the looser sense of "with" or "with reference to." In the strictest possible sense it means "in our place," as indicated by the New Testament prepositions (228–231).

In closer analysis of the event, Barth brings out four aspects of this substitution by Jesus Christ. (1) He takes our place as Judge, abasing himself and liberating us by displacing us, so that we are, as Barth puts it in the English phrase, "displaced persons" (231–235). (2) He takes our place as the judged, becoming our sin in a real exchange, making this sin known to us, answering for it, and leaving to us only the possibility of repentance (235–244). (3) He takes our place in the judgment, that is, in his passion, which is (a) active (244f.), (b) historical, an act of both God and man (245), (c) personal (246), and (d) unique (247), and which is also (a) the content of the Father's act for us (250f.), (b) our reconciliation to God (250ff.), (c) the bearing of sin's punishment (253), (d) the ending of us as sinners (253f.), and (e) an act of satisfaction in the sense of doing what is sufficient (253f.). (4) He takes our place in the establishment of the justice of God, the positive aspect which brings to light the positive nature of the whole action. The Judge, the judging, and the judgment are the justice of God, for Jesus was the just one (257), obedient in his taking of our place (258), vicariously penitent for us from his baptism in the Jordan (259ff.), maintaining his righteousness against the severest temptation in the wilderness and at the cross (260–272).

The fourfold fact of the "for us"—that Jesus took our place as Judge and judged, that he was judged and acted justly—constitutes the center not only of the theology of reconciliation but of all theology. It can be expressed in other ways, particularly in the priestly concepts of Hebrews in which Christ is depicted as the priest offering himself in a perfect offering (273–283). Nevertheless, "if the nail of this fourfold 'for us' does not hold, everything else will be left hanging in the void as an anthropological or psychological myth, and sooner or later it will break and fall to the ground." By this fact everything else "must first be demythologized," as Barth humorously states in total contradiction to Bultmann's suggested program (273).

In the last subsection on the verdict of the Father, Barth raises a question that many people ask. Assuming that Christ died for us so far away and so many years ago, how can that work of his be ours? On the face of it, he comments, we have here a problem of time and space (287). But this is not the true problem; God has already solved it. The serious problem is that of the distance between God and us, between God who is for us and us who are against God (290). This distance of nature makes God's presence something that we cannot face and from which we flee into the chronological and geographical problem. For it involves the disturbing question: Does not Christ for us mean the end of us? In bearing our judgment, has he not definitively displaced us? Has he not put a term to our alienated existence? Does not the "for us" include a terrible "against us"? Can there be anything for us beyond it (294–296)?

If so, Barth suggests, it must fulfil five conditions. (1) It must be an act of the God who judged us in Jesus Christ. (2) It must be a different act. (3) It must be a related act. (4) It must be a historical act. (5) It must be an act done in Jesus Christ (297f.). We know all this because God has performed such an act in raising Jesus from the dead. Barth devotes the rest of the subsection to a discussion of the resurrection—the Father's verdict—as an act that fulfils the following five conditions:

(1) The resurrection, like the execution of judgment, is a free and gracious act of God in which human will and action do not participate (300–304).

(2) It is a new and separate act, following the crucifixion in a definite sequence, answering it, manifesting it, acknowledging the life and death of Jesus, declaring God's verdict on it as a representative fulfilment of the divine wrath in the service of the divine grace (304f.).

(3) It is a related act, for the two acts are the one history of God with us in which he asserts his right against us and yet maintains it over us (310f.). In this new act the temporal being of Jesus becomes and is his eternal being as the Mediator who has made us friends instead of enemies (316f.). Its time as that of God's pure presence sets earthly time in its own light, and separates it from the time of the general resurrection which it anticipates (318ff.; this long passage cannot be adequately summarized and requires careful study if its detailed points are to be mastered).

(4) It is a historical act. Barth strongly affirms this in opposition to Bultmann (cf. III,2, §47,1). He admits that the resurrection itself—the actual raising again—exceeds the possibility of historical depiction

or demonstration in the sense of modern historical scholarship (334f.). The New Testament clearly portrays it as a unique occurrence. Nevertheless, we misunderstand the New Testament if for this reason we interpret the resurrection "as though it had never happened at all, or not happened in time and space . . . or finally had happened only in faith or in the form of the formation and development of faith" (336). Sound exegesis cannot regard the resurrection as timeless truth. If it did create Easter faith, it did so as the Easter event denoted by the empty tomb and the resurrection appearances. We can only affirm this event and not explain it, but we must indeed affirm it (338–342).

(5) It is an act done in Jesus Christ. For this reason the two acts of crucifixion and resurrection are ultimately one, the purpose of the former lying in the grace and mercy of the latter. The one Jesus who was crucified is also the risen Lord in indissoluble unity. Yet the sequence must not be forgotten. The cross happened once and does not happen again. It was followed by the resurrection and Jesus is forever the risen Lord. Fixation on the cross, or a one-sided theology of the cross, must be avoided. The crucifixion of Jesus has made an end for us, and his resurrection has made a new beginning with us (345).

To close the subsection Barth returns to his critical question and answers it in the light of this new act as the other side of the same act. The resurrection demonstrates to us that despite the distance God is ours and we are his (348f.). How this is so may be seen again from the five points, but now in reverse order. (1) All is done in Jesus Christ, so that as we die in him we also live in him (349–351). (2) Since the resurrection too is a historical act—"he is risen bodily, visibly, audibly, perceptibly, in the same sense in which he is dead" (352)—life in him has no less validity than death in him (351–353). (3) The church's existence in the time between that of the resurrection and the coming again attests that God still has time for us and that we are thus included in his work in Christ (353f.). (4) The distinction of the resurrection lies in its being the verdict of the Father, his acceptance of Jesus and of us in him, so that we are called to take seriously the change that has been effected (354f.). (5) As an exclusive act of the same God the resurrection enables us to look confidently at the act of judgment in Jesus Christ. In this divine Yes we can believe we are God's elect because we are. Christ's death for us does not finally put an end to us. We have a new life determined by it (355–357).

2. The Pride and Fall of Man (§60)

From his account of the first aspect of God's reconciling act in Jesus

Christ, Barth in §60 examines the sin from which this act saves us. He opens with a subsection on the sinner in the light of the Son's obedience. In this he first explains and justifies his placing of the doctrine of sin within the doctrine of atonement. To know sin properly, he argues, it is not enough to look at self, for self-knowledge is uncertain and relative. Man "is crooked even in the knowledge of his crookedness" (355–361). Nor is it enough merely to look at the law apart from Jesus Christ. This will give some real knowledge, as one may see from Luther and Calvin. But it suffers from many defects. (1) It presupposes division in God's Word (363). (2) It runs the risk of abstraction (364). (3) It moves, unconsciously at least, toward a fictional God or idolatry (365). (4) It has no adequate defence against rationalistic biblicism (366–368). (5) It departs from the proper hermeneutic that always keeps the true theme in view (368f.; examples in Piscator, Bucanus, Polanus, Wollebius, Leyden Synopsis, Burmann, and Heidegger, 369–372). (6) It tends toward the Pelagian concept of sin as just an evil proclivity (372–374; cf. Wegscheider, Hegel, Schleiermacher, Lipsius, Ritschl, and Troeltsch, 374–387). Barth concludes that man will always end up judging himself unless he learns from Jesus Christ "that man is the man of sin, and what sin is, and what it means for man" (389). The New Testament points in the right direction (cf. Luke 15 and Romans 1–3) and hints may be found in Luther and Melanchthon (391–397).

What does it mean to be brought to the knowledge of sin in Jesus Christ? Barth advances four points in reply to this question. (1) The existence of Jesus Christ is where sin meets us in pure form as deicide, fratricide, and suicide (397–399). (2) Jesus Christ as Judge discloses the sinfulness of sin (400–403). (3) The existence of Jesus Christ shows that sin is the truth of all human being and activity (403–407). (4) Knowledge of Jesus Christ is knowledge of sin's extent and gravity, for although God is superior to sin, this does not mean we can relativize or schematize it. God took it so seriously that he gave up his Son for it, he allowed the Judge to be judged, he caused the man of sin to be put to death in him (407–412).

In conclusion Barth offers the apparent paradox that only the believer can truly know himself as a sinner. The unbeliever will always entertain the illusion that he can overcome his sin. The man who is saved only in another is obviously in himself a lost man. In positive faith alone he has the negative knowledge. The mirror of the Son's obedience compels us to, or liberates us for, the self-knowledge of the man of sin (413).

In the second subsection Barth considers the form of sin that is specifically brought to light by the obedient condescension of the Son.

Very plainly it is the pride of man. Pride is the first concrete form of human unbelief and disobedience. It corresponds to, and contradicts the divine action in Jesus Christ (413–415; cf. Luther, 415) in which the Lord in his love is free to become a servant—God is great enough to be small (417). Barth looks at this contradictory correspondence from four angles.

(1) In Jesus Christ God became man, but in his sin man tries to become God. The attempt is futile but it takes place and betrays man into the threefold error of loving himself, making himself his own standard, and making the God he wants to be a self-centered God (421f.; cf. Genesis 3:5). Barth uses the story of the golden calf in Exodus 32 as an illustration (423–432).

(2) In Jesus Christ the Lord becomes a servant but man as a servant tries to play the Lord. Again the attempt is empty but it has its own reality as an event (cf. Genesis 3:1f.) and for man it entails the threefold error of making himself a self-alienated slave, bringing disorder into earthly relations, and understanding God as a harsh Lord (435f.). The story of Saul in 1 Samuel 8–31 offers a good example (437–446).

(3) In Jesus Christ the Judge was judged; but man, the judged, makes a vain but real effort to be his own judge of good and evil (cf. Genesis 3:5). This ensnares him in the threefold error of misconstruing his own role, doing the bad as though it were the good, and thinking that God needs man's help in the judgment (449–453). Illustration is found in the story of Ahab and Naboth in 1 Kings (453–458).

(4) Jesus Christ became helpless for our sake but helpless man believes that he can help himself and that in so doing he can claim God's help. The attempt to do this has no substance but is nevertheless quite authentic (cf. Genesis 3) (458–463) and produces the threefold error of man's trying to give himself what God gives as a free gift, of his coming into real need and rejecting his only help, and of his misunderstanding God as the true Helper (463–467). The last days of Judah and Jerusalem in 2 Kings provide a fitting example (468–478).

"Pride goes before a fall." Quoting the proverb, Barth discusses in the third subsection the fall that results from human pride. Here again he finds a contrast to Jesus Christ, for whereas the Son of God came down and was raised up, sinful man tried to soar up and fell down (478f.). Before looking more closely at the fall, Barth makes two preliminary points. (1) We must cling very firmly to scripture here, for the real root of rationalistic theology lies, not in intellectual difficulties, but in denial of the fall. (2) We must not take the fall to be a falling out of the hands of God, as though godless man could reduce God to manless God (480f.). In trying not to say too little, we must not say too much (482–484).

What, then, are the implications of the fall? (1) In the light of God's forgiveness it means first that man owes a debt he can never repay, not even in perdition, since nothing he can do will expiate his guilt (484f.). Anselm is our mentor here, though Barth disagrees with his thesis that God cannot forgive by mercy alone (485–487). In his pride man incurs the guilt of resisting God, denying his glory, and disrupting his order. In contradicting God's grace, he comes under the contradiction of his wrath and what can he possibly do to make God gracious again? "To sin is to do that which only God can put right" (487–491).

(2) The falls means, too, that as Christ died totally, so corruption is total. This does not mean loss of humanity, or even of the divine likeness understood as fellow-humanity (§41). But it does not mean either that a relic of goodness remains (492–494). It means that always, everywhere, and without exception, man is sinful to the core, even though acts of sin may differ in form and extent (495–498). This is original sin, not hereditary sin as the German term *(Erbsünde)* suggests, but "the original and radical and therefore the comprehensive and total act of man in which he has imprisoned himself" (499–501).

(3) The fall means finally a unity of man in sin, a racial as well as a historical solidarity. In spite of human achievements, "all" have sinned and come short of God's glory (501–506). Scripture gives the name of Adam to the race in this sense, for his representative sin at the outset is the sin of all. We all follow his law of sin, and his sin and guilt are imputed and adjudicated to us (507–511).

But how do we know about Adam? Returning at the end to the beginning, Barth finds in scripture a parallel between the first man, Adam, and the last man, Jesus. But this is no exact parallel, for it is in the light of the last that the first is known. (Paul "knew Jesus Christ first and then Adam.") The righteousness of the second Adam exposes the unrighteousness of the first. It far outweighs it too, for even as we hear God's sentence on the man of sin we see that this man no longer exists. God has had mercy on all even as he included all under disobedience (513f.).

3. The Justification of Man (§61)

From the man of sin whose judgment is carried and existence done away at the cross, Barth turns to the new man who is introduced by the verdict of the Father in the resurrection. He thus arrives at the doctrine of justification and he deals with it in four subsections, one on the problem, another on God's judgment, a third on the pardon of man, and the last on justification by faith alone.

In a short subsection on the problem, Barth begins with a contrast. Negatively, reconciliation exposes the man of sin who is put to death in Jesus Christ. Positively, it sets before us justified man who has a new and true life in Jesus Christ. The judgment in which we are accused, condemned, and executed is that in which we are also pardoned and raised to life again. The radical transformation thus effected by God is man's justification (514–517).

What, then, is the problem? It is the problem of right both in the sense of seeing the rightness of justification and also in that of saying the right thing about it. How can sinful man be righteous before God? How does God maintain his own righteousness in justification? How can he judge man justly and be gracious? To say the right thing here one must show God's overruling righteousness in his grace and his overruling grace in his righteousness (517ff.). This is the special difficulty of the doctrine that causes Luther to call it a mystery (519f.).

The special difficulty indicates the special function. The doctrine deals with the transition from the old man to the new at the original center of the crisis. It holds, then, a basic position, particularly at certain periods such as that of Augustine and the reformers (521f.). Barth cannot accept the view that for Paul it is only, as it were, a "secondary crater" (522–524). Nevertheless, he cannot agree that justification is *the* word of the gospel and he does not think the reformers treated it as such (524–527). Not justification, but confession of Jesus Christ, is the true article of a standing or falling church, for Jesus Christ is the controlling center of justification and its understanding (527f.).

In the second subsection Barth deals with the question of the justice of God's justifying the unjust in the judgment. The answer, he suggests, depends on acceptance of the higher right of God, which, worked out on man, sets aside man's wrong and establishes his new right (528f.). This higher right is grounded in God himself as right, not arbitrarily, but in his faithfulness to himself (530–532). Against this right man's wrong cannot stand. By setting himself in the wrong, man cannot alter or annul God's right (533f.). This right is the right of grace. It is judgment in relation to man's wrong (535–537), but since the aim of judgment is the overthrow of man's wrong and the restoration of his right, even in judgment God's right is the right of grace (538).

Barth develops this thought as follows: In his judgment God severs man the wrongdoer from man his creature. On the left hand man is the condemned and rejected wrongdoer, on the right he is God's pardoned and upheld possession. This does not mean that the judgment is one of appearance only, or that the sinner does not wholly perish, or that man is statically dualistic, or that one must distinguish between empirical and ideal man (542f.). For everything here takes place as event in a dynamic movement which cannot be seen either speculatively or even empirically as it is lived (544ff.).

How, then, do we see it? We see and know it in Jesus Christ in whose history it is enacted. It is all true and actual in him, and because it is true in him, it is also true in us. The righteousness that is ours is a strange righteousness because first and essentially it is his, and only as his is it ours (548). He as very God and very man takes the wrong-doer's place and sets him aside in his death and passion. In so doing he upholds the right of God in the judgment (550–554). He does it as the righteous man, so that in his enacted work we are set up as new men and the right of grace is also upheld (554f.). In the one reconciling act, in irreversible sequence, Jesus Christ turns the sinner from his sin to God (556ff.).

First and foremost, then, justification is God's justification. His right is done. He justifies himself. His right as Creator is expressed (562f.), the right of his electing grace is fulfilled (563f.), the right of God the Father and God the Son is executed in the justification of the Son by both himself and the Father (564f.). God did not need, of course, to justify himself. In his freedom he willed to do so and he did. In so doing he revealed himself as the God who is just in himself and may be known by us as such (567f.).

By dividing, God's sentence brings pardon to man. Discussed in the third subsection, pardon (1) has to be God's sentence, (2) it can be received and put into effect only as God addresses us in his Word, and (3) as God's sentence and the content of his Word it has total validity (569f.). Involving separation, pardon is naturally a history or movement of transition. It is separation *from*—from the past in which, as man has come to see, he was sinful man always in need of pardon (573–577; Barth expounds here Psalms 32 and 51 from the Old Testament and Romans 7 from the New, 577–591). It is also separation *for*—for the new present and future in which, as man now sees, he is pardoned man, and able to acknowledge his sin (591ff.).

Pardon brings promise, and Barth concludes the subsection by considering three aspects of this promise. (1) It is the promise of complete forgiveness, for present and future as well as past sins, by God's just and mighty non-imputation of sin and endowment with newness of life (596–599). (2) It is the promise of institution into a specific right that replaces the committed but forgiven wrong, the divinely given right of divine worship (599–601). (3) It is the promise of a life in hope in which God has given us the freedom to look for manifestations of our justification and sonship. Barth adduces several passages from the Psalter to support this hope of the justified (605–608).

In the last subsection Barth discusses justification by faith alone. His approach is unusual, for he begins with the question: Who is justified man? Is he a reality? Or is he a myth? (608ff.). The answer is less obvious than one might suppose, for we always run into the problem of self-demonstration. No one looks like justified man (611f.). This is why we are thrust back on faith. Only in faith can it be said that here is justified man, for the reality of justification is God's, not man's (611ff.). Faith is the "absolutely humble but absolutely positive answer to the question of the reality and existence of man justified by God, to the question who and where this man is. . . . The one who can and does believe knows this man well" (614).

What is faith? Barth first says what it is not. It is not a work, whether as knowledge, assent, or trust (615f.). As Calvin said, it cannot contribute to justification (617). Positively faith, as the authentic response to God's faithfulness, is wholly and utterly the humility of obedience (618–620). This is why Paul opposes it to every human work in the two great propositions that no human work justifies and that as believers we are those who are justified by God (621). In a biblical and historical excursus Barth examines the Pauline thesis that works do not justify and then examines its interpretation by the reformers. He concludes that the reformers understood Paul correctly (621–626). Although accompanied by works, the faith of obedient humility excludes justifying works (627).

If in this regard faith has a negative form, this is not because there is merit in self-negation but because faith is the proper response to the crucified and risen Jesus who is the self-demonstration of the justified man (628f.). Faith looks to Jesus Christ, seeing the self in him. This alone is what gives faith its exclusiveness in justifying. This is what necessitates its negative form as an empty hand or vessel (629–631). Faith alone means Christ alone (632). It can utter its Nevertheless on the basis of "the divine Therefore of its object, the existence and reality of the justified man in the one Jesus Christ" (634). On this basis it is a venture of obedient humility that involves the following of Jesus Christ in analogy to God's attitude and action (635f.).

Barth supports his teaching with a brief exposition of Galatians (637–642). He then rounds off the section by quoting the relevant questions and answers from the *Heidelberg Catechism*. His reproduction of these without comment shows that, while his approach has some new features, he follows the reformers closely in this crucial matter, confident that their understanding is true to the teaching of holy scripture.

4. The Holy Spirit and the Gathering of the Christian Community (§62)

What is the effect on fallen and sinful man when this aspect of God's reconciling work in Jesus Christ intersects him? Barth tries to answer this question in the last two sections of chapter fourteen, first from the standpoint of the community, then of the individual Christian. From the standpoint of the community he is led into the first part of a three-fold development of the doctrine of the church, this time relative to its gathering. He has three subsections on this, the first dealing with the work of the Holy Spirit, the second with the being of the community, and the third with its time.

The subsection on the Holy Spirit is short but central. Everything relates to what is done in Christ, but what happens here comes under specifically the third article of the creed: I believe in the Holy Ghost (644f.). The Holy Spirit is he who gathers the community, effecting reconciliation subjectively in a free self-attestation of God to us who in ourselves have no capacity either to know or believe (646). In this work the Spirit is the Spirit of God, the Spirit of the God who acts in Jesus Christ, the Spirit who is sent by the Father and the Son to bear witness to the grace of the Son and the verdict of the Father, and thereby to awaken man to knowledge of the reconciling God (647f.). The manner of this ministry of the Spirit is a mystery for Barth, but it does take place, it did, and it will. If we cannot explain it, we undoubtedly have to state and describe it (649ff.).

A longer subsection on the being of the community opens with the thesis that the church as gathered by the Spirit is a work in history. It exists in its coming together *(ecclesia)*. When this takes place, it is (650–652). This implies visibility as opposed to ecclesiological docetism, but Barth admits that in spite of a general visibility the true being of the church can be known only by believers in the special visibility of faith (654ff.). The outer appearance contradicts the inner reality. Hence no concrete form can be believed as the church, only what it is in the Lord, the primary object of faith (656ff.).

What is this true being of the church as faith perceives it? In its proper reality the church is the earthly-historical form of the existence of Jesus Christ. It is his body created and renewed by the awakening power of the Spirit. Jesus lives in a heavenly-historical form at the Father's right hand. He lives also in the earthly-historical form as the Head of this body of his, which is because he is (661f.). Barth appends a study of the use and significance of the phrase "body of Christ" in the New Testament (662–668).

In further development of his thinking Barth now turns to the traditional notes of the church: unity, holiness, catholicity, and apostolicity.

(1) *Unity* We believe the one church. Various pairs can be suggested, visible-invisible, militant-triumphant, Israel-church, church-churches, but only as forms of the one community (669–674). Thus the churches are valid only as local entities. They are not the church, but the church in this or that place (672–674). Denominations involve a contradiction in terms, for none of them can be the one church and their coexistence has to mean division (675). This is a scandal and ought not to be (676f.). One cannot flee from the visible disunity to an invisible unity. Nor can one restore unity by seeing only religious societies that might coexist and cooperate (678). The only way to unity is for all denominations to take themselves seriously as the church of which Jesus Christ is Head (679ff.). Zinzendorf offers an example. It is for Barth no accident that "the only genuine Christocentric of the modern age (fools would say: Christomonist) must also perhaps be called the first genuine ecumenicist." The unity of the church lies finally in Christ, "who is Himself its true unity" (685).

2. *Holiness* We believe the holy church. Holy means set apart, singled out. While human, the church has a holiness given it by the Holy Spirit (685f.). Barth points out in this regard that we do not believe *in* the church as we do in the Father, Son, and Spirit. Believing in the Holy Spirit, we know the church's holiness by faith, not as its own, but as that of Jesus Christ (686f.). This holiness is infallible and indestructible, for all our human fragility and fallibility (689f.). We do not see, but we believe, and in believing we see the danger as well as the necessity of criticizing the church (691). In the acts of the church its holiness is passive; the church does not make its acts holy (693). The same applies to the members, who are not holy by their assembling, piety, or service, but by the Spirit's ministry. From this we learn to look to ourselves, not to judge others (694–700). Passive holiness, however, does not mean passivity. Believing our holiness as we believe in Jesus Christ, we are summoned to obedience, not in the achievement of holiness, but on the basis of the holiness of the living Lord (700f.).

3. *Catholicity* We believe the catholic church. This is the general or comprehensive church whose identity remains in every difference. In virtue of this identity the catholic church confronts the false church, that is, the heretical or apostate church (701). Catholicity is in space and as such is ecumenicity (702). Yet it is also in time, the catholic church being the true church in every age, not necessarily the most ancient or the most modern, but that which shares in the being of the one church (703–705). Catholicity is in relation to members, entailing

a certain priority of the church over them in conjunction with the Head (705–707). We have to believe it, for we cannot see it without faith, whether in large groups or small (707–710). An alleged catholicity of sight is as such a-catholicity in virtue of its arrogance and impenitence. Real catholicity has its reality as it is grounded in Jesus Christ the Head, so that all watching and obeying takes place in hearing of the living Word of Christ by the Holy Spirit (710–712).

4. *Apostolicity* We believe the apostolic church. This note adds nothing new to the first three but provides a criterion by which to test them (712–714). Apostolicity means in the school and discipleship, and under the authority and instruction, of the apostles (714f.). It has a fuller sense than that of a historical or juridical apostolic succession, which removes it from the sphere of faith and so does despite to the freedom of the Spirit (715–717). It is grounded in the uniqueness of the apostolate and its service (718). Authentic apostolicity lies in agreement with the apostolic witness in a similar ministry of God's Word (720f.). Concretely, conformity with this witness means acceptance of the scripture principle. The apostolic community hears the apostolic witness of the New Testament, and by implication the prophetic witness of the Old Testament too, as direct witness to Jesus Christ. It accepts this as the canon and follows its direction (721f.). The mere presence of scripture does not guarantee apostolicity but its speaking, hearing, and pointing to Jesus Christ does. When this takes place what is done is "the work of the Spirit of scripture who is the Holy Spirit" (723). In an excursus Barth lists some implications of true apostolicity: flexibility of structure, the centrality of Christ, the anchoring of faith and piety in God, a realism that does not make the church an end in itself but finds its end and freedom in service of Christ and the world (723–725).

Finally Barth has a short subsection on the time of the community. He takes up here his thinking on fulfilled time in I,2, on Jesus, Lord of time in III,2, on Easter time in relation to the verdict of the Father in §59,3, and on the mission of the church as the earthly-historical form of the existence of Christ. The time of the community is the time between the first *parousia* of Jesus Christ in the forty days and his second *parousia* when he is manifested as Judge. (In IV, 3 Barth will add a third and middle *parousia* with the coming of the Holy Spirit at Pentecost.) *Parousia* means Christ's direct presence and action. The church lives now between the first direct presence and action and the last in a movement from the one to the other, Christ being present through the Holy Spirit. That it lives in this time and movement is for Barth its weakness and its strength (725).

Living in time and movement is the church's strength because it has Easter behind it, the living Lord, the just Judge for the unjust, the Father's verdict, the justification of the wicked. It has Christ's coming ahead of it, the consummation, the final manifestation of the Lord, the victory of God. Its life has teleological direction from the one to the other. In its gathering in the time between, it has the force and significance of a provisional representation of the humanity justified in Christ (725–727).

Yet living in time and movement is the church's weakness because it must walk by faith and not by sight. Jesus Christ is not present as in the forty days. Easter has to be believed not merely in its simple facticity but in its true facticity as the proclamation of reconciliation (728f.). The *parousia* can be known only in its beginning in Easter. It has to be hoped for in its definitive form. In its own being in the world the church sees itself as a feeble minority (730f.). It can see its true being only by the ministry of the Holy Spirit (732f.).

Nevertheless, this time is *its* time. God in grace has given it this time (733–735). He has given it this time as the time of its work in the world by the Holy Spirit to evoke from man a response of praise and service (738f.). The community has this time for the world's sake, to be in it a provisional representation of justification in Christ. If this time will end with all time, it knows why it has it and can do that which gives meaning to it (739).

Materially Barth will fill all this out when he speaks of the sending and mission of the church in IV,3. Only the first part of his doctrine of the church is presented in this section on its gathering. Yet already some decisive notes are struck. The true being of the church is sought in its Lord. Its unity, holiness, catholicity, and apostolicity are not to be abstracted from Jesus Christ whose body it is. Mission belongs to the core of its reality. God gathers the church, and gives it time to render the service which also means its gathering. It is not left alone in this time, for Christ is present by the Holy Spirit. Nevertheless, it has this time between the comings, not for itself, but for its Lord and the world. In striking these notes Barth achieves depth and penetration in his discussion and avoids the pedantry, futility, and triviality of so many presentations of the church and its nature and function.

5. The Holy Spirit and Christian Faith (§63)

In the last section of chapter fourteen, Barth considers the impact of God's reconciling act on the individual believer. He has in mind the faith which is the basis of Christian existence and which makes someone a Christian (740). In a comparatively short treatment he divides his material into two subsections, one on the object of faith and the other on the act.

In his ongoing rejection of existentialism, Barth stresses first that faith is not the primary datum. This is why he does not follow an earlier fashion and call his dogmatics a doctrine of faith (740f.). Faith plays a vital role but the primary datum is its object, by which it stands or falls. Barth considers three aspects of this.

(1) Faith is oriented to this object, to Jesus Christ, in whom God has reconciled the world to himself. In relation to him it is thus marked by both spontaneity and inevitability (743f.).

(2) Faith originates in its object, in Jesus Christ, who frees man for it, not as mere possibility, but as reality (745f.), with a freedom that is not abstract choice but the authentic freedom of necessity (746f.). This takes place as the root of unbelief is pulled out by the awakening power of the Holy Spirit (748).

(3) Orientation of faith to Jesus Christ and its originating in him mean the constitution of the Christian subject, a new and particular being of man, the new man who can be the individual believer, acknowledging, recognizing, and confessing that Jesus Christ is also and specifically for him (749–757).

In this connection Barth engages in a self-correction. In I,2 he seriously criticized the subjective hymn. He now modifies if he does not withdraw the criticism. The Christian has to say I as well as We. Hence criticism of the I-hymn can be only relative. So long as the I-hymn is a hymn to Christ and not to self it has a valid place. By focusing on Christ one can "demythologize" the I as Paul does in Galatians 2:20. Justice can thus be done to the proper concerns of pietism and even of theological existentialism (755–757).

The second subsection looks at the act of faith, which, from the present angle, must be regarded as *the* act of the Christian life. As intimated already Barth finds in it a threefold act of knowledge *(Kennen)*, acknowledgment *(Anerkennen)*, recognition *(Erkennen)*, and confession *(Bekennen)* (758f.).

(1) *Acknowledgment* This means obedient knowledge. (The stress on it earlier in the *Church Dogmatics* will be recalled.) It comes to expression in our joining the community, not in abstract adherence to its doctrines, but in living commitment to Jesus Christ as the Head of the church and the Lord of scripture (758–761).

(2) *Recognition* This is informed knowledge of Jesus Christ according to the witness of scripture and the community (761f.). It can have different nuances but only within the singularity of its object and the limits of the texts and doctrines (763ff.). As the knowledge of faith, it can never be abstract. While theoretical in relation to its object, it

is practical in the recognition of the self as the one for whom Christ is and acts (766f.). It involves an eschatological decision, not as a repetition of Christ's own death and resurrection, but in an analogous movement of mortification and renewal (767–775).

(3) *Confession* Barth defines this necessary implication of acknowledgment and recognition as a standing to one's faith, or to its object (777f.). The Christian makes confession, not just by what he says and does, but by what he is—the little light reflecting the big light from which it derives and in which it has its being. Confession is a debt of fellowship to others in the world (778). Concretely the summons to it comes through the community which needs the Christian as he needs it in its ministry and common witness (778). It comes also through the world, for the world to which the Christian also belongs needs the message of God's reconciling work which he alone can bring. In face of the world the individual believer has to be, "very humbly but very courageously, a confessing Christian in the confessing community" (779).

CHAPTER XV
The Son of Man

1. The Exaltation of the Son of Man (§64)

HAVING examined reconciliation from the standpoint of Jesus, Son of God, the Lord who became a servant in fulfilment of his priestly office, Barth now turns in chapter fifteen, which comprises the whole of IV,2, to reconciliation as the work of Jesus, Son of Man, the servant who became Lord in fulfilment of his kingly office. He does this in five sections, a first on the exaltation of the Son of Man (§64), then one on the sloth and misery of man (§65), then a transitional one on sanctification (§66). The two final sections are on the Holy Spirit and the Christian community (§67) and the Holy Spirit and Christian love (§68).

In the first section Barth begins with a subsection on the second problem of the doctrine. As chapter fourteen dealt with the first partner in the restored covenant, chapter fifteen deals with man, the second partner (5f.). Its theme, then, is reconciled man, who, in contrast to God in his condescension in Christ, undergoes exaltation in the same Christ (5ff.). Scripture forces this aspect of the doctrine on us. Hence the danger of abstract anthropomonism should not press us into the danger of an equally abstract theomonism (8–10). Barth chooses the example of monasticism to illustrate both the threat and also the valid concern at issue here (11–19). Rooting the doctrine in christology offers the proper safeguard. Man's exaltation is in the man Jesus (19f.).

The second and central subsection presents the Lord who as servant went into the far country but who now comes home as Lord: "The Homecoming of the Son of Man." This time Barth mentions and defends the christological interpretation of the parable of the prodigal son on which his title rests (22–25). In Jesus Christ God is abased and man exalted, for Jesus Christ is both very God and very man. What does it mean that Christ is very man? Here Barth finally examines christology.

The Son of God took our human nature. This involved three things: (1) He took our adamic nature. (2) His nature is like ours and yet unlike ours. (3) The unlikeness lies in its exaltation, in its upward movement, for Jesus is what we are not—faithful, obedient, and true man, in whom all others are exalted (26–31).

Further discussing the exaltation of the humanity of Jesus in which all humanity finds its exaltation, Barth focuses on three contexts in which it has its place and meaning: the basis in election, the fulfilment in the incarnation, and the basis of its revelation in the resurrection and ascension.

(1) *Basis in Election* Having dealt with this in II,2, Barth simply recapitulates. Jesus Christ is the beginning of all God's ways and works. The election of grace is concretely the election of Jesus Christ. In it God made an eternal decision for sinful man. This involves man's fellowship with him as well as his with man. It also involves man's upward movement as well as his own downward movement. In Jesus Christ man is in the divine will and counsel from the beginning. A human history is included in the divine act. The humanity of Jesus has an eternal basis and man's exaltation in him belongs integrally to the election of grace and its execution in reconciliation (31–36).

(2) *Fulfilment in the Incarnation* The incarnation is the historical fulfilment of election. It is the divine act which is the ground of being and the ground of knowledge of the man Jesus (36–39). What is this act? What does it mean that the Creator, God, without ceasing to be such, becomes also creature, man? In answering this question Barth first points out the importance of "also." God does not cease to be God in the incarnation. He is not changed into a man. This is why the concept of assumption has so much to commend it (40–42). This assumption takes place in a once-for-all act of God in his mode of being as the Son. In this act the human being is unified with the divine being (43ff.). In this connection four statements must be made.

(i) God the Son became and is also man. The Son is the existing subject of this act and man the object—not just one man, although the Son does become the man Jesus—but in this specific form, that which characterizes all men, so that humanity as such is exalted into unity with God (46–48). As Barth sees it, the truth and necessity of the *anhypostasis* arise here. Jesus is authentic man only as the Son of God. Barth cannot understand how this destroys his true humanity, as some allege, nor can he regard it as superfluous, since the mystery cannot be described without it (49f.).

(ii) The existence of the Son of God became and is also that of a man, the fellowman of all men. God exists in human being and essence, so that we have to do with God as we have to do with this man (50f.). This involves what theology calls the hypostatic or personal union, the union of the divine and human natures in the one person or *hypostasis* of the Son (51). In an excursus Barth stresses the uniqueness of this union. It is not the same as that of Father, Son, and Spirit in the one God, nor as the immanent union of God with creation, nor as that of two people, nor as that of a man and his clothes, nor as that of heat and light in iron, of form and matter, of body and soul, of sacramental sign and thing signified, of God and man in Christian experience. At most the union of Christ with the members of his body offers an indirect parallel, but in so doing it confirms rather than negates the uniqueness (51–60).

(iii) Divine and human essence or nature—what he has in common with Father and Spirit and what he has in common with us— were and are united in the one Jesus Christ. In view of the divine/human antithesis this might seem to be impossible but what cannot be said metaphysically has to be said because it is a fact in Jesus Christ. There has taken place, not an equation, but a union of natures by mutual participation (60–64). In an excursus on the different emphases of Lutheran and Reformed theology on the union of natures and the hypostatic union, Barth favors the Reformed position (66–69).

(iv) As the Son of God became also man, he raised up human essence into himself in the exaltation which is the second main aspect of reconciliation. Involved here is the determination of the divine nature to the human and the human to the divine (70f.). The human nature is assumed into the divine so that the man Jesus is indeed the Son of God but the human nature is not the divine: The Word was made flesh, not flesh the Word (71f.). The assumption is by mutual but differentiated participation which takes three forms. There is (a) the communication of attributes, which in an extreme form raises the problem of a deifying of humanity or a partial de-deifying of deity (73–83). There is (b) the communication of graces, so that the human essence is totally determined by grace (84–90)—the grace of origin (90f.), sinlessness (92f.), the Spirit (94f.), authority and mediatorship (96f.), and glory and dignity (100f.). Apart from these graces no authentic biography or portrait of Jesus can be achieved, for all we have left is a predicate without a subject (102f.). There is (c) the communication of operations, the union as act, not state—as the one act of exinanition and exaltation (104–111), and the actualization of the union of divine and human essence with a view to the reconciliation of the world with God (113–115). As Barth states, "In the work of the one Jesus Christ everything is at one and the same time, but distinctly, both divine and human . . . the divine and the human work together. . . . But even in their common working they are not interchangeable. . . . Their relationship is one of genuine action" (116).

(3) *Basis of Revelation in the Resurrection and Ascension* How do we know all this? Is it mere theory? Is it just what the church says? Is it myth or fiction? Barth has already given his reply in principle: The ground of being is the ground of knowledge. We do not know it *a priori* nor can we come to know it by demonstration. The divine act has a subjective as well as an objective character. It establishes itself in the knowing subject. It has the character of revelation (119f.).

Noetically we begin with the church and particularly holy scripture, but these lead us to the unique history of Jesus Christ in his self-revelation, which we can read and expound but cannot control. The Holy Spirit opens it up to us in his inner, or, more accurately, his outer testimony. He does it by disclosing what is objectively concealed (125f.). In this witness Jesus Christ is present (128f.) as the one who rose again (131ff.) in an unequivocal self-demonstration intimated already in his life, for example, at the transfiguration (135–140), but fully given only when what is revealed had been effectively completed at the cross (140f.). Corresponding to that death, taking historical form (142) yet also as an act of divine majesty or a miracle (146f.), the resurrection gives us a particular knowledge of the one who first loved us (148f.)—a knowledge which rests on a genuinely historical investigation of the texts (149ff.). In its totality the resurrection includes the ascension, thus telling us where Jesus came from—he rose from the dead—and also where he went to—he ascended to the right hand of the Father. In this exaltation, which is his for us, is manifested also the exaltation of the cross. The incarnation as God's reconciling work exalts humanity in order that we humans might be exalted to God and to life and fellowship with God. The resurrection and ascension give us knowledge of the homecoming of the Son of Man as achieved by the going into the far country of the Son of God (155).

In the third subsection on "The Royal Man," Barth examines the kingly office of Christ (155). In the light of Easter, the New Testament presents Jesus to us as the new and royal man (155f.). A study of Jesus as this man will be a study of the gospel tradition. Barth undertakes such a study in four main divisions.

(1) He looks first at the distinctiveness of Christ's presence as man according to the New Testament. Four points are made. (i) He came into encounter with others (156). (ii) In this encounter he de-

manded decision (157f.). (iii) He was present in unforgettable unique-ness (159–163). (iv) His presence has the irrevocability of the past of him who is still the living Lord, so that the gospels are not biographies or profiles but witness to the royal Son of Man in his identity with the Son of God (163–166).

(2) Barth then considers what it means that the royal man is a reflection of God in correspondence with his purpose and work. Here again he has four points. (i) Jesus shares God's destiny in his dispar-agement, rejection, isolation, and concealment (166–169). (ii) He transvaluates all values by favoring the weak and humble, not the high and mighty (168–171). (iii) His approach to established orders is genuinely revolutionary, cutting across all parties and programs, both conservative and progressive (171–173; cf. his attitude to the temple, family, and political and economic orders, 173–179). (iv) He lives his life for men as Savior, not against them as Judge (180f.; cf. his com-passion on the crowd and also the beatitudes (181–192).

(3) Next Barth tries to understand Jesus in his life-act. This con-sists of interrelated words and works. The words comprehend the works but they are also concrete words, wholly human, yet constitut-ing the powerful Word of evangelizing, teaching, and heralding. The Word places a burden on the community to proclaim to the world what it heard (194f.; Barth adds an excursus on the three decisive terms evangelizing, teaching, and heralding, 195–209). The works are also his Word, yet they are concrete acts which demonstrate his Word and give cosmic history a specific time and place on earth. The acts are extraordinary, such as exorcisms, healings, and nature miracles (212ff.). Even if in some cases there seem to be parallels, these are also un-usual and the similarity is superficial (214f.). The stories show that Jesus never took the initiative, used no particular techniques, did not act in his own interests, and had no general program. He did his mighty works as actualizations of his message with a symbolical qual-ity (216–218). As acts of divine power (i) they are done for the needy (221), (ii) they bring release (222f.), (iii) they express God's covenant concern (224f.), (iv) they involve solidarity with us (225), and (v) they display the freedom of grace in the freeing of man (225–232). Barth discusses the works in John and the Synoptics in this context (226–232) and also the relation of the works to the faith of those for whom they are done (233–242).

(4) All that has been said thus far is controlled and determined by the death of Jesus on the cross (249f.). The cross is no alien element in this royal life. It is not a tragic entanglement or mishap. It is central to the whole (251). In it Jesus received his coronation as the royal man (252). To portray it in terms of despair instead of triumph (as Bach

does) is a mistake (252). The predictions of the passion are important here, as the disciples later saw (253f.). So is the witness of John's Gospel in its positive understanding of the cross (255f.). So is the witness of Pauline theology (256–258). In his pre-Easter life Jesus expected the cross and moved toward it (258f.). He did so voluntarily in fulfilment of the divine predetermination (259f.). He did so in the context of Israel's history, though Pilate acted as executioner when Israel handed Jesus over to him (260f.). He did so in such a way that there is a cross for the disciples too, for whom the cross is light and freedom, but who still stand in its shadow, since "the 'must' of His passion extends to them too" (263).

The extremely long section on the exaltation of the Son of Man includes a fourth and final subsection which forges the link between him in whom we are exalted and us who are exalted in him. What is the power of Jesus' existence for others? To what extent is there a way from him to us? How can that which he was and will be affect us as an act of divine power?

In reply to this question Barth advances a very simple thesis. We are not asking about the fact. Jesus' existence does affect us. We are seeking an explanation. How do we know ourselves as recipients of his direction, set in opposition to our sin and making up his community of service and obedience (264ff.)?

In seeking this explanation of the given fact, we have to remember first that Jesus is a public, not a private figure. He did what he did representatively, in our place, so that we are taken up in him (270) and in him our justification and sanctification have been accomplished (273f.). New Testament evidence from Hebrews, John, and particularly Paul supports this grounding of the Christian in Christ (275–280).

A statement about the being of Jesus is thus a statement about all human beings (280); there is no isolated Jesus or isolated sinner (281). This is an ontological reality, not a value-judgment (281f.). In ourselves we are sinners, but in virtue of Christ's solidarity with us we are now, in him, exalted to fellowship with God, turned from our evil way, and made obedient saints and covenant-partners. We *are* these things, although we can say this only as we look at him and away from ourselves (282f.).

Naturally, it is pointless to say we are these things if we look at ourselves. In ourselves we are not, and believing we are would be believing what we know is not true. Our being in Jesus Christ is hidden. We do not yet exist in such a way as to demonstrate the being of Christ and our being in him. We demonstrate the opposite. Therefore, to see and know Jesus Christ and ourselves, there must be the event which penetrates this hiddenness (286f.).

At its deepest level this hiddenness is not just that of our sin, for our being in Jesus is our justification and sanctification (288). Nor is it a metaphysical mishap, for this would genuinely separate us from Jesus Christ (289). It lies in this: Christ is the royal man under the sign of the cross. His whole life moved toward the cross as the enactment of reconciliation (290f.). His cross was his coronation (292). As the New Testament plainly reveals, we can know the royal man Jesus and ourselves in him, only as the one who was "led by God" and "harried by Israel" to his death. The question, then, is how this cross is "the dominating characteristic of his royal office"—how his death is "the goal of his existence and the new beginning of ours" (292).

Three answers may be given. (1) The cross fulfils the self-humbling of the incarnation (292). (2) At the cross Christ genuinely embraced our situation and radically transformed it (293f.). (3) His determination for the vicarious act of the cross has the character of an act of God, for if death is the goal, it is not the end, for he is resurrected from death (294–296).

When we ask how the reality of Christ's being becomes truth for us, we are led again to Christ as the living Lord who powerfully discloses himself to us even as, in his crucifixion, he is closed to us. In his resurrection he declares himself as the royal man who actualized God's kingdom on earth and by his death interceded for the victims of death (297ff.).

We are told this in the New Testament. Thus our apprehension of it is not self-grounded. It is grounded in the reality and the witness to it (301f.). In telling it to us, the New Testament does not simply pass on information. Those who look to Barth for the odd idea that evangelism is merely informing people that they are saved are misinformed. The New Testament claims us for what is imparted (304) and frees us to appropriate it as our own conversion (304f.). It does this by a power that is greater than itself, the power of Jesus' self-disclosure in his resurrection (305ff.), by which transition is made from him to us. This power has the character of light (310f.), liberation (311f.), peace (314f.), and much else in its total impact on our lives (315ff.). It is the power of the presence and action of the Holy Spirit, to whom the New Testament witness exclusively directs us (319f.), who is separate even as he separates (322), who is Christ's own presence and action (323; excursus on the relation of Christ and the Spirit, 323–330), yet who is called the Spirit of God (332f.), so that we see the Father's will as the eternal background of what is done in the Son, and therefore we see God's own presence and action in this whole history (333–336).

Three features of the history are to be noted: (1) the existence of the man Jesus; (2) community as the goal; and (3) God's self-disclosure as the link between the two (336f.). God is everywhere present as God. All things are from him, by him, and to him (337f.). Thus history points us to the Holy Trinity, in whom the Holy Spirit, who mysteriously and miraculously makes the transition between Jesus and us, is eternally transition in distinction in the partnership of the Father and the Son (341ff.).

From the Spirit we learn (1) that the antithesis in the humiliation of the Son of God reflects a transcended differentiation in God's one but twofold will (348ff.). We learn (2) that the antithesis in the exaltation of the Son of Man rests on the one divine act of the mercy of the Father and the majesty of the Son (353ff.). Hence the antithesis forms no paradox, no juxtaposition of a divine No and Yes, but the puzzle of a No for the sake of the Yes which the Holy Spirit solves "by causing the work and wisdom of God to be known in it" (359).

How does the Spirit do his work? How does he meet, touch, and move us? What does it mean to have the Spirit?

In the last few pages of the subsection Barth characterizes the work of the Spirit as a giving of direction. The German word here *(Weisung)* is connected with the two other words "wise" and "way." By the Holy Spirit Jesus gives us direction as the wise man, or wisdom, who tells us in what way we should be and think and will and act (360ff.). The transition from Jesus to us entails our determination by this direction.

The direction takes three forms:

(1) It is indication. It points us to the place of freedom where we must start. The Holy Spirit does not leave us with open options but directs us to a fixed place. We are to be what we are in Jesus. An imperative is issued resting on the indicative (363–367).

(2) The direction is also correction. The Holy Spirit distinguishes between the possibilities of freedom and those of unfreedom. He permits no compromise. He marks off the new man from the old. He allows no cheap grace. He does this on the basis of effected sanctification. But he does it in order that this may be just as real in us as it is in itself. Here is the corrective element in the direction (367ff.).

(3) Finally the direction is instruction. The Holy Spirit reveals and writes on our hearts and consciences the will of God as it now applies to us. The instruction is a concrete assignment demanding obedience. It has a unique sovereignty. The Holy Spirit—the Spirit of Jesus—speaks *to* us, not *from* us. He now tells us to advance, to use our freedom. When we need to be corrected he tells us to halt, to stop not using it. He calls us to the good works we must do because we are not our own but Christ's (372–374). The main lines of this instruc-

tion, as indeed of the correction (370–372), may be found in the apostolic admonitions of the New Testament (374–377).

2. The Sloth and Misery of Man (§65)

In chapter fourteen Barth developed the doctrine of sin in the light of the self-humiliation of the Son of God. In chapter fifteen he now looks at it from the standpoint of the exaltation of the Son of Man. He is thus led to see the plight of unaltered man, determined by sin, as one of sloth and misery. His section on this topic (§65) is divided into three subsections, a first on the man of sin in the light of the lordship of the Son of Man, a second on man's sloth, and a third on his misery.

The procedure of the first subsection corresponds to that in the parallel subsection in §60. Barth recalls his principle that man cannot properly know his sin except as he knows God in Jesus Christ (378–380). Knowledge of sin is more than knowledge of sins. It is insight into the human situation. The substance and center of the biblical message gives this insight (381f.).

Now when the human situation is set in contrast with the exaltation of the Son of Man, it is pinpointed as one of immobility or inertia. This involves our total shaming (383f.). This shaming is not caused merely by the disclosure of individual offences. Often we can find excuses for these and evade their shame. It is caused by comparing ourselves with God. This comparison brings us to the point where we know ourselves in our loathsomeness and are ashamed in the same manner that Peter was ashamed (384–389).

Four points stand out in relation to this shaming. (1) We do not escape it even if we have done no extraordinarily bad things. When measured by Jesus Christ, all of us, however mediocre and trivial our offences, are shown to fall far short of him and to be opposed to him with our doubting, rejection, and betrayal (389ff.).

(2) Although unbelievers find it hard to accept this, mediocrity or triviality is itself to be described as sin. Jesus Christ has taken our place in liberating power, so that there is no more reason for mediocrity. He calls us to himself and a failure to respond is wrong. Excuses for the failure do not relieve the shame; they confirm it. When Jesus confronts us, all differentiation from him entails our disqualification as sinners (391–393).

(3) We cannot detach ourselves from our sin as though it were a defect or accident. In our sin we are sinners. This is decided by Jesus Christ. He has taken our place as Judge. He has become for us new, different, exalted man, and is with us in our sin. If we will accept our disqualification as sinners we may be this new man in him. If we will

not, the only alternative, as Barth very sharply states, is that "we want to be in hell" (393–397).

(4) We cannot plead the inevitability of sin, for in his death and resurrection Jesus Christ has overcome sin in such a way that, not in smooth transition but in implacable opposition, the new man has replaced the man of sin. In Jesus Christ God acted to this end, thus exposing the seriousness as well as the absurdity of sin. We did not accomplish the death of the old man and the life of the new. We can share in it only with our exit as sinners and our entry as disciples "in the gratitude which corresponds to God's free and unmerited grace" (401–403).

Looking more closely at sin in the light of the new man introduced in Jesus Christ, Barth works out in the second subsection his initial point that in antithesis to the upward movement of the Son of Man, immobility characterizes the man of sin. Sin is sluggishness, indolence, slowness, inertia, or sloth (403). Here is the unheroic aspect of sin expressing disobedience, unbelief, and ingratitude in rejection of the man Jesus (403–407). Sloth is man's refusal. It works itself out in the fourfold relation to God, others, self, and time (cf. III,2; III,4).

In relation to God, sin as sloth involves a futile but true refusal of God's gift due to sheer stupidity and folly (409–411). In this respect the fool as defined in scripture is an apt term for the man of sin (411–412). The refusal is a silly one but it is also powerful and dangerous (414ff.). It is all the more dangerous because it hides under the guise of worldly wisdom and cannot easily be unmasked (417). In and with the rejection of God it entails a break in the other three relations, to others (420f.), self (421f.), and time (422f.). Again taking his illustrations from the Old Testament, Barth offers in support a detailed analysis of the story of Nabal, the man who is as his name is—a fool (427–432).

In relation to others, sin as sloth involves a useless but factual inactivity and inhumanity (432–436). This, too, is dangerous, for it can lead to secret or blatant oppression and exploitation (436f.). Its concealment as philanthropy or activism only increases the danger (437–441). It carries with it a break in the other three relations, to God (441–443), to self (443f.), and to time (444f.). The Old Testament provides a striking example in the society that came under the prophetic castigation of Amos (445–452).

In relation to self, sin as sloth involves futile but no less real dissipation (453–455). This is also dangerous, for it means self-destruction (455–458). It hides itself in the appealing forms of freedom and naturalness (459f.), but this does not prevent it from disrupting the other three relations, to God (460f.), to others (461f.), and to time (462ff.).

The Old Testament story of David and Bathsheba is aptly recounted in illustration (464–467).

Finally, in relation to time, sin as sloth means futile but factual care or anxiety (461–467). Although apparently feeble, anxiety has its own power and for this reason it, too, is dangerous (470ff.). It conceals itself in different forms, particularly frantic activity on the one side or contemplative passivity on the other (472–475). It breaks the other three relations, to God (475f.), to others (476f.), and to self (477f.). To illustrate this aspect of sloth Barth examines the response of Israel to the report of the spies whom Moses sent out to investigate the promised land (478–483).

Barth closes the section with a shorter subsection on the false and inauthentic existence that the slothful man or sinner creates for himself by his stupidity, inhumanity, dissipation, and anxiety. It may be described, he thinks, as the misery of man, his exile as the sum of human woe. Man's misery is his corruption in the choice of inertia (483f.). If this state of corruption is not outside the sphere of divine grace, the man of sin must suffer God's grace as wrath and judgment (484f.).

Set in relation to the being and work of the man Jesus, the misery of man takes three forms. (1) Since it can be cured only by Christ's death, it is in itself incurable. Not yet death, it is a plunge into death whose terrible future is that of existence in radical perversion (486–488). No relic of goodness escapes the plunge. If man's good is the totality of his God-given nature, his downward movement has the same totality. Scripture calls this perversion the flesh, in the bad sense of the term (489f.).

(2) Since Jesus brings in a new man, man's misery may be seen as that of the old being—of the original sin that gives rise to actual sins. If no actions are evil in abstraction, they all take place in the endless circle in which the sinner is what he does and does what he is. That he moves in this circle is his misery (490f.). In a short excursus Barth considers the classification of actual sins: sins of commission and omission, sins of infirmity and ignorance, voluntary and involuntary sins, and so forth. He recognizes the value of these distinctions but has to reject that which is made between mortal and venial sins (491–493).

(3) Since Jesus Christ in royal freedom has set us free, the misery of man entails the bondage of the will (494f.). This bondage does not mean determinism. Man has abstract choice between sinning and not sinning. But freedom to sin is no freedom. The only true freedom is that of not being able to sin *(non posse peccare)*. The choice of sin excludes freedom. Asserting a freedom to sin, the man of sin chooses,

but has lost his freedom. Sin excludes freedom, freedom sin. Freedom can be had only by the new man in Christ, and inasmuch as this man is still the old man, even as the new he has his freedom in ongoing conflict, not in synthesis with the old bondage.

Barth concludes the subsection with a brief but important discussion of the Tridentine teaching on man's cooperation in justification. This view, he believes, undercuts the bondage of the will. It thus hampers a full appreciation and affirmation of the seriousness of sin.

3. The Sanctification of Man (§66)

Having characterized the old man who is exposed and set aside by the exalted Son of Man, Barth has a look at the new man who is exalted in him. He does this in a study of sanctification, not as a struggle on our part to become new people, but as our conversion to be the new people we already are. He divides his material into six relatively short subsections, beginning with a discussion of the relation between justification and sanctification.

Having first equated sanctification with regeneration, renewal, conversion, and penitence, and having pointed out that this, too, is God's work (499f.), Barth urges (1) that we understand justification and sanctification, not as two successive acts of God, but as two moments of the one act of reconciliation in Christ. This leads him to a criticism of the whole idea of an order of salvation as an arbitrary and artificial schematization which almost ineluctably involves a descent from theology to religious and moral psychology (501–503).

If justification and sanctification are not to be separated, Barth warns also (2) against confusing them. The one is not the other. The one cannot take the place of the other. Participation in Christ is a twofold grace. If Roman Catholic theology tends to subsume justification under sanctification, Evangelical theology must not make sanctification no more than a paraphrase of justification (503–505).

For all that, Barth argues (3) that the inseparability of the two must be upheld lest we fall into the error of quietism ("cheap grace") on the one side or that of self-justification on the other. He commends Calvin in particular for the force and clarity with which he distinguishes and yet relates the two moments (505–507).

Finally Barth discusses (4) the proper order of the two. Questioning a temporal order, he also doubts whether there is a clear material order. If justification comes first as basis and sanctification follows as goal, sanctification might be said to come first as aim and justification to follow as consequence. He again finds Calvin particularly helpful in this area (507–511).

The second subsection deals with the relation between Jesus Christ, the holy one, and those who are holy in him (the saints). The divine transformation applies *de facto* to the holy people, to the saints in the plural (511–513). In this transformation God is subject, and he alone is originally and properly holy, so that originally and properly only one man is holy, the man who is separate from all others, the holy one in the singular (513f.). He, Jesus Christ, is our sanctification, so that it is by participation in him, not intrinsically in ourselves, that we, too, are holy ones, the saints (514ff.).

Barth makes a critical distinction here. Christ has taken the place of all. *De iure,* then, he is the sanctification of all (518–521). What he is *de iure* for all becomes an event, *de facto,* in those who are redirected by him through the Holy Spirit (522ff.). In themselves these people, the saints, are like all the rest (524). The difference is that in their *de facto* sanctification they are disturbed out of sleep (524f.), a limit is set to their sin (525f.), they are called to lift up their heads to the exalted royal man (526f.), and they are raised to conformity with him (529ff.). In Jesus Christ, and by the Holy Spirit, they thus receive a decisive liberation for obedience (529ff.).

Working out the implications of *de facto* sanctification, Barth devotes the third subsection to the call to discipleship. Following constitutes the substance of the call in whose power Jesus Christ makes us saints (533). In the call Barth (1) sees the grace of God as his command to us to follow (534–536). He then characterizes the call (2) as something that binds us, not to an idea, but to the person of Jesus Christ (536–538). The call demands (3) a first step of self-denial in faith involving a specific act of obedience (538–542). Finally, Barth argues (4) that this act involves a break with mammon which God has already made for us (543) but to which our obedience bears witness as we become nonconformists (544ff.) in relation to possessions (548), fame (548f.), force (549), family (550f.), and religion (551). The New Testament requirements in these areas are not to be regarded, Barth thinks, as evangelical *counsels* but as evangelical *mandates* demanding a response of decision and action (553).

The call awakens, and so Barth entitles his fourth subsection "The Awakening to Conversion." *De facto* saints are those who have been jolted awake out of the slothful sleep of death (553–555). God is the origin and goal of this awakening (556), which is an awakening to conversion effected by God through holy scripture (557–559). But what is conversion? It is turning around and renewing, halting and proceeding (560f.). Embracing the whole man, (1) it includes the relation to others as well as to God (563f.), (2) involves the person and not just the acts (564f.), (3) is public and not just private (565f.), (4) is ongoing and not restricted to a single moment (566f.). In it we are put at odds with ourselves in a struggle between the old and the new man in which we are always both saints and sinners but are determined as saints and not as sinners (570–574). John is cited here, as well as Calvin and Kohlbrügge, although Barth deplores the undue stress on mortification at the expense of renewal (574–577). In the dynamics of conversion Barth contends (1) that the compulsion is that of liberation (578), (2) that the basis is God's decision for us (579ff.), and (3) that in the power of the Holy Spirit the reality lies in Christ's conversion for us, which we know in faith and enter into in our own movement of conversion (581–584).

Sanctification means works, and Barth considers these in a short subsection on the praise of works. The works of awakened and converted saints entail praise both in the sense that God praises works and also in the sense that works praise God. Works are obligatory though they do not justify, as one may see from Paul and James (585f.). God works first and in so doing makes our works possible. Our works follow, declaring his, but with no claim to merit (590). These works of ours have, astonishingly, a part in God's works, so that we are called co-workers with God by his gift (594f.). They are distinctive in the sense of being done both by God's command and in the freedom he has given, so that they are the works or fruits of love (594f.). There can be in this sense Christian works that are truly good, praised by God and praising him (596f.). By God's empowering, Christians do them as works of faith, conversion, and love, not in praise of self, but with and to the praise of God (597).

Barth closes the section with a meditation on the dignity of the cross. In this last subsection he notes that the cross marks the limit of sanctification, the point at which it reaches beyond itself to the last things (598). It also characterizes the moment of sanctification as that of the people of Jesus Christ whose cross is his crown (599). Our cross rests on his cross. He alone bore this, so that our cross does not reenact his, but corresponds to it (599f.). We must not try to evade this cross of ours. It means our crossing out. We bear it by accepting this negation and we can do so because we see in Christ's cross our goal and glory (603ff.). Bearing our related but dissimilar cross fulfils sanctification because (1) it keeps us humble (607f.), (2) it chastens us (608), (3) it is a powerful disciplinary force (608f.), and (4) it offers specific verification by testing and purifying (609). The cross takes the three specific forms of persecution, sharing common afflictions, and temptation (609ff.). In relation to it, two things must be kept in mind. First, it is not to be sought; self-sought suffering has nothing to do with the participation in Christ's cross which is our sanctification. Second, it is not an end in itself. It is penultimate and provisional. It has an end, the future eternal life to which Christ's cross points us in the power of the resurrection. Hence "there cannot lack a foretaste of joy even in the intermediate time of waiting, in the time of sanctification, and therefore in the time of the cross" (613).

4. The Holy Spirit and the Upbuilding of the Christian Community (§67)

What does sanctification effect? Barth has both a corporate and individual answer to this question. In the power of the Spirit Christ's direction brings about the upbuilding of the Christian community and the love of the individual Christian. Defending this order, Barth points out that although loves makes an individual Christian, this takes place only in the context of the community and its upbuilding (614ff.).

Barth opens his discussion of this upbuilding with a subsection on the true church. In the time between Christ's resurrection and return the church, while a human work, is always first the result of the divine upbuilding. To be seen in its truth it must be seen, not in isolated abstraction, but in this relation to God's work. Its reality and visibility as the true church are those of grace (616ff.).

As the true church in this sense, the community is no end in itself. It has the goal of being a provisional representation *de facto* of the *de iure* sanctification of humanity in Jesus Christ. God gives it this goal and God equips it in order to achieve this goal (cf. Ephesians 4:12–15) (623–626). This equipment is for its upbuilding or edification, to use the New Testament term which embraces corporate as well as individual upbuilding (626ff.). God does this building through Jesus Christ and in the power of the Spirit ("I will build my church," Matthew 16:18). Jesus Christ embraces the community, so that it, too, has a role in its upbuilding (632ff.). Upbuilding means integration in mutual love with the specific work of common worship at the center (635–641).

A first and obvious aspect of upbuilding is growth. Dealing with this in the second subsection, Barth equates upbuilding with communion as an action in which many people, on the basis of union, engage in common movement toward this union. The communion at issue is that of the saints but also a communion in holy things: relations, gifts, tasks, and functions (641–643). Upbuilding in this communion means growth, a complementary metaphor from the organic world. Growth implies extension externally and intensification internally (645–647). Internal growth is for Barth the true secret, but it carries with it external growth, not as an end, but as a by-product

(648ff.). Growth is not just a matter of human planning, effort, and direction. Its power is that of the community living as the holy communion. More accurately, it is the power of Jesus as that of the life immanent and acting within it in and by the Holy Spirit (650f.). Exalted at God's right hand, Jesus acts by remote power; however, working by the Holy Spirit he acts also by immanent power (652). Jesus creates and rules the community on earth as his earthly historical form of existence (653). He is self-attested in the Holy Spirit, so that even in its growth as a human operation the church sees itself only in relation to him as the being of the church and also of the kingdom, which, even if the church is not the kingdom, is itself the church (655f.). At the end of the subsection, Barth surveys the relation of Christ and the kingdom, suggesting that Christ is the kingdom in person to whom, as to its head, the church is to grow (651–660).

Upholding forms an important aspect of upbuilding. Barth examines this in the third subsection. Having its life and strength in Christ, the community is preserved in spite of its weakness (660f.). It needs protection, for, as a human society, it faces outer and inner danger (661f.). The outer danger consists of the pressure that the world exerts to check or destroy it by restriction, domestication, or the supreme intolerance of tolerant indifference (662–665). The inner danger consists of impatience with grace and the desire to grow like any other society. This can take the two forms of alienation by secularization and self-glorification by sacralization (667–670). On its own the church has no defence against these dangers. It must look to God for help. When it does, it is indestructible. It is upheld, according to the promise of Matthew 16, because scripture remains as God's living Word and Christ remains as its living content (670–676). Confident in Christ, the church has no real or possible need for concern or despair concerning its upholding (676).

The fourth and last subsection deals with the order of the community. Upbuilding has to be orderly. It thus poses a need for right or law, for example, in worship, work, discipline, and church relations (676–678). Since the community is as Christ is, being the body of which he is head, the only possible basis of its order is christological. Barth criticizes Sohm and Brunner for their failure to see this (679f.). A christologico-ecclesiological view of the church implies (1) that its nature as a brotherly christocracy, in which Christ commands and the community obeys, imposes order on the church (here again Sohm and Brunner miss the point with their opposition to church law) (680f.); (2) that this is a unique order, since Jesus Christ, as the acting subject, gives his community living and spiritual law, that is, law established and administered in the fellowship of the Holy Spirit (681f.). The voice of this acting subject is heard in holy scripture, so that to listen to him the church must listen to scripture, and scripture must have a normative role in relation to its law. In this connection Barth addresses five searching questions to Brunner, whose *Misunderstanding of the Church* he thinks to be very aptly named (684–686).

Before characterizing the church's christological law, Barth interposes a short discussion of secular approaches to the church. The world views the church as merely one sociological construct among others. While the church cannot stop this, it must certainly resist it. A real difficulty arises in the relation of the church to the state, to which the church accords particular theological significance. The state may well give the church a defined station, but the church cannot afford to let itself be secularized by the law of church and state. It must always maintain its ultimate freedom under the rule of Christ (686–689).

In the rest of the subsection Barth expounds four presuppositions of christological church law. This law is (1) ministering, (2) liturgical, (3) living, and (4) exemplary.

(1) As ministering law, church law may be defined in three ways. First, it is unequivocal and irreversible; service cannot become a reason for dignities, claims, or privileges. Second, it it total; it applies to every sphere and activity. Third, it is universal; it embraces all Christians in all functions, with no discharge or leave of absence (690–695).

(2) As liturgical law, church law has its seat in worship, in the order of divine service, which expresses the church's existence as history or event, not just as institution or establishment. Barth again sees three aspects. First, church law is ordered by divine service, common confession, trust, edification, and prayer. Second, it is found in divine service, in which Christ's lordship, according to the normative witness of scripture, is discerned in the fourfold occurrence of confession, baptism, the Lord's supper, and prayer. Third, it has its proper theme in divine service and therefore has the task of securing and protecting this by truly ordering it in obedient regard for ordering by the Lord according to scripture's witness (695–710).

(3) As living law, church law has a dynamic, not a fixed and static quality. This, too, may be seen in three features. First, it is open law, open to investigation and instruction, ready for new answers. Second, it is law engaged in constant transition from the worse to the better. Third, it is tolerant but not relativistic law, which can respect even if it does not accept different forms in different times and churches, assuming that here, too, the living voice of the living Lord has been sought and heard so that the chance of authentic ecumenical encounter arises (710–719).

214 / The Doctrine of Reconciliation

(4) As exemplary law, church law, for all its particularity, bears outward responsibility as an indirect pattern for all law. Again three aspects are noted. First, the purpose will be that of witness to the gospel. Second, the basis will be the analogy between secular and ecclesiastical law. Third, the possibility will be that of helping to improve secular law. Church law certainly cannot set up God's kingdom on earth. God himself has done this. Nevertheless, it can give a provisional representation of God's law and thereby exert a corrective influence. "In this way it will show that its law is true law, a law which on the basis of the Gospel proclaims the Gospel" (719–726).

5. The Holy Spirit and Christian Love (§68)

What does the sanctification effected in Jesus Christ mean for the individual Christian? In his answer to this question Barth turns again to the three things that abide according to 1 Corinthians 13, and this time to love. In four subsections he examines Christian love under the headings of the problem, the basis, the act, and the manner of love.

Looking at the problem, Barth considers first the relation between faith and love. In the power of the Spirit faith can be called the living and active reception of God's work in Christ. From this angle being a Christian consists wholly of the act of faith. But not exclusively! In answer to our exaltation in the Son of Man, there is, in the power of the same Spirit, a second and related act of self-giving in confirmation of what is received in faith. This act of self-giving is Christian love— faith and love being two inseparable but distinguishable moments in the one movement that constitutes Christian existence (728–731).

Love as self-giving entails a specific relation to others. It is self-giving to and for them (733). It thus differs from forms of love that have a possessive character involving self-love (734f.). These forms find a representative in eros, the self-giving form in agape. Barth expands here his earlier comparison and contrast of the two. He begins with a biblical differentiation (736–740). He then takes seven important steps in development of the antithesis. (1) Both relate to man. (2) Both determine his nature. (3) Both express his nature. (4) Both express the same man. (5) Agape corresponds to his nature, eros contradicts it. (6) Agape accepts God as man's eternal counterpart, eros closes itself off from him. (7) Agape respects fellow-humanity in the I-Thou encounter, eros rejects it (736–746). This development of the antithesis clarifies Christian love, but Christian love exists in and not by the antithesis, as Barth shrewdly observes (746f.). Coming from God, agape excels eros in dignity and power. Hence a conciliatory word may be ventured. God loves erotic man. Hence erotic man, although not his erotic love, is to be affirmed in and with agapic love. God seeks to bring erotic man to his true self by releasing him from self-seeking in agapic self-giving. In this self-giving, eros is made superfluous and pointless. That self-finding lies in self-giving is the declaration of those who love as Christians to those who do not (748–751).

What about the basis of Christian love? Barth points out in the next subsection that the basis of love corresponds to the object of faith. We believe "in," we love "because." Because of what? Because of God's prior love (751f.). If our love is a free action, it is neither primary nor without basis (752f.). God's love comes first as grace and forms the basis of our love as gratitude (754f.). To say God's love is to say first the inner love which is his essential being: "God is" and "God loves" are synonymous (755), for "God is love" (756f.). It is also to say that the love of the God who is love for us is revealed in the covenant according to the understanding of the Old Testament (761–764) and the New (764–766). This covenant love is to be defined in three ways as (1) electing love (766–771), (2) purifying love (771–776), and (3) creative love, initiating love in the loved (776–783).

The Christian love based on God's love has an active quality. The theme of the third subsection, then, is this active love—what the Christian does. As Barth states, he does what he has the freedom to do as one who is loved by God: he loves (783). This act is (1) highly unusual. It is also (2) free, not just an extension of God's love, but an act of the human will in the full sense (785f.). It has (3) the character of an impartation, a giving of energy and time, but supremely of the self (786). It means (4) exaltation and joy for those who love, not as a goal, but as a necessary and confirmatory by-product.

But what precisely is this activity? First it is love for God, or Jesus. It is so as a response and correspondence that are not without their own mystery and miracle of freedom (789ff.). It implies an interest in God, a constraining interest comprising trust and obedience (793–795). Against the idea of, for example, Kant and Ritschl, that direct love of God may be eliminated, and in spite of the fact that in practice love of God means love of neighbor, Barth argues that scripture teaches direct love of God, that the story of the anointing illustrates it, and that if this source dries up the stream of neighborly love will dry up as well (795–797). Notwithstanding the dangers of enthusiasm, we do better to follow the older mystics, pietists, and hymn writers in this regard (797).

Second, the act of Christian love is the love for neighbor springing out of love for God. Already in I,2 Barth gave an unusual account of this, and again he adopts an unorthodox approach. Asking who the neighbor is, he argues that in scripture no general love for humanity is taught, for love needs proximity. Instead, what is taught is a specific love for neighbors and enemies in salvation history (802ff.). Yet this does not mean exclusiveness, for no line is drawn between those who are and those who are not to be loved, as the stories of Rahab and Ruth show (807f.).

With this clarification, Barth asks why love for God should demand love for neighbor. Salvation history, as the history between God and man, is also the history between man and man. Those with whom God has his history are brought together in it in a relation of mutual love. Liberation for God carries with it liberation for others (809ff.). But why? Barth finds the simple answer to this question in the word "witness." The neighbor is a witness to me and I to him.

Barth develops this concept in the rest of the subsection. Neighborly love bears active testimony to God's own love as a reality (812f.). Christians cannot be such without giving this witness. As God's children, loved by him, and loving him in return, they are set under this law of their common life and mission (814). Witness to God's love is not, of course, identical with it but it expresses and reflects it (815f.). The great realities of grace and the work of the Spirit do not render it superfluous, for grace demands brotherly love and the Spirit gives freedom for it (817f.). What this witness requires, in reflection of God's love, is a standing surety, or accepting of responsibility for the other in the form of self-interposition on his behalf as a pledge of God's love and the freedom to love God (819f.). But who can do this? The man Jesus has done it, fulfilling the law, performing the act of love in both its dimensions. In him, however weak and imperfect, we can also do it. As he is the great witness, we can be little witnesses representing him. In his discipleship, looking to what he has done and doing likewise, we can achieve, in great and little acts, genuine actualizations of love (821–824).

Barth devotes his fourth and last subsection to what he calls the manner of Christian love—the manner in which it determines life in the community, the manner in which community life is lived under its determination, and the manner of the promise that is peculiar to this life. Basing his thinking on 1 Corinthians 13 he is thus led to a meditation on what he takes to be the three dominant themes of the chapter: (1) that love alone counts, (2) that love alone conquers, and (3) that love alone endures.

By way of introduction Barth outlines the situation in which Paul is writing. The Holy Spirit gives the life and gifts underlying individual life in the community. Those in whom he works are human and sinful.

They treat the Spirit's riches as an endowment which they can claim and play off against the endowments of others. They use the gifts for themselves and not for the common good. They thus dissolve the community, changing its life into that of a religious society. In this situation, what reality must characterize action under the Holy Spirit as authentically Christian? Paul answers this question in the hymn to love in chapter thirteen which he interposes between the discussion of gifts in chapters twelve and fourteen (826–828).

(1) *Love alone counts* No matter how great and varied and important spiritual gifts may be, these are not in themselves the relation of the community and its members to the living Lord. Whether what takes place in them is real is decided not merely by derivation from the Holy Spirit and dependence on him, but by life in the Holy Spirit in the discipleship of Jesus Christ. This is the true reality without which even the most imposing achievements cannot be called truly Christian. It is the decisive reality of love (828f.). The biblical foundation may be found in 1 Corinthians 13:1–3 (829–831).

(2) *Love alone conquers* As the action of love, human action overcomes all the powerful forces that resist the fulfilment of love as self-giving. It thus reflects the resurrection of Jesus and prefigures the general resurrection. It witnesses to the existence of the royal man in whom it has its source. It "serves to promote the edification of the community and its equipment for its mission in the world" (831f.). Support for this may be found in 1 Corinthians 13:4–7 (832–835).

(3) *Love alone endures* Only in the form of love does Christian action have indestructible content and certain continuance, that is, participation in the life of God. Gifts are for ministry on the journey toward the future of the final manifestation of God's dominion in Jesus Christ. Love is the continuing form in which this ministry will outlast the time of pilgrimage. Faith and hope endure also, but only, Barth thinks, because they are themselves the act of love, or because love is the form of the life-act accomplished in them. Love alone retains the form it has now. "It is . . . the promise already fulfilled in the present," the future eternal life shining in the present. It therefore needs no change of form (837f.). This is the teaching of 1 Corinthians 13:8–13 (837–840).

CHAPTER XVI
The God-Man

1. The Glory of the Mediator (§69)

IN chapter thirteen Barth proposed to work out the doctrine of reconciliation in three parallel sequences. He has completed two of these, the former dealing with the Son of God, the Lord as Servant, fulfilling the priestly work, the other with the Son of Man, the Servant as Lord, fulfilling the kingly work. He now takes up the third: the God-Man, the true Witness, fulfilling the prophetic work. Following the pattern of the two previous chapters, he divides his material into five sections: the glory of the Mediator, man's falsehood and condemnation, vocation, the Holy Spirit and the sending of the community, and the Holy Spirit and Christian hope. In this case he has too much to say for a single book, so he divides the part-volume (IV,3) into two halves with §§69 and 70 in the first half and §§71–73 in the second. Since the division is artificial, the table of contents covers both halves and the indexes for both halves come together at the end of the second half.

The first section on the glory of the Mediator (§69) is extremely long (IV,3, 3–366) and consists of four subsections. The first serves as a link and deals formally with the third problem of the doctrine. The next two depict Jesus Christ successively as the light of life and as victor. The fourth plays the same transitional role as the parallels in IV,1 and IV,2 on the verdict of the Father and the direction of the Son. It bears the title "The Promise of the Spirit."

The so-called third problem arises because of the difference between the priestly and kingly offices on the one side and the prophetic office on the other. The first two sequences deal with the two aspects of the material work and it might seem that no more is needed. What remains, however, is the revelation of the material work, which, as Barth understands it, occurs in and with reconciliation and is still the work of Jesus Christ, this time as prophet (3–8). In this connection expositions are given of John 1:4, 1 Timothy 2:6, 2 Corinthians 1:20, and the Amen sayings in John (11f.). These rightly led the early church to the discerning of a third office which is worked into the threefold scheme in Roman Catholic, Lutheran, and Reformed theology (13–15).

Barth finds five difficulties, uncertainties, or limitations in the traditional formulation, but he does not regard these as fatal and thus is prepared to attempt a reconstruction. He closes the subsection with an analysis of post-reformation church movements of retreat but more particularly of advance, that is, in the six areas of emphasis on the Word, missions, evangelism, biblical study, lay action, and ecumenism. These have all helped us to restore the doctrine of the prophetic office (18–38).

As reconciliation, revelation is also accomplished in Jesus Christ. Barth takes up this theme in the second subsection on the light of life (38f.). The first point is a simple one: Jesus lives. He lives as God and man (39f.). His life is act or self-actualization (40f.), and is thus personal. It is also life for us (41f.). He lives as the subject of salvation history, the Lord as Servant and the Servant as Lord (42f.).

Barth offers three preliminary explanations at this point. (1) From scripture we learn about this living Jesus Christ. (2) We say that he not only has lived and will live but also lives now. (3) We say that he lives in the confession of faith.

Descriptions of this life of Jesus Christ follow. It shines out radiantly—this is the glory of the Mediator. It is life under a name. As history, it manifests itself. It thus brings its own incontestable verification. In its combination of words and acts it is Logos, the Word of life and therefore the light of life, embracing both the glory of God and also the glorifying of man by God (47).

At four points, Barth suggests, the prophecy of the life of Jesus transcends Old Testament prophecy. (1) Jesus is himself the Word he speaks. (2) He addresses all people. (3) He speaks of the fulfilled covenant. (4) As prophet he is also Mediator (49–52). Nevertheless, if Israel's whole history is prophecy, this does in a sense compare with the prophecy of Jesus at the four points listed (52–65). It may thus be called the pre-history of his prophecy, the fore-word to his Word. When he comes, he sums it up as the one prophet with whom the witnesses of both Old and New Testament are concerned (66–71).

Is all this just a value-judgment? Do we ourselves "ascribe" to

Jesus his titles as light, truth, revelation, glory? No, says Barth, for what competence have we even to ask whether Jesus is these things? The point is rather that we ourselves are asked whether we are those to whom he has shown himself as light and truth. The question is asked: Are we of the truth? If we can answer positively, we confess the reality (72–76). Far from asking for authentication, we are asked for our own authentication which we give by true and obedient life, and more specifically by true and obedient thought and speech (77–79). The reality of Jesus as light and life is self-authenticated because in him we have to do with (1) God's own presence and action, (2) God's gracious covenant addressed to man, and (3) the fellowship of one who even as a stranger is our fellow and neighbor (79–83).

When Jesus is called the light, the definite article expresses exclusiveness; he is the one and only light just as his life is the one and only life. This is a difficult saying that the church has always been tempted to relativize and soften in view of the charges of arbitrariness, presumption, and obscurantism that are brought against it. Nevertheless, it has to be upheld. Christian freedom is freedom for the confession of Jesus Christ as the one prophet on the basis of Jesus Christ as the object of the confession and the biblical witness to him (86–95; biblical references, 93–95).

Made on this basis and according to this witness, the statement (1) is a christological one, referring to Jesus Christ alone, not to scripture, or to church life or teaching apart from him. Thus, although other lights and words exist in scripture and the church, and even outside them, none of these can challenge, supplement, or replace Christ as the one light and Word (96–99). The statement (2) describes Jesus as the full, total, and definitive Word of God, whose prophecy can be rivalled by no other, combined with no other, and transcended by no other (99–103). It can be ventured (3) only because he shows himself to be the unique Word with this unique content (103–110). It allows us (4) to call other words true, particularly those of scripture and the church, but only (a) as they conform to the one Word, (b) recognize their distinction from it, and (c) have the acknowledgment of the one Word. The New Testament parables serve as prototypes of words of this kind (110ff.).

That there are these other lights and words in scripture and the community raises no difficulty, but can we really say that true words and lights are found outside as well? In a long discussion Barth concludes that on the basis of Jesus' work for the world we should indeed expect them, not as the results of natural theology, but as attestations of the divine self-impartation that are accredited by their agreement with the biblical witness accepted in the church (114ff.). They may even be found in pure secularism (more often in mixed secularism), but they are no more than attestations (118ff.) and must always be tested by the criteria of scripture, the church's confession, their fruits, and their significance for the community (125–130).

How, then, is the church to receive these "free communications," as Barth now calls them? It must be neither too receptive nor too resistant. Whereas scripture has a constant and universal authority, free communications come at specific times and in specific situations and will be accepted only by some. Hence they will be extraordinary words with no normative character (130–135).

Before closing the subsection, Barth reconsiders the question of a second and subsidiary line or strand which he considered in II,1. In addition to the statement about Jesus Christ as the one light, another statement has to be made about the light or lights that relate indirectly, not directly, to Jesus Christ. These are the lights or truths or words of creation. Creation, too, speaks to man, and also speaks through him. It is both a text and also its own reader or expositor. What the text speaks of is the constancy, continuity, and rationality of created being in its existence, dynamic, inner contrariety, law, freedom, and depth (135–150). While this second statement differs from the first, it also stands in relation to it. Since creation is God's work, its lights form a luminous sphere for the light of the self-declaration of Jesus Christ, although, as God and creation cannot be equated, neither can the lights of creation and the light of Jesus Christ (150f.). Avoiding both dualism and monism, we must understand that the truth of God institutes and integrates that of the creature because it is binding, total, and final (151–163). For Barth this is the critical but positive relation between the light of life and the lights of creation that God has given us in his eternal goodness. It should be noted that Barth makes what is perhaps his only reference to general or primal revelation in this context. So long as this is distinguished sharply from natural theology, he has no objection to it.

In another long subsection Barth examines the shining of Jesus as the light of life. This shining takes the form of a history in which opposition is faced and overcome (165f.). From this standpoint an apt title for the subsection is, he thinks, the slogan "Jesus is Victor," which the elder Blumhardt took over from the defeated spirit that had plagued his parishioner Gottliebin Dittus (168–171).

The event or history of Jesus as the light of life has a specific direction. It moves on to triumph. This is not the triumph of grace. Barth replies here to Berkouwer's evaluation of his theology under that title (173–180). It is Jesus' own triumph in his prophetic or revelatory work (180–183). In this work Jesus (1) mediates a specific knowledge of himself (183–185, with a discussion of the meaning of knowledge in scripture). In so doing he (2) provokes the opposition of man and the world (185–191, with a discussion of the parable of the sower, 188–191). In his prophecy, then, Jesus (3) impinges on all history (193–196). The opposition, however, does not have the same force or solidity as the prophecy and so Jesus (4) moves on to victory over it (196f.; Paul's conversion serves as a dramatic illustration, 198–211).

Jesus' work as revelation takes historical form as the knowledge established by it. In his prophecy Jesus "creates history, namely, the history enacted in Christian knowledge" (212). (1) This knowledge differs from the event of reconciliation as the *nosce* (knowledge) following the *esse* (reality) (213f.). (2) Yet the two are closely related, for reconciliation implies knowledge as its consequence, and knowledge implies reconciliation as its presupposition (214–216). (3) The knowledge is not neutral, but with its awakening reconciliation takes place as God's work on and in us with the presence and action of Jesus Christ (216–218). (4) Hence knowledge is no mere acceptance, no purely subjective attitude; it is authentic reconciliation as Jesus Christ is present and the whole person is grasped by its object (218–220).

Characterizing Christ's prophetic action as the disclosure of completed revelation, Barth speaks first of its commencement. It begins with a fact, the distinctive, once-for-all fact or history of Jesus Christ (221ff.). This history that occurred then and there is also an ongoing history here and now (223f.), being posited by God in divine freedom as a gift of grace (225–231). Barth finds all the points that he makes here in the fourth Gospel, "the Gospel of the Gospel itself, i.e., of the prophetic work of Jesus Christ" (231–237).

From the commencement of the action Barth turns to its course. This is one of conflict. The light of Christ attacks the darkness of the world. Barth stresses that light, not darkness, has the initiative. The revelation of reconciliation sets the world in a new light. It tells it that it is the reconciled world (239f.). It thus proclaims an altered situation (241f.). It describes as totally outdated the world's own thinking, for example, about its supposed freedom (242f.). It declares the reality (not the illusion) of the new man and the new freedom that Christ has introduced in his vicarious work (246ff.). Resistance arises because the world in unbelief clings to its old reality as though Christ's prophetic revelation were illusion, or, at most, a promised future and not a present fact (249ff.). It continues on its wicked and stupid way (253f.). To the Word of grace it opposes its own world-views, which offer an escape because they involve distance and are panoramic, general, comparative, and accommodating (255ff.). As a last resort it takes refuge in religion, even a form of Christian religion, which imitates Christ's prophecy but evades its true force (258f.). Barth appends here a brief reply to Wingren's criticism that there is "no active power of sin" in his theology (260f.).

Finally a word is said about the conclusion of Christ's victorious prophecy. In a sense there is no conclusion. The conflict goes on and Christ will speak the last Word at his coming. Nevertheless, the prophetic Word carries with it certainty of victory, not because it is a word of progress, or of the church, or of faith, but because it is the Word of Christ (263–265). It will win out by reason of the unconditional superiority of Christ as (1) the Word of God and (2) the Word of the act of God who (3) makes a direct appeal to the real man over and beyond the resisting element, whether this takes the form of a sham church, world-views, or the massive reaction of simple indifference (267–274).

As in the two previous chapters, Barth feels the need for a transition from the work of Christ—this time as prophet—to the work in us who are *de facto* his in faith, knowledge, and service. Where is this movement from christology to anthropology located? Barth takes up this question in the fourth subsection on the promise of the Spirit.

As so often, he opens with a simple point. Jesus makes the transition as the risen Lord manifesting what he was and did (281ff.). This means three things. (1) When we have said all, we still have to count on him (285f.). (2) Our answer has force only when we are astonished that we can give it (286f.). (3) We can and should be sure of our ground in giving it (287ff.).

What does it imply that in the Easter event Jesus Christ has declared himself? It implies the new coming of him who came (291). There is, of course, only one coming again *(parousia)* of Jesus Christ, but this one coming again, Barth thinks, has three forms: the coming at Easter, at Pentecost, and at the end (293f.). Each is distinctive, each eschatological, and each related to the other two in perichoresis (293–296).

What is distinctive about the Easter form of the new coming? (1) It is a once-for-all and irrevocable self-manifestation in which God has committed himself to man (296–301). (2) It is a total, universal, definitive redetermination of man (301–308). (3) It is an authentically and radically new and particular coming from the dead involving "the concrete, visible, audible, tangible presence of the man Jesus" and carrying with it God's eternal life, so that the world is no longer lost but also cannot go on as it is (308–316). In this passage Barth goes out of his way to resist a docetic view of the resurrection, insisting on "the psycho-physical totality of His temporal existence familiar from His first coming" (312). He also stresses the impact of Christ's prophetic self-manifestation in this event. People cannot hear that they are reconciled in him and carry on as usual. They are given a new future and are thus summoned to advance into it (315).

Why does not the new future made present in that event immediately engulf the world and renew it? To this question Barth has three answers. (1) It does, but we do not yet see it (317f.). (2) It does, but only in the first, not the final stage (318ff.). (3) It does, in its visible impact on the church (320). In sum, Jesus Christ is still on the way from the beginning to the end, and we are on the way with him, being given space and time to share and witness (326–332).

Barth is thus led to reflect again on the time between, which he earlier called the time of the community. This is the time of the advance of Jesus' prophecy. It is the time of our human freedom under the conditions of our effected but not yet fully manifested reconciliation (334–337). It is the time of the solidarity of Christians with non-Christians in ignorance and imperfection (340–342) but also the time when Christians see Christ's prophecy in the light of the Easter event (342f.) and live in the tension of movement from the first form of the *parousia* to the last (343). They do so in the dynamic of the teleology of Jesus Christ (343f.) as a public people in virtue of Christ's call and commission (344f.).

Christian life in the time between is not life in a vacuum (346f.). In it Jesus himself is the common hope shining among us here and now, the subject of his Word "at the place where we are on the day which is our day" (348f.). He is fully present and active in the second form of his coming again, that is, the promise of the Spirit (350). The promise of the Spirit denotes two things: (1) that the Spirit promises the coming again of Christ in its final form (351–353); and (2) that the Spirit is promised, that his presence has yet to be fulfilled among certain people (353ff.). This fulfilment occurs as Jesus Christ comes in the second form in and by the Holy Spirit.

Barth feels it necessary to stress that this second form must not be disparaged. He makes three points in this regard. (1) The coming again in the Spirit is no less genuinely the direct and personal coming of Christ (356f.). (2) In this form of his coming he is no less Son of God and Man, the Mediator. (3) His work in this form of his coming is qualitatively no less than in the first and third forms. In relation to our Christian present, then, we need not sigh "because it is no longer the time of Easter and not yet the time of the end, but only the time of the Holy Ghost" (359).

Why does there have to be this time? Partly to give the creature time and space for the expression of freedom, but more specifically that Christ's glory might be manifested in his prophetic work (360f.).

For all the ambiguities of this time for us, we are to praise God for it and to use it for life in hope and in the power of the promise (362). What does life in the power of the promise mean? With the answer to this last question Barth closes the subsection and the section. Life in the power of the promise means supremely (1) that this day of ours is also the day of the living Jesus Christ (362ff.). By implication it thus means (2) that our day is that of mission to non-Christians (364ff.). This means further (3) that our day is the day when we are not just objects of his work but also subjects in his service, placed on a way that may be one of difficulty but is also one of resurrection and glory (366f.).

2. The Falsehood and Condemnation of Man (§70)

As in the previous part-volumes, Barth turns next to the man on whose behalf Jesus Christ does his work. He sees him first as the man of sin exposed by what he has done. In this case the prophetic work of Christ is at issue. In the first subsection, then, Christ is presented as the true witness. In contrast, the man of sin is shown to be guilty of falsehood and this leads to his condemnation. An ongoing exposition of the Book of Job provides the Old Testament illustration.

Full knowledge of sin, Barth reiterates, is gained from a knowledge of Jesus Christ (369f.). In this connection Barth has a brief excursus on Lutheran objections to his supposed confusion of law and gospel (370f.). When Jesus Christ is known as the true witness, sin is unmasked as untruth (371f.). By way of falsehood man tries to evade and obstruct the reality of God, opposing his own word to God's Word (372f.). The truth manifests itself to man but he does not want it, advances his untruth against it, and is thus shown up as a liar.

What is the truth that unmasks him? It is not (1) a mere idea, not even correct doctrine (375f.). Nor is it (2) a directly illuminating and pleasing phenomenon (376–378). It is truth as the true witness himself, the living Jesus Christ present in the promise of the Spirit, the historical person of a specific man.

How is Jesus Christ the true witness? Barth offers in reply to this question a threefold characterization. (1) Jesus Christ is a unique person enjoying an unparalleled relation to God whereby he stands on an equal footing with us and yet may accuse and condemn us (379f.). In this distinctive relation in which God is authentically God and man is authentically man, he lives a life that is given up to God and thus is distinguished by him in an act of freedom on both sides, the reciprocal freedom of coronation and commitment (380–383). The relation between God and Job, particularly at the beginning and end of the book, serves as an illustration.

(2) Jesus Christ as the true witness is also a suffering person. He performs the task of reconciliation in the alien form of the passion (389f.). In his present mission he still works in a dark and difficult sphere (392f.). He is even now with us as the crucified Lord (395f.). Yet as such he is in unity with the Son or Word of God, and vice versa, so that even as the suffering Jesus, victorious in his suffering, he pursues his prophetic task, witnessing to the truth of God's own suffering with us in him. The sufferings and questionings of Job offer a remarkable comment on this aspect.

(3) Jesus Christ as the true witness is finally a speaking person in whom the truth speaks for itself (408f.), even though this speaking be out of the great silence that only God can break (410f.). The Word he speaks is God's Word spoken by him who was crucified, dead, and buried. It is the Word of reconciliation, of the vicarious bearing away of sin in fulfilment of God's will (413–417). He speaks this Word whether he is heard or not (418). If he is heard, it is not in virtue of human possibility but of the work of the Holy Spirit by whom he is present in our time and history as this speaking Subject (419–421). The speeches of God to Job, and Job's response, elucidate this aspect (421–434).

The falsehood unmasked by the true witness forms the theme of the second subsection. As a spiritual phenomenon, falsehood consists of a movement of evasion (434), especially in the form of an apparent espousal of the truth (435–437). Differentiation is thus needed which only God's Word can effect (437–439). It does this by showing up the evasion for what it is at four sensitive points. (1) For all its pretended love of truth the evasion will not accept the identification of truth with Jesus Christ (440f.). (2) It will not accept truth as the Word of the cross (441f.). (3) It will not accept truth as God's Word of grace and pardon to the sinner pledging him to gratitude and obedience (443–446). (4) It will not accept truth as God's free Word that endows us with the true freedom of a free cleaving to the free God and a free following of his free decision (446f.).

Starting back from this truth, the man of sin attempts to establish another kind of truth. He systematizes the event of God's encounter with man and thus brings it under the control of a principle (448). He does away with God's freedom by making him a mere supreme being (448f.). He establishes a false and foolish freedom of man to do as he likes, even to the point of imagining his own god, who may even be a supposedly Christian god served by supposedly Christian man (448–450). A false Christian offers a far more mature and dangerous form of untruth than one who is simply caught in superstition or error.

This is why, Barth thinks, lying has not diminished but, if anything, increased with the coming of Christianity. Becoming a liar in encounter with Jesus Christ, man becomes a liar at every point. The pious lie gives rise to the secular lie as we now see it in every sphere of life and on the grandest possible scale. If ordinary falsehood is to be dealt with, this will not be by moral accusation or exhortation, but by authentic committal to the truth as it meets us in Jesus Christ the true witness (451–453). The three friends of Job are apt examples of men who evade the truth by pious falsehood (453–461).

A brief subsection follows on the condemnation of man. False-hood carries with it implicit condemnation, for it puts the sinner under the threat of being nailed to his lie (462). The truth to which Jesus Christ bears witness is that in him we are reconciled to God. We start back from this. We refuse the offered pardon. We treat the truth as untruth (462–464). Naturally we cannot change the truth into untruth but in calling it untruth we set ourselves in the shadow of the sinner who is dead in Jesus Christ, in other words, of damnation (464f.). Fortunately the condemnation has not yet fallen. God still gives time. But there is no guarantee that the threat will not finally be executed (465f.).

Barth sees a need for distinction here. Many people have not even heard the truth. They are in "the lost and false situation of living as though Jesus Christ did not exist." Others have heard the truth and disregarded it. These, too, are in a lost and false situation but by their own falsehood (466). With it they do harm to others as Jonah did (468). Most of all they do harm to themselves. Falsehood twists the whole being (468). It gives a false image of reality with no center or periphery. It rules out coexistence with others and with the cosmos. It involves an ongoing disintegration of the person (470–473). Yet, as Barth insists again, it cannot overthrow the truth. The truth attacks it (474f.). God's reality opposes its pseudo-reality. Hence even under the threat of condemnation the unexpected work of revelation and grace may be known.

Barth concludes with a typically ambivalent statement on universalism. The threat of condemnation might finally be withdrawn. If it is, this is not due to any logical necessity but solely to God's free and gracious gift. We may not count on this even though we hope for it. On the other hand, Barth thinks, there is no reason not to hope for it. The reality which limits the situation points in its direction. Recognizing that we have no claim, we should cautiously hope and pray for it.

3. The Vocation of Man (§71)

As the man of pride is replaced by justified man, and the man of sloth by sanctified man, so the man of falsehood is replaced by called man. Vocation in the theological sense corresponds at this point to justification and sanctification in chapters fourteen and fifteen. Barth looks at six aspects of it in six subsections of the long section (§71) devoted to the theme.

He begins with a discussion of "Man in the Light of Life." In this light the sinner is seen to be foreordained for divine calling, that is, for institution into Christ's fellowship and his people's service (482f.).

Calling implies distinction. Not all are called. Naturally, vocation is not based on the self. It is based on God's election (484f.). Christians are called because they are elect. This basis in election means basis in the work of Jesus Christ in history by which all people are set in the light of life in the realistic biblical "universalism" that forms the presupposition of calling (485–490). Not by inherent capacity but by divine ordination fulfilled in Jesus Christ every human heart has a predisposition to respond to the call of God by the Holy Spirit (491). This does not exclude specific calling but protects it against any appearance of accident or caprice by grounding it solidly in the reconciliation effected by Jesus Christ as priest and king.

Barth shows the practical relevance of this under three heads. (1) If not all are called, but all are oriented to calling, Christians must be open to all and avoid premature differentiation of the called and the uncalled (493f.). (2) If vocation is the universal *telos,* Christians should address all people on their responsibility to him who calls them (494–496). (3) If vocation is the determined future of all, Christians must understand themselves as the called only in the light of the prophetic as well as the priestly and kingly ministry of Jesus Christ (496f.).

Having examined the basis, Barth discusses next the event of vocation. His first point in this second subsection is that the event as such, in the form of conversion, must not become an independent focus of attention apart from election and reconciliation. Nevertheless, it does take place in specific histories outside the time of Israel and Christ (497–500). As such an event, vocation is historical (500f.), spiritual or "pneumatic" (501f.), and personal: the call of Christ in the power of the Spirit (502f.). Within the one total process of vocation many things happen: illumination, conversion, new birth, and renewal. Some theologians have tried to arrange these in an order of salvation *(ordo salutis)* but with only partial success (505f.). Barth thinks the process can be comprehensively described as illumination (508f.), new creation (509f.), and awakening (510–514; on awakenings, 513f.). He concludes the subsection with a consideration of the traditional distinctions between direct and indirect vocation, external and internal, once-for-all and continuous (515–518). He regards these as valid so long as vocation is understood as the work of Jesus in his prophetic ministry (518–520).

What is the goal of vocation? In the third subsection Barth argues strongly that the goal is simply to be a Christian (521)—only a secularized Christianity fails to see this—and not to be a particular kind of Christian, that is, a monk, or minister.

But what does being a Christian mean? Generally Barth defines Christians as those who, in a special way, belong to Jesus Christ, not in mere continuity with the situation determined by him, nor in his adoption as a symbol, but in confession of him as Lord through the freeing power of the Word (526–530). This belonging to Christ within the general union of humanity to him involves divine sonship in the fellowship of discipleship and obedience to his call (534–536). Vocation is effective, not because it constrains, but because it liberates from self-ownership for the fellowship in which Christ is Lord (536–538).

Fellowship, however, is too broad a term. Perfect fellowship means union with Christ—a concept Barth has not previously developed—as the true goal of vocation (540ff.). Union with Christ is to be understood primarily as his uniting of himself with us (he in us) (541ff.). In the reality and power of this union Christians then unite themselves with Christ (we in him) (543ff.). In this union Christ speaks, acts, and rules as Lord, and Christians gratefully accept this speaking, acting, and ruling. As the goal, the union is not, of course, something toward which we strive. It is that which makes us Christians. Since the goal of vocation is Christianity as attachment, fellowship, and discipleship, we become and are Christians as Christ unites himself with us and we with him. Barth quotes John and Paul to back his presentation (543–547) and in development of the topic he offers a critical analysis of the contributions of Luther, Calvin, and Reformed theology.

The fourth subsection is an important one for Barth, for in it he works out the content of the goal of vocation from the standpoint of the Christian witness. What is the new structure of the Christian life as one of union with Christ? First, it is a life in the eschatological tension of being in the world as though it were already past (557). But while this is true—we cannot contradict Paul—Christian distinctiveness is also that of the new ethos of obedience to Christ (558–561). Behind this lie the new and special characteristics of the Christian: illumination, conversion, peace, and freedom (561–563). Even these, however, cannot be the final answer. To these things there might be secular parallels or they might depend on our own awareness or sense of assurance (564–566). Materially, too, a discordant note of self-interest can be struck when the blessings of the gospel, real though they are, are regarded as the essence of life in union with Christ (566–568). Pious egocentricity, both individual and collective, always couches at the door (568–571).

What, then, is the alternative? Scripture supplies the answer with its clear indication that vocation is not just to salvation but also to service, to the task of witnessing to others (571ff.), to serving God by serving the world (576). The prophetic callings of the Old Testament and the calling of the disciples and Paul in the New offer ample illustration (577–592).

The primary answer in scripture is confirmed by a second answer, the implication of union with Christ as vocation's goal. For union with Christ does not just mean enjoying his benefits. If it did, it would be only a means and Christians would not be oriented to Christ (595ff.). While his benefits are certainly enjoyed, union with him means union with him in his work, commitment to his cause, cooperation with him in his ministry (597–603), not, of course, in its priestly or kingly form, but in its prophetic form as the ministry of God's Word (603–606). Christ does not need our cooperation but he associates us with him in his ministry in demonstration of his grace and mercy and in the form of an accompanying and confirmatory sign consisting of the witnessing act of our whole existence (607–610). Barth appends a discussion of the terms used by Paul in Romans 1:1 and of the New Testament use of the word for witness (610–614).

If witness is one distinctive mark of Christian life in union with Christ, affliction is another. Looking at this in the fifth subsection, Barth characterizes it as the pressure which, as a secondary determination, arises out of witness (614–616). In some form this pressure unavoidably comes on all Christians (618f.).

How does it arise out of witness? Barth answers this question in three ways. (1) As Christians bear witness, the world and its situation bring pressure on them (620–625). (2) As Christians are under constraint to witness, they bring pressure on themselves and they cannot evade this by flight, by softening the message, or by seeking worldly strength (626–633). (3) Since the world is what it is, and Christians are what they are, in virtue of who Christ is and what he has done, Christ brings pressure on Christians as he who was afflicted, who is still afflicted in his people, and in and with whom his people are afflicted (634–640).

Although unpleasant, affliction has a bright background and Barth closes the subsection with six positive theses. (1) Affliction is for us a good, since in it we are at God's side and he at ours (641). (2) It arises in the warfare of Christ which has the Easter assurance of triumph (641f.). (3) It takes place in a forward movement toward the definitive revelation of reconciliation in Christ (642f.). (4) It is accompanied by provisional fulfilments anticipating and indicating the great and comprehensive fulfilment (643f.). (5) It cannot remove or destroy the security of the life that is hid with Christ in God (644–646). (6) It is imperiously demanded in the fulfilment of the task imposed by the gift of fellowship with Christ (646). Barth appends a brief note on perseverance as the essential content of the Christian attitude in affliction (647).

The last subsection deals with the personal aspect of being a Christian. This must be neither ignored nor overemphasized. It accompanies the ministry of witness which makes us Christians. Barth calls it the liberation of the Christian.

From the personal standpoint vocation means liberation to see Christ's self-revelation with a view to witnessing to it (649f.). More intimately this entails a distinction and alteration of the being of the called (650). The alteration does not take place for its own sake. It has an outward reference to God and neighbor. The self loses itself in self-rotation. Finding self occurs as a by-product when serving God and neighbor becomes the first and only concern (652ff.). The blessings enjoyed by the Christian play an important part in the witness he bears, for without them, as in dead orthodoxy, the witness lacks truth (655–657).

In this light Barth finds Christian liberation indispensable for three reasons. (1) It brings out the facticity of the light of God's act and revelation in Jesus Christ (658f.). (2) It conveys the urgency of the need to respond to this light (659f.). (3) It presents and confirms the self-witness of Christ to what God has done in him and to the liberation whereby we can accept it (660–662).

The concrete implications of liberation are listed next. Since the state of grace is no static thing but a movement with Christ, liberation means transition. This transition may be described as (1) a pulling out of solitariness into fellowship (664), (2) a transferring from the sea to the rock (665f.), (3) a movement out of the realm of things into that of people (666f.), (4) a shift from desiring and demanding to receiving (667ff.), (5) a deliverance from indecision, for action (669f.), (6) a replacing of the rule of the moral by that of forgiveness and gratitude (670f.), and (7) a release from anxiety, for prayer (671f.).

By way of emphasis and confirmation Barth adds four further points. (1) Liberation is an ongoing event, never complete in this life (673f.). (2) It has exemplary significance, anticipating both its own completion and also the final general liberation purposed in what God has done and revealed in Jesus Christ (674f.). (3) It is an indispensable presupposition of the ministry, although not the content of witness

(676f.). (4) It raises the pressing and critical question of personal liberation, although only in the context of the even more urgent question of vocation to discipleship and the service of witness (677–680).

4. The Holy Spirit and the Sending of the Christian Community (§72)

In accordance with the general plan of Volume IV, the impact of vocation on the community forms the next topic of the chapter. As justification means the church's calling and sanctification its upbuilding, vocation means its sending. Barth deals with this in four subsections, a more general one on God's people in world occurrence, a transitional one on the community for the world, and two more specific ones on the task and ministry of the community.

Clesis means *ecclesia;* calling means church. The church is the company of the called (681f.). The church, however, is in world history, of which Jesus is Lord (684ff.). Three questions are thus raised: What is world history? How does the people of God see itself in it? How does it live and persist in it?

(1) What is world history? World history is a very different history. The world is plunging to ruin in its contradiction of God and yet it is upheld by God in his overruling providence (cf. III,3). This is demonstrated by the role of the Old Testament nations in their coexistence with Israel (687–693). World history presents a picture of human confusion and divine providence (693–696). We are not to interpret this in terms of a relativizing of the one by the other (696–700) nor of a dialectic of thesis and antithesis leading to synthesis (701–705). We are to interpret it in terms of the grace of God addressed to the world in Jesus Christ (706ff.) as the new thing or person that is the hidden reality of world history (710ff.), visible now in signs (714f.), known in faith, and to be fully manifested at the *parousia* (715f.). Seeing world history in this light, God's people may confidently and resolutely follow the divine decision concerning it in hope (716–721).

(2) But how does the people of God see itself in world history? It sees itself as the people that knows the new and true reality of this history (721f.). By essence it is, phenomenologically, a visible entity and yet by essence it also is a unique and invisible entity pressing for visibility (722ff.). In this sense it corresponds to Jesus Christ in his incarnation, although only by confusion can one call it an extension of the incarnation (728f.). Its uniqueness lies in its election and calling by Jesus Christ to be with him and to share in his self-declaration. The people that understands itself thus is the one people of God in both the Old Testament and the New (730–734).

The visibility and invisibility of this people entail two things. (a) The first is its total dependence on its environment and yet also its total freedom from it (734–742). Barth illustrates this in the two spheres of speech (735–739) and sociological structure (739–742). (b) The second is its total weakness in relation to world occurrence and yet also its total strength (742–751). Questions of place (742–746), work (747), and success (747ff.) arise in this regard. In the last analysis, God's people lies under no ultimate pressure because the results of its work are in God's hand and its only concern is responsible obedience. Here is the secret of its strength (750f.).

(3) How, finally, does God's people live and persist in world history? In general it does so in virtue of its ontic and noetic basis in Jesus Christ and the Holy Spirit (751f.). This general answer may be subdivided into its christological and pneumatological components, which cannot be separated, but each of which elucidates the other.

(a) Christologically, the community called into existence by Jesus Christ in the power of the Holy Spirit, exists as Jesus Christ exists (752f.). It is a predicate, dimension, and form of existence of his being (754). Primarily he exists alone, he alone being the eternal Son. Secondarily he exists as the one he is with his community (and thirdly perhaps with all creation, 754–756). Hence the community exists as the Head is not without his body but is also with his body, the community being the body of the heavenly Head (757f.).

(b) Pneumatologically, the community called into existence by Jesus Christ in the power of the Holy Spirit, exists as the Holy Spirit puts forth the creative power of God whereby the community exists as Jesus Christ exists (758ff.). The Holy Spirit is the power, and his action the work of the coordinating of the being of Christ and the distinct but included being of his people. The Holy Spirit holds together God's working on the one side and man's on the other, so that God's creative freedom finds an equivalent in human freedom and Jesus Christ, preceding his people, is received and reflected in it. By the action of the Holy Spirit the Head lives in and with the body and the body in and with the Head, so that God's people lives and persists as his witness in world occurrence.

The community is for the world—this is the theme of the second subsection. The community is for the world because it is for God (762ff.). Barth even finds a gap in reformation teaching here. Christ's sending of the disciples offers a basis for his own view (768f.). The essential elements in this being for the world are as follows. (1) To members of the community it is given to know the world and people as they really are, that is, as God sees them. Here is a sign or note by which the true community may be infallibly known (771f.). (2) To members of the community it is given to know and practice exemplary solidarity with the world and people (772–776). (3) To members of the community it is given to be under obligation to the world and people, to come under responsibility for them and their welfare (776–780).

Three elucidations are needed in relation to these statements. (1) It must be stressed that all these things—the knowledge, solidarity, and obligation—are given to the community. (2) It should not be missed, however, that they are given to its members and not to a collective automatically including the members; hence the members must receive and practice what is given (780–783). The question of distinctions among members arises in this connection (783–785).

A basis is also needed for the statements. That the church is for the world is said in faith. We thus believe the church when we believe in Jesus Christ (784–786). This knowledge of the reality of the church in faith implies four things. (1) The church knows it has its origin in God's power through the speaking of the Word in the mighty operation of the Spirit (786f.). (2) It knows that what it can do involves confessing Jesus Christ as God acting in and for the world and revealing himself to it (787–790). (3) It knows its confession of Jesus Christ can be only a free but obedient response to Christ's confession of it, he being the primary and proper subject acting in and with it (790–792). (4) It knows itself only as a likeness or reflection of Christ, a provisional and imperfect representation of his prophecy with a prophetic character of its own, so that it cannot possibly be for itself but has to be for the world as is the prophecy of Christ (792–795).

In the third subsection Barth examines the task of the community in its being for the world. Three questions arise: What is the content of this task? To whom is it directed? What about its purity?

(1) The answer to the question of the content of the task lies in Jesus Christ as the great Yes of God. The community is to confess Jesus Christ, his person, work, name, and prophetic Word. It is to confess him as God with man and for him. Confessing him in his affirmation of man, it finds in man, too, the content of its task, man as the one on whom God has set value in spite of his intrinsic lack of value. In short, the gospel is the content of the task (796–801).

(2) As regards the recipient, the answer lies in man, but in man only as seen from the standpoint of the gospel. It lies, then, in man in terms of God's will and work for him and not of his own ignorance and revolt. This man whom the community addresses in fulfilment of its task undoubtedly suffers from self-misunderstanding and self-contradiction. Nevertheless, he is a designated Christian, a Christian in hope. As such he is the target of the church's task (801–812).

(3) The question of the purity of the task relates to both content

and recipient. (a) Purity is achieved in content when the gospel is seen and proclaimed as both the living Word of the living Lord—a call—and also as the one Word of the one Lord—the unchanging and always relevant truth of God not shackled by our presuppositions or manipulated as though it were a dumb object (812–824). (b) Purity is achieved in relation to the recipient when he is not neglected, when the community does not break solidarity with him or commitment to him, but when it also does not patronize him, manipulate him, propagandize him, or impose itself upon him (824–830). "If the community may serve the Word [of Jesus Christ], then it can only try to serve and not to control the world" (830).

Coming finally to the ministry of the community, Barth opens the fourth subsection by characterizing this ministry as definite, limited, and full of promise. It is (1) definite because the community is for the world and has been given by Jesus Christ the task of witnessing to it (830–832). It is (2) limited because it is very strictly a ministry (to both God and man), and materially a ministry of witness—no more, no less, no other (834–838). It is (3) full of promise because even under pressure it can exert the counterpressure of the promise of Christ, of which specific fulfilments may already be seen, but whose true fulfilment is Christ (838–844).

Looking next at the nature of the ministry Barth again adopts a threefold grouping. The ministry is essentially (1) the declaring of the gospel, the making known of the divine grace and covenant, and the proclaiming of the reconciling life, death, and resurrection of Jesus Christ (844–846). It is no less essentially (2) the explanation of the gospel, the disclosing of its rationality, the actualizing of its intelligibility, the showing of the perspicuity and coherence of its content (846–850). Here Barth clarifies that for him, even though we can apprehend the gospel only by the Holy Spirit, the gospel as such "is generally intelligible and explicable . . . rational and not irrational" (849). The ministry is also essentially (3) the application of the gospel, evangelical address or appeal, the dispelling of the illusion that it is only for the few or for others, the bringing home of its reference to all those to whom it is declared and explained (852–854).

What are the forms of the ministry? How does it function? In answering these questions Barth first points out that in unity, differentiation, and irreversible order there are two basic forms—speech and act (854–863). He then devotes the rest of the subsection to a consideration of the more detailed forms and arranges these in two groups (although numbering them successively), first the six ministries of speech, or of action by speech, and then the six ministries of action, or of speech by action.

(1) The first ministry of speech is obviously praise of God, a total action which culminates in the specific ministry of word and song.

(2) Preaching comes next among the speech ministries. Its central importance throws doubt on the validity of art, which has no ability to portray Christ and ties us to a single conception (867f.). In contrast, preaching is event, action. It is not just exposition, instruction, or the expression of opinion, but proclamation of Christ (867–870).

(3) Teaching has its place and Barth puts it next in the first series. Though more than a school, the community is also a school. It instructs its members and also the world. Only indolent, not modest Christians can claim to be just lay people and not theologians. Every Christian should be taught scripture, history, and doctrine even to the point of studying the catechism and memorization (870–872).

(4) Evangelism follows in the sense of bringing the gospel to those who call themselves Christians but do not know what is at issue. Evangelism awakens the sleeping church. It takes place on the frontier of true and nominal Christians, showing the latter what their true place is and inviting them to occupy it (872–874).

(5) Mission in contrast means movement to the pagan world. The necessary presuppositions of true mission are Christ's finished work, the community as subject, exclusive commitment to God's glory and man's salvation, esteem for other faiths even in opposition to them, and teaching and service as well as preaching and witness. Barth has reservations about the Jewish mission (876–878).

(6) Theology as biblical, dogmatic, and practical theology comes last in the first series. It is necessary as the ongoing self-criticism that positively serves the community and its cause. Barth again commends theology as a "singularly beautiful and joyful science" and repeats his conviction that good dogmatics is the best apologetics (879–882).

(7) With no break in numbering, Barth goes on to list the ministries of action. Surprisingly he begins with prayer. The community prays as it works and in praying it works. Prayer constitutes the basic element in all action (882–884).

(8) Cure of souls comes next as a general activity which includes service to individuals. Secular techniques can be used in this, for example, psychology, but it actually begins where these break off and one should be aware of its distinctive function as a service of both God and man (885–887).

(9) Barth finds a place for the personal example of Christian life and action, possibly in exercise of the charism of faith. Exalting personalities must be avoided but "the Holy Spirit is not a friend of doctrinaire democracy." Some Christians represent a special action of God and therefore of the community (887–889).

(10) Diaconate in the more special sense of material service needs and receives longer treatment. In it the community accepts solidarity with the helpless and gives a sign of the cosmic sweep of reconciliation. Three points must be recognized: (a) that individual needs arise out of a basic disorder; (b) that the diaconate must supplement schemes of public welfare; and (c) that the whole community bears responsibility for it (889–895).

(11) Prophetic action is the fifth of the action ministries. Barth sees this as the relating of events in church and world to the imminent kingdom of God. From it a call goes out to advance into the emerging situation, though this might be hampered both by the world and by a significant number of Christians (895–898).

(12) Last in the action series comes the establishing of fellowship. This fellowship is that of the gospel transcending, although not necessarily removing, all differences of nationality, race, culture, and class. Baptism and the Lord's supper play an important role here, for after the pattern of God's own action they are powerfully significant actions establishing fellowship. They thus bear simple but eloquent witness to peace on earth among those in whom God is well pleased (898–901).

5. The Holy Spirit and Christian Hope (§73)

In the fifth and last section (§73), Barth investigates the impact of Christ's prophetic work on the individual Christian. As in the corresponding sections on faith and love in the two preceding chapters, he again turns to the Pauline triad in 1 Corinthians 13 and proposes hope as the term to describe this impact. He examines his proposal in two subsections, the first on the subject of hope and hope, the second on life in hope.

Hope arises because Jesus Christ has begun but not yet finished his prophetic work (903f.). The basis of the Christian life is to be found in the resurrection of Jesus Christ as grasped in faith. Its present essence is in love as the outworking of the sanctifying ministry of the Holy Spirit. But what about its future, seeing that the *parousia* has yet to come and the Christian's place in it has yet to be decided? Hope in the sense of sure and certain expectation provides the answer to this question (905ff.).

In this connection Barth again presents his concept of the threefold *parousia*. The *parousia* embraces an already—the resurrection; an even now—Pentecost; and a not yet—the coming again. Faith relates to the already, love to the even now, and hope to the not yet (910ff.).

But what is the power of hope? As in the case of faith, the power resides in the subject, Jesus Christ, who is objectively the hope of the believer, and the theme, goal, and basis of his subjective hope (914). Barth criticizes Calvin for failing to stress this, though he commends Calvin's fine description of hope and its role. The Christian does not have to help out his feeble faith and love with a little hope. Although the veil remains, hope can be strong, for if Jesus Christ is objectively his hope, his witness is possible and his future secure (915ff.).

Certainly the world's contradiction of hope is daunting in the absence of Christ's final manifestation. Nevertheless, one does not set hope in man or the church but in God (918f.). Certainly, too, the contradiction of Christian life and witness appalls us, but assurance of the removal of the contradiction is given (919f.). Even more challenging is the dubious nature of Christian existence and service in view of Christ's coming as Judge, but hope sees this judgment to be the judgment of grace (922f.). Most alarming of all is the sure and certain end of earthly life, whether with death or with Christ's return, but the end is Christ who brings a new beginning, so that the Christian can move on even to his end in hope, having the freedom not to fear it, but to rejoice in it (924–928).

Describing hope in the second subsection, Barth points to three main aspects. (1) Hope is individual but not private. The individual is a member of the community. His hope has a universal context, that of God's kingdom. It is also given a public ministry, that of the witness to Christ in which the Christian is a watchman representing God on the one side and awakening humanity on the other (930f.). For this reason the Christian must not delay to live in the hope for which he has been liberated (933f.).

(2) Hope, even though it faces the veil of present appearance, must never become hopeless in relation to the present—a purely otherworldly hope (935f.). Hoping for and intimating the ultimate, it hopes for the penultimate too (937f.). Avoiding foolish optimism on the one side, it also shuns foolish pessimism on the other (938). It takes an active, not a passive form. It is not a private hope for the self but a responsible hope of witness that looks and works for indications of the new creation in the present world (938f.).

(3) Life in hope has its origin in God and not in man (939ff.). It comes into being through the mighty action of the Holy Spirit, who awakens the Christian to it. As *Spirit,* the Holy Spirit wakens man to freedom, so that hope, like faith and love, is his own. As *Holy* Spirit, he does this in his own freedom, so that man must constantly seek his hope from him. It is as he is constant in prayer, then, that the Christian will be found serving the Lord and rejoicing in hope (941f.).

APPENDIX
Holy Baptism

BARTH planned to finish Volume IV with a chapter on the ethics of reconciliation. He prepared a draft of this chapter (published separately under the title *The Christian Life,* Eerdmans 1980), but deteriorating health and vigor prevented him from revising and completing it. He did, however, work through one of the sections, that on baptism, and published it independently as "The Christian Life (Fragment)," with the subtitle "Baptism as the Foundation of the Christian Life." He divided this section into two subsections, a shorter one on baptism with the Holy Spirit and a longer one on baptism with water.

The opening theme of the first subsection is that the new life has its foundation in God (3f.), not by supernatural infusion, nor the kindling of innate powers, but by the change in God's free grace, whereby we become what we were not, that is, faithful to God (5f.). The New Testament presents this change in terms of newness: new robes, the new man, the new heart, the new birth (6–10).

In contrast to other new beginnings, this is unique, for the freedom to be faithful rests on the free act of divine and human faithfulness in Jesus Christ (13f.). All the new things spoken of in the New Testament bear a reference to Jesus Christ. It is his robe we put on, his birth that is ours, and it is in his death and resurrection that we die and rise again (14–17).

Christian life, then, is possible only in union with Christ. The change is neither outside us alone, in a kind of Christomonism, nor in us alone, in a kind of anthropomonism (17ff.). It is both outside and inside us in Christ, who, as faith for us, frees us for faithfulness in an event whereby the "outside us" is efficaciously "for us" and therefore "in us" (22f.).

Two aspects call for notice. (1) Christ as risen Lord has the power to be this for us all (23ff.). (2) It is by the Holy Spirit that he has the power to work it out, so that his history becomes the event of our renewing (26–29). The becoming here and now of what is there and then is the baptism with the Holy Spirit (29–31).

Barth concludes the subsection by summing up in five points what he has just said about the divine act that is constitutive for the beginning of the Christian life. (1) It takes place in a direct self-impartation of Jesus Christ (31–33). (2) It is the active and actualizing grace of God, reconciling grace as specific address (33–35). (3) As giving grace it demands obedient gratitude, so that one must adopt a position toward it (35f.). (4) It brings a new beginning of life in distinctive fellow-humanity and therefore in personal service (36–38). (5) It is and remains a true beginning, never complete or definitive, developing as God's work, yet moving toward a goal that comes to meet it, so that the power of the life to come is that of the new life here (38–40).

The counterpart of the divine change is the human decision of an obedient life, and it is with this in view that Barth considers baptism with water in the second subsection. Obedience, which originates in the divine change and embraces the total life-act, begins with baptism (43f.). Barth makes seven initial points concerning this. (1) It is a bodily washing with water (44). (2) It is important as such (45). (3) It parallels Jewish proselyte baptism (45f.). (4) It is self-evident in the New Testament church (46f.). (5) It is not a major theme in the New Testament (47f.). (6) It is indebted to God's resolve and work as well as man's (48f.). (7) It is not self-given, and in giving it, the community acknowledges the faith of the baptized (49f.).

Going now to the heart of the matter, Barth divides his discussion into three parts dealing with the basis, the goal, and the meaning of water baptism.

(1) *The Basis (50–68)* In a relatively short treatment Barth traces water baptism to the command of Christ (50f.). Behind the command, however, stands the baptism of Jesus (52ff.). In this he (a) began his mission (54ff.), (b) confessed God and man (58ff.), and (c) took up his work as mediator in subordination to God and in solidarity with man (60ff.). In an excursus Barth comments on the Baptist's message about Jesus and on the heavenly acknowledgment of Jesus at his baptism (61ff.).

(2) *The Goal (68–100)* The goal, Barth suggests, is to be found beyond the act itself in God's own act—we are baptized *into* the name of Father, Son, and Holy Spirit—as the act of reconciliation and change that is confessed in the obedience of faith (68ff.). While the goal of John's baptism is the same, a difference between it and Christian

baptism arises because (a) Christ has now completed his history (75f.), (b) the Spirit has now been poured out (76f.), (c) there is a heavier stress on fulfilled judgment (78–80), (d) there is also a stronger emphasis on forgiveness (80–82), (e) Christian baptism has a unitive character (82–84), and (f) it is baptism into the one church of Jews and Gentiles (84f.). In all these things the goal of both is the one divine act of salvation but this goal is depicted in different ways, not in the sense that Christian baptism may be directly equated with that of the Spirit, but in the sense that the work of Jesus Christ, the basis of both, is only beginning with John's baptism and has already been done in Christian baptism (85–90). Barth closes this part of the investigation with a discussion of the verses that relate baptism to the name of Christ and also to the trinitarian formula in Matthew 28:19 (90–100).

(3) *The Meaning (100ff.)* This receives more extended treatment. Barth begins by considering the interpretation of baptism as an immanent divine work—a view that he finds in different forms in Roman Catholic, Lutheran, and Reformed teaching (101–107). Since this sacramental understanding claims biblical support—and Barth acknowledges that we must not oppose scripture (107)—the biblical references demand examination, beginning with the word "mystery" of which "sacrament" is a translation (108f.). Barth bases what he has to say on two hermeneutical principles: (a) that scripture is its own interpreter, and (b) that all exposition is interpretation (110f.). He adds that there are allusions to baptism in the New Testament as well as direct references, but that it rarely comes up as an independent subject and we must always ask whether the basis, goal, or meaning is in view (111f.). A detailed examination of the relevant New Testament passages follows (111–127). From this Barth concludes that, biblically, baptism has no sacramental significance (127f.). "Its meaning is to be sought in its character as a true and genuine human action which responds to the divine word and act" (128–130; cf. Zwingli).

Three emphases, Barth thinks, are needed if its meaning is to be understood. They are emphases (a) on the form of the baptismal act; (b) on its social character; and (c) on its freedom (130–134). But what occurs in this act to make it Christian baptism? In correlation with God's act, yet in distinction from it, what takes place is an act of obedience and hope (134f.); an act of conversion, not just to the community but to God (136ff.). On the basis of knowledge of the divine word and act this conversion is a free and responsible decision (141f.). It achieves visibility in water baptism (144f.) and its confession (148), so that baptism may be regarded as the first step that the person who has come to see Jesus Christ takes with the community (149) after receiving instruction in Christian faith and conduct (151f.).

What is involved in the free and responsible act of baptism? It is (a) an act of obedience to a command, although this command is not, of course, absolute in the sense that its fulfilment is essential to salvation (153–158). It is (b) an act of renunciation and committal answering the basic work of remission and renewal accomplished in Jesus Christ (158–163).

All this corresponds, Barth believes, to what may be found in the New Testament. Hence the discussion might close here were it not for a factor with which church history confronts us from a very early period, that of infant baptism, first as a practice, then as a doctrine (164–167). Barth regards infant baptism as an erratic block that does not belong to authentic baptismal teaching and practice (164–194).

He first lists what he understands to be the requirements of a proper defence of infant baptism. (a) One must show its necessity, as Luther and Calvin fail, he thinks, to do (169f.). (b) One must present the case calmly, unlike Luther and Calvin (170ff.). (c) One must not shift to other ground, as Luther and Calvin do (171–175). (d) One should prove what has to be proved and not something else, as the reformers tend to do (175–178).

Barth then presents his criticism of reformation teaching. (a) Exegetically the New Testament passages cited do not provide explicit evidence for infant baptism (179–185). (b) Dogmatically the ideas of vicarious faith and real infant faith have little cogency (185–189). Furthermore, while infant baptism does no doubt depict the objectivity of grace and declare the baptism of Christ and the Spirit, Barth is not persuaded that this justifies an administration to infants in whom no human act of obedience and conversion takes place (189f.). The appeal to good Christians who have been baptized as infants, or to the pharisaism of some Christians baptized as adults, carries no dogmatic weight, however true it may be in fact (190ff.).

To round off his own presentation Barth returns to the positive task of describing baptism as the first step of the Christian life. Thus far he has seen this mainly as a step of obedience. He now depicts it as a step of hope (cf. Romans 6:1–11) with the risen Christ as its object and content (195–198). This hope has a place in the divine teleology, for by it Christians live, not just with an eye on their own future, but in co-responsibility with the community for a prophetic and proleptic ministry of God's word and work to those outside (199f.).

Baptism in this sense is a beginning, the initiation of the Christian life. As a first act, of course, it is to be followed by others (202f.). This ongoing is guaranteed, not by human power, but by its basis in God's Word and command and Christ's finished work and ongoing presence (204–207). In hope, the community allows Jesus Christ to be its future.

In this way baptism is an act of hope. But what precisely does one do in hope? The deed of hope, and hence the meaning of baptism, consists and can consist only of the baptizing community and those baptized by it, praying together that God will answer for them (208). This prayer, which recognizes God's sovereignty, but which is also confident of being heard, constitutes the final meaning of baptism as a humble but bold act of prayer in Luke 3:21; Acts 22:16; 1 Peter 3:18–22 (210–213). He concludes that "as asking and praying which is ventured in hope in Jesus Christ, in obedience," baptism "is a constitutive action which makes a beginning and which is a model for all that follows" (213).

Conclusion

BARTH never brought his *Church Dogmatics* to a conclusion. How, then, can there be a conclusion to this introductory précis? Perhaps there cannot be. Since Barth did not finish his work, what is said about it must always be in some sense tentative and incomplete. One certainly cannot try to construct the missing eschatology of Volume V from hints and anticipations in Volume I-IV. Nor can one know for certain how the eschatological teaching might have shed new light on the themes already presented. Definitive appraisal of an unfinished work can hardly be made.

Nevertheless, even an incomplete work has a certain finished character. It must be considered for what it is. What Barth might or might not have said in the last volume can now have no bearing on what he did say in the existing volumes. Thus, even though the tentativeness of what is attempted may be granted, certain things can and should be stated in relation to the material available. Conclusions may be drawn, points of weakness discerned, and merits recognized.

Difficulties arise even in the evaluation of the finished volumes of the *Dogmatics*. The mode of approach is perhaps the chief of these. To some degree approach, like method, is arbitrary. One can come at a work in many different ways, all of them abstractly legitimate. Nevertheless, as was pointed out in the Introduction, certain approaches can, in fact, more or less rule out in advance any possibility of valid assessment. Thus it serves little purpose to label Barth an existentialist, neoorthodox, or dialectical theologian and then evaluate the *Church Dogmatics* according to this presupposed schema. Equally futile is the approach of the doctoral dissertation which proposes to look at Barth's view of, for example, truth, history, or transcendence, and ends up by interpreting the whole work in the light of the selected concept. Of dubious value, too, is the method whereby Barth is simply measured against a traditional theology and his attempt at biblical and historical rethinking is dismissed from the outset. At the same time naive and uncritical acceptance of Barth as a quasi-infallible authority has nothing to commend it. It even runs contrary to Barth's protested adherence to the scripture principle whereby the purity of all theology, his own included, must come under the biblical test.

Is there, then, a proper course to take? In detail, endless variety is still possible, but in general, certain things seem to be essential to an authentic approach even though they cannot be put in a definitive order. For one thing, introductory studies, particularly of all Barth's earlier works, obviously have to be consulted before there can be true understanding and evaluation of the *Dogmatics*. Again, sooner or later the main task of reading, and then rereading, the whole of the *Dogmatics* will have to be shouldered. An analysis of the whole is also called for in which, with the help of the indexes, it may be seen how the various themes are integrated and the complementary discussions of individual topics can be set in relation to the main presentations. To be included, too, is a minute examination of the biblical materials that Barth adduces in support of his teaching: Does he have for this the solid ground in scripture which he claims? Does he engage in legitimate exposition? The historical materials require similar treatment: Has Barth produced sound evidence for his positions? Does he properly interpret past theologians and theological movements? Does he correctly relate historical developments both to the pertinent biblical teaching and also to one another? Once these investigations are concluded the way opens up for a discussion of some of the larger issues raised by the *Church Dogmatics*.

To what general conclusions might one be led by this type of investigation? Here again the field is as wide as the *Dogmatics* itself. Hence any selection, and any attempt to group such a selection, will inevitably suffer from some measure of abstractness and artificiality. Nevertheless, as a tentative proposal, an assessment might be undertaken relative to the formal and material weaknesses and qualities of Barth's dogmatic work. It will be remembered, of course, that form and matter do not stand in disjunction from one another in this enterprise but form displays adaptation to matter.

Formally the *Church Dogmatics* suffers from some obvious defects. It often takes a rhetorical rather than a more strictly scientific path. This leads to overstatement and imprecision, even to the point of leading unwary readers to think that Barth supports what he is negating. The complicated sentences, while not without cumulative force, hardly make for clarity of utterance. In inner arrangement, too, the *Church Dogmatics* leaves much to be desired. The outlines give evidence of careful and imaginative planning, even down to the sub-sections, but within the general scheme Barth's subtle movements of thought can give difficulty to readers, particularly when he does not have numbered subheadings. A certain patchiness also marks his use of supporting biblical and historical materials. In some parts of the work they seem to follow a definite scheme or come in naturally and smoothly. Elsewhere one can never be sure whether to expect abundance or poverty or even total absence. Although these materials ought to form the foundations, the body of the work can be built up irresistibly regardless of their strength or weakness.

Even formally the *Church Dogmatics* also has striking qualities. Barth as rhetorician can achieve magnificent flights. The freshness and vigor of his statements add to his theology the force and vitality of holy scripture and the best reformation writing. His thinking, too, displays perspicacity and fertility of the highest order, so that the reader is shaken out of humdrum habits. Nor does the *Dogmatics* in its totality lack order and structure. The general outline, like the style, arises naturally out of the material. The individual volumes give evidence of considerable thought and skill in the interweaving of various themes, such as the Word of God or reconciliation. Barth certainly allows himself some freedom in the subsections. This corresponds to freedom under the Word. Nevertheless, closer analysis will show that these passages too are by no means unstructured. On a larger scale Barth has achieved a balance and beauty of arrangement seldom if ever excelled in theological history. The uneven distribution of supporting materials, which derives in some degree from their availability, is counterbalanced by the ability with which Barth manages not only to use and exegete so much of scripture but also to introduce all the most important matters of debate in the history of dogma.

Materially Barth can sometimes be the victim of his own architectonic skill and inventive mind. He escapes systematization in one sense but cannot wholly escape the problems of systematic integration. He flees speculation but some of his more brilliant insights leave the impression that he might be making up what is not actually there. Sometimes, too, he falls into the common theological trap of allowing positive statements to be too strongly shaped by negative reactions. Indeed, he seems at times to be fighting shadows, exaggerating the weaknesses in historical or contemporary positions and overcompensating on the opposite side. For some of his own theses Barth can produce only the thinnest biblical support. This applies particularly in his discussion of evil. In spite of his vigorous statements in self-defence, and notwithstanding his commendable zeal to avoid dualism, he has little biblical backing for his elaborate development of nothingness or for his demonology. Indeed, in the matter of fallen angels he deliberately will not accept the fairly plain hints that scripture gives because they do not fit his total picture. The same seems to be true in the question of universalism. Barth will not commit himself to this. He rightly perceives that his theology does not force him to do so. Yet he insists on leaving the matter open when, according to most exegetes, scripture clearly seems to close it. Barth speaks bravely about the scripture principle but like most theologians he can turn a blind eye to scriptures he does not greatly care for. His lack of emphasis on the inspiring of the authors of scripture perhaps belongs to this category, although in this instance he reinterprets the relevant passages rather than ignores them, and does so in the interests of genuine biblical concern.

The material weaknesses, of course, are counterbalanced by considerable material strengths. Barth's magnificent understanding of dogmatics and the dogmatic task opens the way for the rehabilitation of theology and its liberation from the humanities that have so long enslaved it. Few if any theologians have ever even contemplated, let alone undertaken, so comprehensive a study of the Word of God in its various aspects. A serious reexamination and restatement of the doctrine of the Trinity goes hand in hand with this, along with an authentically dogmatic exposition of the virgin birth. The objectivity of God receives proper recognition, as does also the objectivity of reconciliation and the corporeal reality of the resurrection. Commitment to holy scripture comes out strongly not only in the discussion of authority but also practically in Barth's thinking on male and female or on the vicarious nature of Christ's reconciling work. Nowhere has the scriptural centrality of Christ found more convincing exposition, although not at the expense of the divine triunity, since, as Barth constantly reminds us, all the persons are at work in all God's outward operations, so that to say Christ is to say God in all his fulness. Many of the fashionable complaints about Barth dissolve on closer material acquaintance with his actual statements; for example, that he finds no truth outside revelation, that he subjectivizes the gospel, that he makes faith too cognitive, that he finds no place for obedience, that he gives scripture only a spasmodic existentialist role and allots it no controlling function. Similarly many unrecognized points of strength emerge: the helpful thinking on election, the interrelating of dogmatics and ethics, the fresh approach to anthropology, the fine treatment of providence, the challenging expositions of scripture, the valuable historical surveys, the concentration on mission, and the ultimate orienting of theology to worship.

Is there anything comprehensive one might say by way of a final word? Various things suggest themselves. Barth's theology constitutes no static complex of clear-cut and supposedly definitive theses. It has always a personal and responsive quality. Without undergoing essential change, it grows as different aspects of God and his word and work unfold. As Barth once said, its general course is constant but its detailed movements are always changing. Its vitality—and here perhaps is an important clue—derives from its nature. This is not the theology of a man and his thoughts about God. It is the theology of a man meeting God and responding to him. In contrast to so many religious writers, Barth takes God seriously as real object and real subject. His *Dogmatics* is neither anthropology disguised as theology nor theology as a codification of beliefs about God. It is a scientific attempt to study God as he is and as he has revealed himself to be in word and deed. Whether right or wrong in detail, it is always authentic theology. Here perhaps is the secret of its greatness and its power.

Indexes

I. Scripture References

Genesis
1–2:3   113ff.
1:1   114
1:2   114
1:3a   114
1:3b-5   114
1:6-8   114
1:9-13   115
1:14-19   115
1:20-23   115
1:24-31   115
1:26   117
2   130
2:1-3   116
2:4   141
2:4b-7   117
2:8-17   117
2:18-25   117f., 162
2:23   117
2:24   160
3:1f.   186
3:5   186
22:14   141

Exodus
3:4   79
32   30
32:30   186

Leviticus
14   94
16   94

1 Samuel
25   206

2 Samuel
11   207

1 Kings
13   94f.
21   186

2 Kings
25   186

Job
1ff.   225ff.

Psalms
18:25ff. 79
32   62
51   62
113-116   62

Proverbs
16:18   186

Song of Songs
1ff.   118, 130, 162

Isaiah
7-8   176

Ezekiel
37   117

Amos
1ff.   206

Jonah
1ff.   227

Matthew
1:26   176
16:18   211
19   161
25   136
28:19   241
28:20   121

Mark
1:14f.   135
3:16   177
6:13   163
12:29-31 32

Luke
1–2   26
2:41-51   163
3:21   243
15:11ff. 180, 198

John
1:1f.   87
1:14   25
3:6ff.   60
3:16   177
11   219
14:18   136

Acts
2:37ff.   103
3:19f.   136
17   62
22:16   243

Romans
1–3   185

1	62	*2 Corinthians*		*1 Timothy*	
1:1	230	1:20	219	2:6	219
6:1-11	242	3:14	37		
7	189	5:19ff.	177	*2 Timothy*	
7:1f.	130	11:2f.	130	3:16	37
8:18f.	166				
9:1-5	91	*Galatians*		*Titus*	
9:6-29	92	1ff.	190	1:3	135
10	92	2:20	195		
11	92	3:26f.	130	*Hebrews*	
12–13	104	4:1	135	1:1	135
12–15	104			11:3	109
		Ephesians		12	164
1 Corinthians		1:9f.	135	13:8	135
1:30	77	5:10	161		
2:6-16	37	5:22ff.	130	*1 Peter*	
6:12-20	130	5:34	160	1:20	135
6:16	160	6:4	164	3:18	22, 243
7	130, 161				
11:1-16	130, 161	*Philippians*		*2 Peter*	
13	214, 216f.	2	181	1:10-21	37
13:1-3	217				
13:4-7	217	*Colossians*		*Revelation*	
13:8-13	217	2:3	77	1:8	135
13:13	237	3:21	164	4–5	153

II. Proper Names

Ames, W.   157
Anselm   3, 11, 187
Aquinas   29, 47, 72, 85,
   87f., 93, 109f., 116, 141f.,
   146ff., 152, 157
Arianism   19
Aristides   110
Arminianism   85
Athanasius   18, 87f.
Augsburg, Confession
   of 46
Augustine   19f., 23, 27,
   79, 81f., 88, 117f., 123,
   142ff., 151, 155, 188,
   201f.

Bach, J. S.   46
Barmen Declaration   41,
   64
Barth, P.   90
Bartmann, B.   35
Basil of Caesarea   47, 115
Bauer, W.   152
Beauvoir, S. de   161
Berdyaev, N.   161

Berkouwer, G. C.   221
Beza, T.   88
Biedermann, A. E.   70
Blumhardt, C.   166, 221
Boettner, L.   85
Bonaventura   141
Bonhoeffer, D.   157
Bovet, T.   160ff.
Bretschneider, K. G.   152
Brockes, B. H.   120
Brunner, E.   26, 93, 112,
   114, 125, 157f., 161f.,
   164, 212
Bucanus, W.   86, 123, 185
Buddaeus, J. F.   29
Bullinger, H.   6
Bultmann, R.   135, 175,
   183
Burmann, F.   144, 185

Calixtus, G.   47
Calvin, J.   12, 19, 23, 26,
   29, 32, 35, 41, 45, 47, 72,
   85, 93, 110ff., 115ff., 127,

   141, 151, 185, 190, 208,
   210, 229, 238, 242
Cocceius, J.   86, 88, 145,
   177

Descartes, R.   119
de Wette, W. M. L.   100
Dittus, G.   221
Dorner, I. A.   113, 152
Dort, Synod of   85
Drey, J. S. von   39

Feuerbach, L. I.   70
Fichte, J. G.   125

Gerhard, J.   8, 86, 141,
   143
German Christians   64
Gess, W. F.   181
Goethe, J. W. von   144
Gogarten, F.   8
Gomarus, F.   88
Grotius, H.   39
Grünewald, M.   25

Haering, T. 152
Hagenbach, K. R. 100
Harnack, A. von 25, 31
Hegel, G. W. F. 70, 185
Heidanus, A. 79, 141, 143
Heidegger, J. H. 144, 185
Heidegger, M. 149
Heidelberg Catechism 90
Herder, J. G. 25
Herrmann, W. 100
Hollaz, D. 41, 86

Infralapsarianism 88f.
Irenaeus 23

Jaspers, K. 125
John of Damascus 27

Kaftan, J. 152
Kähler, M. 49
Kant, I. 71, 103, 215
Kierkegaard, S. 32
Kirn, O. 100, 152
Kohlbrügge, H. F. 210
Kyburtz, A. 120

Lactantius 111
Leenhardt, H. 160
Leibniz, G. W. 120, 149
Lesser, F. C. 120
Leyden Synopsis 185
Lipsius, R. A. 79, 111, 143, 152
Lombard, Peter 27, 141
Lotze, H. 70
Lüdemann, H. 70
Luther, M. xii, xiv, 7, 11, 19, 23, 26, 32, 36, 41, 45, 47, 85, 110, 114, 117, 185f., 188, 229, 242

Manicheism 124
Marcion 118, 124
Martensen, H. L. 152
Martyr, Peter 86

Marx, K. 132
Mastricht, P. 79, 81, 89
Maury, P. 89
Mayer, E. W. 100
Melanchthon, P. 19, 47, 86, 111, 185
Möhler, J. A. 39
Molinism 80
Mozart, W. A. 149
Müller, H. M. 149
Musculus, W. 177

National Socialism 64, 142, 165, 168
Nicene Creed 19f., 112
Nietzsche, F. 128
Nitzsch, C. I. 49, 152

Origen 151
Otto, R. 125

Pelagia 167
Perkins, W. 157
Piscator, J. 185
Polanus, A. 75, 85f., 109f., 111, 125, 185
Portmann, A. 125
Pseudo-Dionysius 82, 152

Quenstedt, J. A. 27, 67, 75, 79, 86

Reinhard, F. V. 152
Rhaetican Confession 86
Ritschl, A. 70, 111, 158, 185, 215
Rothe, R. 152

Sailer, J. M. 39
Sartre, J. P. 149
Scheeben, M. J. 39
Schlatter, A. 152
Schleiermacher, F. E. D. 10, 38, 47, 79, 100, 149, 152, 160, 162, 185

Schopenhauer, A. 118
Schubart, W. 160
Schwarz, A. 160
Scots Confession 89
Seeberg, R. 79, 152
Siebeck, H. 70
Siegfried, T. 8
Simon, R. 39
Soe, N. H. 157
Sohm, R. 212
Stephan, H. 152
Strasser, C. 160
Strauss, D. F. 38, 70, 142
Supralapsarianism 88f.

Tertullian 111
Theophilus of Antioch 109
Thirty-nine Articles 86
Thomasius, G. 181
Titius, A. 125
Troeltsch, E. 152, 185
Turrettini, F. 27, 86, 88

Ursinus, Z. 177

van de Velde, T. 160
van Til, S. 29
Vatican I 39
Vischer, W. 94

Wegschneider, J. A. L. 185
Wendt, H. H. 49
Westminster Confession 86
Wingren, G. 223
Wolff, C. 120
Wollebius, J. 79, 81, 157, 185

Zinzendorf, N. L. von 192
Zöckler, O. 125
Zwingli, H. 86, 133, 142, 177, 185